St Antony's Series
General Editor: **Jan Zielonka** (2004–), Fellow of St Antony's College, Oxford

Recent titles include:

James Milner
REFUGEES, THE STATE AND THE POLITICS OF ASYLUM IN AFRICA

Motti Golani
THE END OF THE BRITISH MANDATE FOR PALESTINE, 1948
The Diary of Sir Henry Gurney

Demetra Tzanaki
WOMEN AND NATIONALISM IN THE MAKING OF MODERN GREECE
The Founding of the Kingdom to the Greco-Turkish War

Simone Bunse
SMALL STATES AND EU GOVERNANCE
Leadership through the Council Presidency

Judith Marquand
DEVELOPMENT AID IN RUSSIA
Lessons from Siberia

Li-Chen Sim
THE RISE AND FALL OF PRIVATIZATION IN THE RUSSIAN OIL INDUSTRY

Stefania Bernini
FAMILY LIFE AND INDIVIDUAL WELFARE IN POSTWAR EUROPE
Britain and Italy Compared

Tomila V. Lankina, Anneke Hudalla and Helmut Wollman
LOCAL GOVERNANCE IN CENTRAL AND EASTERN EUROPE
Comparing Performance in the Czech Republic, Hungary, Poland and Russia

Cathy Gormley-Heenan
POLITICAL LEADERSHIP AND THE NORTHERN IRELAND PEACE PROCESS
Role, Capacity and Effect

Lori Plotkin Boghardt
KUWAIT AMID WAR, PEACE AND REVOLUTION

Paul Chaisty
LEGISLATIVE POLITICS AND ECONOMIC POWER IN RUSSIA

Valpy FitzGerald, Frances Stewart and Rajesh Venugopal (*editors*)
GLOBALIZATION, VIOLENT CONFLICT AND SELF-DETERMINATION

Miwao Matsumoto
TECHNOLOGY GATEKEEPERS FOR WAR AND PEACE
The British Ship Revolution and Japanese Industrialization

Håkan Thörn
ANTI-APARTHEID AND THE EMERGENCE OF A GLOBAL CIVIL SOCIETY

Lotte Hughes
MOVING THE MAASAI
A Colonial Misadventure

Fiona Macaulay
GENDER POLITICS IN BRAZIL AND CHILE
The Role of Parties in National and Local Policymaking

Stephen Whitefield (*editor*)
POLITICAL CULTURE AND POST-COMMUNISM

José Esteban Castro
WATER, POWER AND CITIZENSHIP
Social Struggle in the Basin of Mexico

Valpy FitzGerald and Rosemary Thorp (*editors*)
ECONOMIC DOCTRINES IN LATIN AMERICA
Origins, Embedding and Evolution

Victoria D. Alexander and Marilyn Rueschemeyer
ART AND THE STATE
The Visual Arts in Comparative Perspective

Ailish Johnson
EUROPEAN WELFARE STATES AND SUPRANATIONAL GOVERNANCE OF SOCIAL POLICY

Archie Brown (*editor*)
THE DEMISE OF MARXISM-LENINISM IN RUSSIA

Thomas Boghardt
SPIES OF THE KAISER
German Covert Operations in Great Britain during the First World War Era

Paradorn Rangsimaporn
RUSSIA AS AN ASPIRING GREAT POWER IN EAST ASIA
Perceptions and Policies from Yeltsin to Putin

Ulf Schmidt
JUSTICE AT NUREMBERG
Leo Alexander and the Nazi Doctors' Trial

Steve Tsang (*editor*)
PEACE AND SECURITY ACROSS THE TAIWAN STRAIT

St Antony's Series
Series Standing Order ISBN 978–0–333–71109–5 (hardback) 978–0–333–80341–7 (paperback)
(outside North America only)

You can receive future titles in this series as they are published by placing a standing order. Please contact your bookseller or, in case of difficulty, write to us at the address below with your name and address, the title of the series and the ISBNs quoted above.

Customer Services Department, Macmillan Distribution Ltd., Houndmills, Basingstoke, Hampshire RG21 6XS, England.

Refugees, the State and the Politics of Asylum in Africa

James Milner
Assistant Professor of Political Science
Carleton University, Canada

palgrave macmillan

In Association with
St Antony's College, Oxford

First published 2009 by
PALGRAVE MACMILLAN

Palgrave Macmillan in the UK is an imprint of Macmillan Publishers Limited, registered in England, company number 785998, of Houndmills, Basingstoke, Hampshire RG21 6XS.

Palgrave Macmillan in the US is a division of St Martin's Press LLC, 175 Fifth Avenue, New York, NY 10010.

Palgrave Macmillan is the global academic imprint of the above companies and has companies and representatives throughout the world.

Palgrave® and Macmillan® are registered trademarks in the United States, the United Kingdom, Europe and other countries.

ISBN: 978–0–230–21504–7 hardback

This book is printed on paper suitable for recycling and made from fully managed and sustained forest sources. Logging, pulping and manufacturing processes are expected to conform to the environmental regulations of the country of origin.

A catalogue record for this book is available from the British Library.

A catalog record for this book is available from the Library of Congress.

10 9 8 7 6 5 4 3 2 1
18 17 16 15 14 13 12 11 10 09

Printed and bound in Great Britain by
CPI Antony Rowe, Chippenham and Eastbourne

In loving memory of my father,
William Stephenson Milner

Contents

Illustrations

Maps

Figures

Tables

Abbreviations

ADFL	*Alliance des forces démocratiques pour la libération du Zaïre/ Congo* (Alliance of Democratic Forces for the Liberation of Zaire/Congo)
AFP	*L'Agence France-Presse*
AFRC	Armed Forces Revolutionary Council, Sierra Leone
AI	Amnesty International
ANC	African National Congress
BMS	*Brigade Mixte de Sécurité* (Mixed Security Brigade), Guinea
BNCR	*Bureau National pour la Coordination des Refugiés*, Guinea
CCM	*Chama Cha Mapinduzi* (Party of the Revolution), Tanzania
CIREFCA	International Conference on Central American Refugees
CNISR	*Commission Nationale pour l'Intégration et le Suivi des Réfugiés*, Guinea
CPA	Comprehensive Plan of Action for Indochinese Refugees
CRS	Centre for Refugee Studies, York University
DRC	Democratic Republic of the Congo (formerly Zaire)
ECOMOG	ECOWAS Monitoring Group
ECOWAS	Economic Community of West African States
ECRE	European Council on Refugees and Exiles
EPAU	Evaluation and Policy Analysis Unit, UNHCR
ERP	Economic Recovery Programme, Tanzania
EU	European Union
ExCom	Executive Committee of the High Commissioner's Programme, UNHCR
FDD	*Forces de la démocratie*, Burundi
FGoR	Former Government of Rwanda
FRELIMO	*Frente de Libertaçao de Moçambique* (Front for the National Liberation of Mozambique)
GDP	Gross Domestic Product
HEP	Humanitarian Evacuation Programme for Kosovar Refugees
HRW	Human Rights Watch
HTP	Humanitarian Transfer Programme for Kosovar Refugees

ICARA I	First International Conference on Assistance to Refugees in Africa, 1981
ICARA II	Second International Conference on Assistance to Refugees in Africa, 1984
ICG	International Crisis Group
IDP	Internally Displaced Person
IFI	International Financial Institution
IMF	International Monetary Fund
IOM	International Organization for Migration
IRIN	UN Integrated Regional Information Network
KANU	Kenya African National Union
KLA	Kosovo Liberation Army
LAP	Local Assistance Project, Kenya
LCHR	Lawyers Committee for Human Rights
LURD	Liberians United for Reconciliation and Democracy
MPLA	*Movimento Popular de Liberaçao de Angola*, Angola
NARC	National Rainbow Coalition, Kenya
NATO	North Atlantic Treaty Organization
NCCR	National Convention for Construction and Reform, Tanzania
NEP	North Eastern Province, Kenya
NESP	National Economic Survival Programme, Tanzania
NFD	Northern Frontier District, British East Africa
NGO	Non-Governmental Organization
NPFL	National Patriotic Front of Liberia
OAU	Organization of African Unity
OSCE	Organization for Security and Cooperation in Europe
PAC	Pan-African Congress, South Africa
PANA	Pan-African News Agency
RCK	Refugee Consortium of Kenya
RCMP	Royal Canadian Mounted Police
RPF	Rwandan Patriotic Front
RUF	Revolutionary United Front, Sierra Leone
SADF	South African Defence Force
SPRAA	Special Programmes for Refugee Affected Areas, Tanzania
SWAPO	South West Africa People's Organization of Namibia
TCRS	Tanganyika Christian Refugee Service, Tanzania
ULIMO	United Liberian Movement for Democracy
UNAMSIL	United Nations Assistance Mission in Sierra Leone
UNDP	United Nations Development Programme

UNEP	United Nations Environment Programme
UNGA	United Nations General Assembly
UNHCR	United Nations High Commissioner for Refugees
UNICEF	United Nations International Children's Emergency Fund
UN-OCHA	United Nations Office for the Coordination of Humanitarian Affairs
UNOIOS	United Nations Office of Internal Oversight Services
USAID	US Agency for International Development
USCR	US Committee for Refugees
USRP	US Resettlement Programme
WFP	World Food Programme
ZANU	Zimbabwean African National Union

Acknowledgements

The origins of this book date back to my experience in Malawi in 1992. While my time in Malawi was not directly connected to the presence of refugees, I will never forget my first visit, however brief, to a refugee camp. That exposure put a human face on what had previously been an abstract and distant issue for me. I will be forever grateful for the experience of that summer, and for the patience of David Barrie, who helped me ask some challenging questions in Malawi, and Gordon Beaton, who helped me make some sense of the experience after my return to Toronto.

My interest in displacement and refugee issues became clearer in the mid-1990s. Like so many, I watched, naively and from a safe distance, the television footage of the Rwandan genocide and the subsequent 'humanitarian catastrophe' in the refugee camps in the Kivus and around Ngara. My interest in refugee issues has its origin in these events, especially Tanzania's decision to expel tens of thousands of Rwandan refugees in December 1996. I found it hard to understand how Tanzania could so clearly turn its back on its long tradition of being one of the most generous asylum states in Africa, if not the world. This left me with the simple question: why?

This book is the result of my effort to answer this seemingly simple question. It has been a long process, and I have been supported, encouraged and inspired by so many friends, colleagues and strangers over the years. While I am solely responsible for any shortcomings of this book, I would like to thank a number of people who have played key roles in helping me reach this point.

My appreciation for research that engages with real problems through direct experience, and my willingness to work in ways that do not always fit into neat disciplinary silos, was fostered through my wonderful undergraduate experience with the Peace and Conflict Studies Programme at the University of Toronto. While I was fortunate to be taught by some exceptional professors and belong to a vibrant and engaged community, I reserve special thanks for Tad Homer-Dixon. Tad's intellect, leadership and example motivated, and sometimes terrified, so many students. I am especially grateful for his engagement with my independent research on displacement in Kenya, and the Programme's support for my fieldwork there in 1996. The lessons I learned from that experience continue to guide the way I ask questions and try to answer them.

But my ability to engage with the politics of asylum, in Africa and elsewhere, was most clearly developed through the unforgettable experience of my graduate studies at St Antony's College, Queen Elizabeth House and the Refugee Studies Centre at the University of Oxford, and my work with the United Nations High Commissioner for Refugees (UNHCR). These experiences will always have a very special place in my heart and have left me with so many wonderful memories and treasured friendships.

St Antony's College was, and in many ways remains, my home away from home, and it is an honour to be publishing this book as part of the Palgrave Macmillan / St Antony's series.

My framework for engaging with the case of Tanzania and my understandings of burden sharing and the security implications of refugee movements were developed through my master's research. I remain deeply grateful to Michael Barutciski, then at the Refugee Studies Centre, for his sustained engagement with my research and insistence on precision in my argument. I am also grateful for the support of the Chevening Scholarship and the British Council, which enabled me to spend time at the Centre for the Study of Forced Migration at the University of Dar es Salaam in 1999. *Asante sana* to Khoti Kamanga for his hospitality during my time there.

I was then privileged to work with UNHCR in India, Cameroon, Guinea and in the organization's Geneva headquarters. This experience remains the foundation of my practical understanding of the role that politics can play in the daily challenge of refugee protection. I cannot imagine completing this project without the benefit of this experience and the guidance and encouragement I received, and continue to receive, from friends and colleagues in the organization. In particular, I would like to thank Mamadou Dian Balde, Jeff Crisp, Debbie Elizondo, Brian Gorlick, Augustine Mahiga, Sumbul Rizvi and Yasser Saad.

This practical experience with the complexities and realities of refugee protection served as a challenging, and sometimes distracting, foundation when I returned to Oxford for my doctoral studies. I am grateful for the patience and support of Matthew Gibney and Neil MacFarlane who nurtured the development of this project and challenged me to find the balance between the work of practitioner and researcher. The development of this book also benefited enormously from comments provided by colleagues and friends, including David Anderson, Leah Bassel, Alexander Betts, Christopher Harding, Emma Samman, Nicholas van Hear and Roger Zetter.

I am very grateful for the support of the Pierre Elliott Trudeau Foundation. While the Foundation's financial support both allowed me to complete my doctorate and undertake extensive fieldwork in Kenya, Tanzania and Guinea, I am also grateful for the encouragement I have received from many of the Foundation's members. I also wish to acknowledge the support of the Holly Wyatt Walter Scholarship and the Cyril Foster and Related Funds.

My fieldwork took me to capitals and camps, through the early rains and around potholes the size of a school bus. I am profoundly grateful for all those who got me there and back in one piece. I am indebted to all who took the time to be interviewed in Geneva, Nairobi, Dadaab, Dar es Salaam, Kibondo, Conakry and N'Zérékoré. I am especially grateful to the support of UNHCR in all three countries and to a number of colleagues whose kind assistance and patience made all the difference. In Kenya, my special thanks to: Peter Kimanthi, Alex Kishara, George Okoth-Obo and Rossella Pagliuchi-Lor. In Tanzania, my special thanks to: Chrys Ache, Mzee Joseph Butiku, Annette Nyekan and Duane Poppe. In Guinea, my special thanks to: Louise Aubin, Sani Chaibou, Moustapha Condé, Stefano Porretti and Stefano Severe.

I am also indebted to the generosity of the many refugees I met in Nairobi, Dagahaley, Dar, Kanembwa, Conakry, Lainé, Kola and Kouankan. Their courage continues to inspire me.

I do not have the words to fully express my thanks and gratitude to Gil Loescher. His writing and research has been a significant influence since the early 1990s, largely shaping my approach to the question of refugees. Since 2001, I have been privileged to know him and learn from his vast knowledge, unfailing conviction, and gracious humility. He and his family have welcomed me into their home, and made me feel that I belong. Since 2003, they have all taught me the true meaning of heroism and resilience, and it has been a profound honour to know them, and call them friends.

I was fortunate to have the time and space to substantially revise the text of my doctoral thesis and refine its argument during my time as a Postdoctoral Fellow at the Munk Centre for International Studies at the University of Toronto from 2006 to 2008. I am very grateful to the Social Sciences and Humanities Research Council of Canada (SSHRC) for its support and Janice Stein for her guidance. I am also grateful for the support I received from friends and colleagues at the University of Toronto and the Centre for Refugee Studies at York University for easing my repatriation and reintegration to life and work in Canada.

I am also very grateful for the welcome that I have received since arriving at Carleton University in the summer of 2008. Colleagues in the Faculty of Public Affairs, the Department of Political Science and the Institute of African Studies, especially Katherine Graham, Ted Jackson, Laura Macdonald and Blair Rutherford, made me feel immediately welcome and have encouraged me to expand this area of work through my teaching and future research.

I have also been very fortunate to be encouraged by a wider community of colleagues in Canada who are committed to findings solutions for the world's refugees. My particular thanks to: Howard Adelman, Michael Barutciski, Wenona Giles, Elissa Golberg, Barry Halliday, Jennifer Hyndman, Susan McGrath, Michele Millard and Jessie Thomson.

I would also like to thank UNHCR for permission to use the tables, figures and maps from the *Global Report* in this text, and for permission to use the photograph on the cover of this book. Images depicting refugees have a tendency to deny them agency, to portray them as passive victims, and to reinforce a range of stereotypes. My hope is that this photo, entitled 'a returnee youth in Rwempasha, Rwanda looks towards the future', speaks to the determination, strength and resilience of refugees.

My greatest thanks are due to my friends and family, who endured my angst, absences and distractions. Very special thanks are reserved for friends who have sustained me since long before I embarked on this adventure. You know who you are. And through it all, there has been my family, especially my Mum and Dad. While my father was not able to see the final product, his spirit, determination, love and humour have sustained me throughout. He was a grand lad. My mother's faith, hope and love seem to have no limits, and have seen me through many dark times. I will be forever grateful for everything she has done for me.

And finally, I could not have taken this final step without my wife, Laurie. She has graciously accepted my work into our life with more love, patience and support than I could have ever dreamed possible. Her nook has been my refuge through so many changes. Her smile has warmed me on even the coldest Ottawa mornings. Her reassurance has sustained me to finally call this book done. Her love has changed my life. I cannot thank her enough, or show her how much I love her in return – but I will spend the rest of my life trying.

JAMES MILNER
Ottawa

Maps

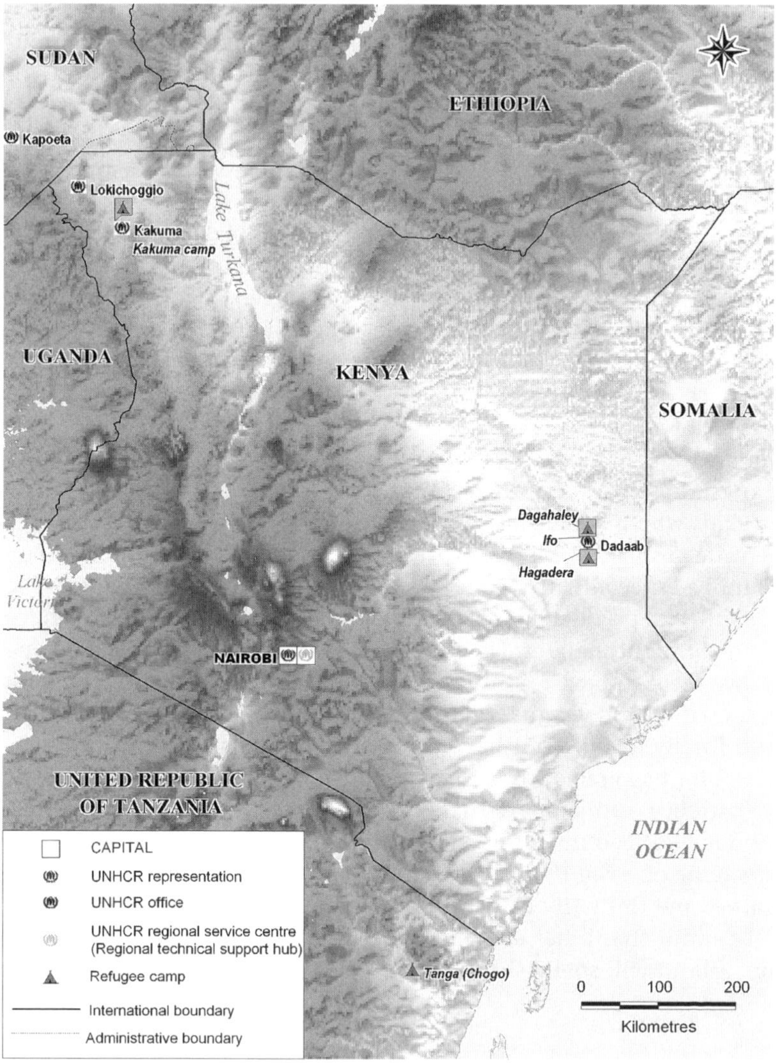

Map 0.1 UNHCR operations in Kenya (31 December 2006) (UNHCR 2007a)

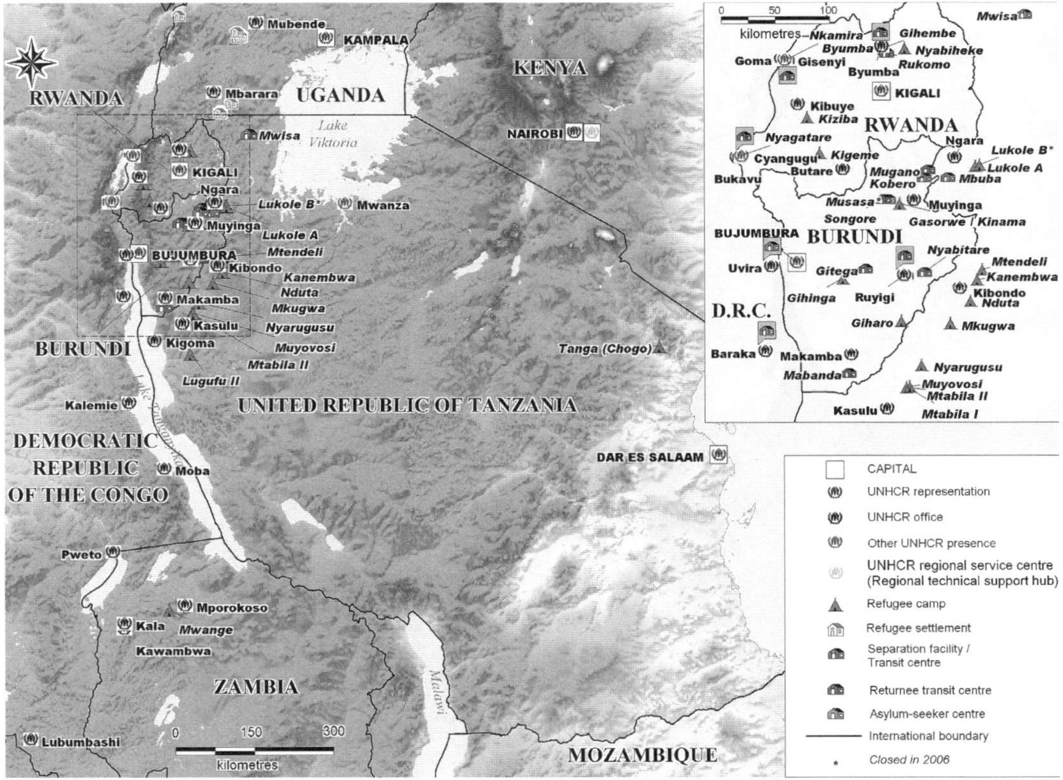

Map 0.2 UNHCR operations in Tanzania (31 December 2006) (UNHCR 2007a)

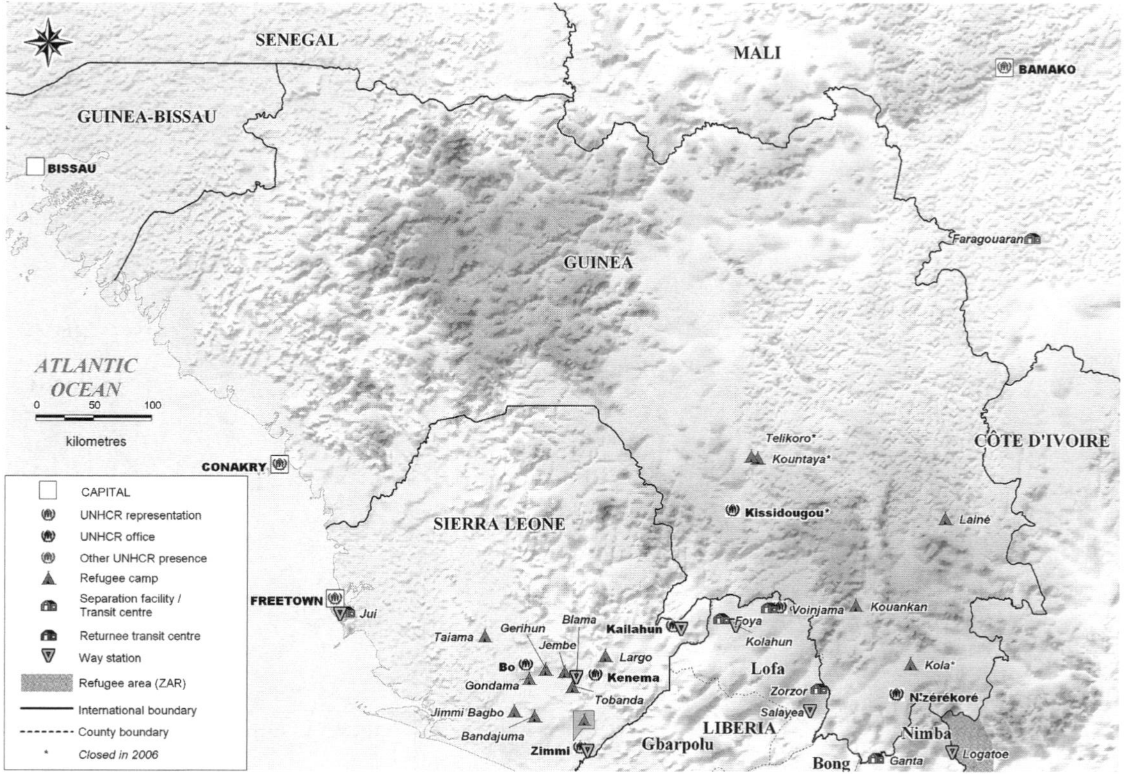

Map 0.3 UNHCR operations in Guinea (31 December 2006) (UNHCR 2007a)

1
Understanding the State and Asylum in Africa

The plight of refugees in Africa has been one of the most visible consequences of the conflicts that have plagued the continent for the past fifty years. Images of refugees pouring across borders to escape persecution, mass human rights violations and conflict, huddled in camps and surrounded by the flags of international aid agencies, have put a human face on issues as complex and abstract as the collapse of a state. This was especially true in the 1990s, as millions of African refugees fled conflict and state failure in many regions of the continent. The world looked on as scores of refugees fled conflicts in Burundi, Liberia, Rwanda, Sierra Leone and Somalia, to name but five of the more notorious. Shocked by the scale of human suffering, there were demands for action. In response, Western governments gave hundreds of millions of dollars to humanitarian agencies like the Office of the United Nations High Commissioner for Refugees (UNHCR) and dozens of other international and non-governmental organizations (NGOs).

But interest in these refugee situations soon faded, and international attention shifted to conflicts and humanitarian challenges elsewhere. Dozens of refugee situations were left unresolved, and millions of refugees trapped in camps across Africa. By 2004, there were some two million refugees living in camps across the continent, some of whom had been in exile for decades. In the late 1980s and early 1990s, one of the more iconic images of African refugees was that of a refugee mother, recently arrived in a camp, trying to feed her child. Many of those children have grown up in refugee camps and are still in exile. There is a lost generation in Africa, living in limbo in dozens of camps spread across the continent.

In the absence of sustained and effective action to resolve the conflicts and human rights violations that forced these refugees to flee, it may seem inevitable that refugees will continue to languish in camps.

Such pessimism, however, overlooks the fact that African refugees have not always been treated as they are today. During the 1960s and 1970s, the vast majority of African refugees did not live in camps, but lived in rural settlements, were provided with agricultural tools and training, and encouraged to be self-reliant. Many refugee settlements produced surplus crops, thereby contributing to local markets and regional development. During this time, the hosting of refugees was a source of pride for African states, and refugees were seen to bring many benefits to the communities that hosted them.

By the end of the 1990s, however, the perception of refugees by African states was profoundly different. African states hosted a third of the world's refugees in 2000 (UNHCR, 2007c). Many of these refugee populations were large and protracted, received dwindling donor assistance, and were seen to be the cause of a range of security concerns. In response to the scale of these challenges, and in stark contrast to the treatment of African refugees in the 1960s and 1970s, a significant number of host countries across the continent placed restrictions on the asylum they offered to refugees. Some states limited the *quantity* of asylum they offered by closing their borders to new asylum seekers, promoting early repatriations, and, in exceptional cases, carrying out mass expulsions. Other states limited the *quality* of asylum they provided by denying refugees a range of basic social and economic rights and containing them in isolated and insecure camps, on the periphery of the state and cut off from local communities.

African states have generally pointed to three justifications for adopting these restrictive asylum policies. First, they highlight the scale and enduring nature of the problem. They argue that the sheer number of refugees on their territory makes the problem simply too big for their limited resources and state capacity. States also point to the prolonged stay of many refugee populations, stretching into decades for many groups, and argue that they are unable to cope with such a protracted problem. Second, many African states have pointed to a perceived lack of assistance from the international donor community, so-called burden sharing, as a justification. They argue that the mass arrival and prolonged presence of refugees has placed a strain on the environment, economy and public services in refugee-populated areas, and that they have carried this burden for too long. Coupled with declining support from donor countries to fund assistance programmes across Africa, states now feel justified in geographically isolating refugee populations until a solution can be found outside of their country. Third, states claim that the presence of refugees has resulted in a number of security concerns for the host state. These concerns include the presence of armed groups within the refugee population, the spillover of conflict, and crime and insecurity in refugee-populated areas. Given their limited capacity to resolve such security concerns, a number of states have responded by attempting to 'contain' the refugee 'problem' in remote border areas, on the periphery of the state, and far from the core of political power in the capital city.

This response further exacerbates the challenge of asylum in Africa. UNHCR estimates that, by 2004, there were over 2.3 million refugees in Africa who had been in exile for five or more years, typically contained in geographically isolated camps or segregated settlements (UNHCR, ExCom, 2004b, 10). According to UNHCR, 'the consequences of having so many human beings in a static state include wasted lives, squandered resources and increased threats to security' (UNHCR, ExCom, 2004b, 2). Given the interplay of these human rights, development and security implications, the global pressures on asylum, and the significant share of the global refugee burden borne by Africa, the pressing need to develop a more rigorous understanding of asylum in Africa becomes more apparent.

Asylum and the state

In contrast with their more open approach to refugees in the 1960s and 1970s, events of the 1990s suggest that African states have generally become more reluctant to host refugees. The objectives of this book are to ask why, to critically examine the factors cited by host states in Africa as a justification for limiting asylum, and to develop a more rigorous understanding of the range of factors that shape the asylum policies of major African host states. Drawing on the cases of Kenya, Tanzania and Guinea, this book considers three related questions. First, how have African states responded to the mass arrival and prolonged stay of refugees? Second, which factors have played the most significant role in determining the state's response to refugees? Third, how have these factors and responses changed over time?

Contrary to the rhetoric of many African states, this book argues that a state's asylum policy is only partially the result of factors such as numbers, the responsiveness of the donor community and a range of security concerns perceived to be associated with the presence of refugees. Crucially, asylum policies are also the result of a number of factors unrelated to the presence of refugees, but stemming from broader changes in the African political landscape since the 1980s. These changes have resulted in new internal and external constraints on the state in Africa, including democratization, economic liberalization, and the increased imbalance in power relations between African states and the international donor community. It is a combination of these factors, both related to and separate from the presence of refugees, which motivates African states to adopt particular asylum policies.

Any examination of asylum policies in Africa should consequently be rooted in an approach that recognizes the politics of asylum in Africa. Taking Africa's perceived place on the periphery of the international system as its point of departure (Ayoob, 1995; and Clapham, 1996), such an approach illustrates how many regimes in contemporary sub-Saharan Africa have a prevailing sense of vulnerability to external and internal challenges. This sense of vulnerability, in turn, leads many regimes to view the arrival and presence of refugees as a potential threat to their survival. Facing such threats, but under pressure from the international donor community to provide asylum to refugees from neighbouring conflicts, African states balance a number of often contradictory priorities when formulating their asylum policies.

Recent commentators on asylum in Africa have not given sufficient consideration to the relationship between the restrictive asylum policies adopted by states during the 1990s and broader political forces in Africa. In fact, there has been very limited consideration of the state and factors motivating their asylum policies. As argued by Jacobsen (1996, 656), 'much of the refugee literature...focuses on the refugees themselves, rather than the effects of refugee movements on host countries and communities.' Indeed, the predominant perspective of the literature on refugees in Africa in the past decade has been to examine the causes of refugee movements, catalogue violations of refugee protection standards and examine specific aspects of particular refugee populations. This literature has made important contributions to the debate on root causes and prevention, advocacy efforts on behalf of refugees, and understandings of the realities and dynamics of the refugee experience. Such approaches, however, are limited in their analytical utility when trying to explain the response of states to refugee movements.

Two decades ago, Loescher (1989, 4) highlighted how 'less than adequate treatment...has been accorded to the process of refugee policy-making at the national or international level.' Instead, he argued that additional attention needed to be paid to 'national interest, domestic and foreign policy constraints, and ideological concerns of states which must be taken into account together with legal and humanitarian principles in order to understand both the reasons for and the response of states to refugee crises' (1989, 5). While Loescher's appeal has been followed by a number of works on individual asylum countries, with the case of Tanzania being especially well represented in the literature, such factors have rarely been considered in a comparative perspective. Indeed, with the exception of recent work by Asres (2007), Crisp (2000), Rutinwa (1999) and Veney (2007), no scholarly work in the past decade has attempted a comparative analysis from the specific perspective of African host states. As argued by Harrell-Bond (1986, 13), this lack of engagement with the host state may be due either to the assumption that host government institutions are too weak to be a determining factor in the response to refugees or to the belief that the 'main business [of the state is] to oppress and exploit the poor within their own societies', and that engagement with the state should consequently be avoided. Either way, researchers have, by accident or design, generally avoided engagement with the host state when considering the problem of refugees in Africa.

As illustrated by the cases of Kenya, Tanzania and Guinea, however, host states have played a significant role in determining asylum policies on their territory. This book consequently focuses on the African state and its response to the arrival and prolonged presence of significant refugee populations and develops a more critical understanding of the range of factors that affect the asylum policies of African states. While criticisms of the African state as a social construct persist (Asres, 2007, 33–64), it would be highly problematic to exclude it entirely from our understanding of asylum and refugee protection. As Veney (2007, 65) highlights, 'even in poor countries the state is more than able to exercise sovereignty by deciding who to let in, who to keep out, how to treat those who are let in, and who to kick out when they are no longer wanted.' In considering the asylum policies of Western states, Gibney (2004, 13) argues that 'how much any state – or to be more specific, any *government* – can do for refugees will be determined largely by the possibilities afforded by its domestic political environment, and that environment will be shaped by a changing array of social, institutional and economic forces, both domestic and international in origin.' A similar approach is required to understand asylum policies in Africa.

This focus on the perspective of host states is not, however, intended to excuse state behaviour or to justify restrictive policies. Instead, at the core of this approach is a belief that a more critical understanding of state behaviour can not only help reveal the interests behind the rhetoric of African states, but also contribute to more effective responses to the plight of refugees in Africa. As argued throughout this book, states play a central role in the formulation and implementation of particular asylum policies. These actions, in turn, are motivated by the interests and priorities of states. Engaging with state interests does not necessarily mean agreeing with state action. Instead, a more critical engagement with the interests of states could provide the basis for encouraging a shift back to the more open asylum policies of the 1960s and 1970s. As outlined in Chapter 2 of this book, a number of key host states in Africa have recently taken tentative steps towards adopting more open asylum policies. States like Guinea, Uganda, Zambia, and, most recently, Tanzania, have demonstrated a willingness to pursue more open asylum policies that could lead to a solution for refugees through naturalization and local integration. While these developments present a potentially exciting opportunity to find solutions for many refugees in Africa, this willingness can best be encouraged and replicated in other states by engaging with the interests of host states in Africa, and expanding the space within which more open asylum policies may be formulated and implemented. In this way, a more critical understanding of the actions and interests of African states could contribute to a solution for African refugees.

Key concepts: Refugees, asylum policy and the African state

Given the objectives of this book, it is important to begin by explaining how the terms 'refugee', 'asylum policy' and 'African state' are employed. Arguably the most influential definition of 'refugee' is contained in Article 1(A)2 of the *1951 Convention relating to the Status of Refugees* (1951 Convention), which applies the term 'refugee' to any person who

> [a]s a result of events occurring before 1 January 1951 and owing to a well-founded fear of being persecuted for reasons of race, religion, nationality, membership in a particular social group or political opinion, is outside the country of his nationality and is unable or, owing to such fear, unwilling to avail himself of the protection of that country...

This definition was developed specifically in response to the refugee situation in Europe after World War II, and 'from the outset, it was recognized that, given its various limitations, the Convention definition would not cover every refugee' (Goodwin-Gill, 1996, 19). It was not until the adoption of the *1967 Protocol relating to the Status of Refugees* (1967 Protocol) that the temporal and geographic limitations of the definition were removed, making the definition more universally applicable.

A central feature of this definition remained, however, its exclusive reference to individualized persecution. According to the 1951 Convention definition, only persons who could demonstrate that they were individually the victims of persecution could be recognized as a refugee. This raised two particular concerns for newly independent African states in the 1960s. First, as outlined in Chapter 2, the majority of refugees in Africa at the time were not fleeing individualized persecution, but generalized violence, either as a result of the ongoing wars of national liberation or as a result of conflicts in newly independent states. Second, application of the 1951 Convention requires individual refugee status determination procedures. Even given the number of refugees in Africa in the 1960s, such procedures were found to be too resource- and time-intensive for many African states.

In response to these and other concerns, and in response to a number of political concerns outlined in Chapter 2, African states adopted an additional refugee definition under the auspices of the Organization for African Unity (OAU). The OAU's *1969 Convention on the Specific Aspects of Refuge Problems in Africa* (1969 OAU Convention) contains two definitions of the term 'refugee'. The first, in Article I(1), is identical to the definition in Article 1(A)2 of the 1951 Convention. Article I(2) of the 1969 OAU Convention, however, states that,

> The term 'refugee' shall also apply to every person who, owing to external aggression, occupation, foreign domination or events seriously disturbing public order in either part or the whole of his country of origin or nationality, is compelled to leave his place of habitual residence in order to seek refuge in another place outside his country of origin or nationality.

Through this definition, the 1969 OAU Convention introduced two important innovations. First, the term 'refugee' in the African context now applies to individuals fleeing both persecution and generalized violence. Second, by making refugee status contingent on generalized situations in the refugee's country of origin, the 1969 OAU Convention allows states to recognize entire groups of individuals as refugees on the basis of shared characteristics and common cause of flight. This procedure, known as *prima facie* refugee status determination (Rutinwa, 2002b), is the basis upon which the vast majority of refugees in Africa are recognized today. In fact, of the 2.7 million refugees in Africa at the start of 2006, 2.1 million (77 per cent) were recognized on a *prima facie* basis (UNHCR, 2007c, 181).

With the arrival of individuals or groups of individuals claiming to be refugees, states must decide how to respond to these claims and how to accommodate refugees for the duration of their exile. Taken together, this response is the state's 'asylum policy'. As outlined by Jacobsen (1996), states receiving refugees, called 'host states', must adopt policy responses to three sets of questions. The first set relates to what Jacobsen terms 'the legal-bureaucratic response', involving the position states take on the legal status of those individuals seeking asylum, the adoption of procedures to determine refugee status on a group or individual basis, and the allocation of responsibility for the refugees within the state bureaucracy. The second set of questions relates to the nature and level of cooperation between the host state and the international donor and humanitarian community.[1] The third set of questions relate to the 'admission and treatment of refugees'. In this way, the host state's asylum policy will determine whether refugees are allowed to enter the state's territory, where and in what manner they are allowed to settle, what rights they are afforded while in exile, and the division of responsibility between the host state and international actors such as UNHCR.

If a host state applies international and regional refugee protection standards, allows access to and cooperates with international organizations, and grants refugees the full range of social, economic and political rights contained in international refugee law, such as freedom of movement and the right to seek employment, they may be said to have adopted an *open asylum policy*. If, by contrast, a state prevents or frustrates the arrival of refugees, does not apply international and regional refugee protection standards, does not cooperate with international organizations, and denies refugees the rights they are afforded by the 1951 Convention, they may be said to have adopted a *restrictive asylum policy*. As Chapter 2 will illustrate, the position of African states on these questions has changed considerably in the past fifty years, moving from a 'very generous attitude towards refugees' in the 1960s and 1970s to a marked decrease in their commitment to asylum in the 1980s and 1990s (Rutinwa, 1999, 1). Explaining this shift is a core objective of this book.

While there is general agreement on the legal definition of 'refugee', notwithstanding its potential conceptual and operational limitations (Zetter, 1991), there is significant debate on the definition of the 'state', and particular debate on the meaning of 'the African state'. The objective of this section is not to resolve these debates, but to present a general overview of the origins and evolution of the African state. While recognizing that the post-colonial experiences of individual states have been very different, it is possible, and indeed important, to emphasize those characteristics shared by the majority of post-colonial states in sub-Saharan Africa. It should, however, be emphasized that the argument of this book is limited to sub-Saharan Africa, and excludes the question of refugee movements in North African states bordering the Mediterranean.

From the early uses of the term 'state' by Jean Bodin and Thomas Hobbes in the sixteenth and seventeenth centuries (see: Gibney, 2004, 198–201), to characterizations developed by Migdal (1988) and Weber (1994), a 'state' has generally been taken to consist of a territory, a population that inhabits that territory, and an authority that governs that population and which has a monopoly over the use of force to exercise its authority. To these domestic characteristics must be added the international characteristics of the state, namely recognition by other states and sovereignty. As such, understandings of the state should include both domestic and international characteristics, with a conceptualization broad enough 'to encompass not only the relationships between the internal dynamics of individual territory-government-society packages, but also the larger systemic dynamic of the way in which these packages relate to each other' (Buzan, 1991, 60). Such a conceptualization of the state is particularly important in the context of refugee movements, which are, by their very nature, both domestic and international events.

To this end, Buzan (1991) proposes a conceptualization of the state based on three components. The first is the physical basis of the state, including its population, territory and resources. The second is the institutional expression of the state, comprising 'the entire machinery of government, including its executive, legislative, administrative and judicial bodies, and the laws, procedures and norms by which they operate' (Buzan, 1991, 83). The final component is the idea of the state, rooted both in the nation, especially in those rare instances where the territory of nation and the state coincide, and in organizing ideologies, which can take for form of 'some fairly general principles, like Islam, or democracy, or some more specific doctrine, like republicanism or communism' (Buzan, 1991, 79).

As Chapter 2 will argue, pan-Africanism and solidarity with liberation movements were central elements of the idea of many African states in the 1960s and 1970s. This idea of the state contributed to open asylum policies for refugees fleeing wars of national liberation, even when such policies resulted in retaliation by the colonial power and attacks on the host state. Buzan's characterization of the state helps explain this willingness to host refugees, despite attacks on the physical base of the state. As Buzan (1991, 95) argues, 'since the state ultimately rests on its physical base, the protection of territory and population must count as fundamental national security concerns, though they may be sacrificed in considerable measure to protect the other two components of the state.' As Chapter 6 will argue, for example, this helps explain Tanzania's willingness to host refugees from Mozambique in the late 1960s and early 1970s despite attacks by the Portuguese Air Force: the hosting of refugees was seen as a tangible expression of the idea of the pan-Africanist Tanzanian state under the regime of Julius Nyerere.

In this way, it is also important to understand the difference between the 'state' and the 'regime'. According to Job (1992, 15), the term regime 'refers to the small set of persons who hold the highest offices in the state and/or are the elite that effectively command the machinery, especially the coercive forces, of the state.' While Buzan incorporates the regime into his conceptualization of the institutional expression of the state, he notes that the 'state' and 'regime' are not always the same. In fact, regimes 'can be assumed to have their own interests, both organizational and individual, apart from the state interests which they represent' (Buzan, 1991, 89). As illustrated in the case studies, differentiating between the interests of the state and the governing regime is 'both possible and necessary' in the African context (Harbeson and Rothchild, 2000, 7).

Underlining Buzan's three components of the state is sovereignty. States are, by definition, sovereign, and in the post-1945 international order enshrined in the Charter of the United Nations, all sovereign states are equal. To paraphrase Orwell, however, while all states are equal, some are more equal than others. Accordingly, it is important to consider the nature of weaker states in the international system, which Jackson (1990) refers to as 'quasi-states'. Jackson argues that the rapid process of decolonization following the end of World War II brought into existence a significant number of states. These states came into being in an international system that both guaranteed their existence and bestowed upon them sovereign equality. In reality, however, these states were far from equal with other states in their capacity to provide the 'concrete benefits which have historically justified ... sovereign statehood' (Jackson, 1990, 21). Jackson consequently argues that while these states may have juridical statehood, their empirical statehood was not yet fully established, making them 'quasi-states'.

While Jackson argues that this juridical statehood has ensured the survival of many otherwise weak states, especially in Africa (Jackson and Rosberg, 1982), Ayoob (1995) argues that the 'negative sovereignty' conferred upon weak states has not made them more secure, but is at the core of their 'insecurity predicament'. Ayoob believes that many 'Third World'[2] states share a common predicament stemming from their late or delayed state-making and their late entry into the international system. As a result of these pressures, Ayoob argues that Third World states can be characterized by their weakness and vulnerability. This view is echoed by Krasner (1985, 58), who has argued that 'the international and domestic weaknesses of Third World states make them vulnerable to systemic shocks, which they cannot control.' As a result, the primary objective of these states, and the regimes that govern them, is to 'reduce the deep sense of insecurity from which Third World states suffer domestically and internationally' (Ayoob, 1995, 2–3). While the concept of vulnerability will be central to the examination of the relationship between refugee movements and security in Chapter 4, it is also useful for understanding the nature of the state in Africa.

While recognizing the tremendous diversity of African politics (Chazan et al., 1999, 5–13), it has been argued that 'to talk about politics in Africa is virtually to talk about the state' (Chabal, 1994, 68). Domestically, the post-colonial African state has been characterized as 'weak in foundations, structurally deficient, without deep legitimacy and generally lacking the political means of its putative power over civil society' (Chabal, 1994, 74). Internationally, the African state is 'at the bottom of any conventional ordering of global power, importance and prestige' (Clapham, 1996, 3). To this characterization of the African state must be added the artificiality of its borders, which were drawn mostly in the late nineteenth century by European colonial powers with little or no regard for local particularities. As argued by Davidson (1992, 163), 'the colonial partition ... inserted the continent into a framework of purely artificial and often positively harmful frontiers.'

Notwithstanding the weakness and artificiality of the African state, gaining control of the state and preserving it were the twin priorities of African nationalist leaders, both in the run-up to independence and in the early post-colonial period. Leaders subsequently agreed not to revisit the colonial boundaries, a principle enshrined in the Charter of the OAU, signed in 1963. It is also significant that African independence was achieved in the early phases of the Cold War, during which 'diplomatic, economic and military support was often given to individual African leaders who allied themselves (sometimes interchangeably) with either the United States or the Soviet Union' (Taylor and Williams, 2004, 6). While the dynamics of the Cold War will be discussed in greater detail in Chapter 2, it is important to note here that a number of African leaders were able to use superpower rivalry to 'fend off political opponents at home' (Taylor and Williams, 2004, 7).

The assurance of sovereignty did not, however, ensure domestic stability and security. The weight of expectations at independence, coupled with the scarcity of resources available to the newly independent state, created fierce domestic competition over the authority to allocate those scarce resources. Regimes in Africa in the 1960s and 1970s became increasingly centralized either around a single political party or the military, and domestic opposition was either constrained or eliminated (see: Clapham, 1996, 56–62). This centralization of power allowed a number of regimes to pursue ambitious state-led development programmes, such as those in Tanzania (Chapter 6) and Guinea (Chapter 7). It also allowed several regimes to pursue refugee policies irrespective of domestic support, especially in the context of refugees fleeing Cold War proxy conflicts (Chapter 2). These models of governance did not, however, prove sustainable and 'by the late 1970s and early 1980s most, if not all, African states were undergoing an organizational crisis' (Chazan et al., 1999, 65). This crisis was characterized by deteriorating relations between the state and society, high levels of graft and corruption, and the collapse of many basic services.

This organizational crisis was mirrored by an economic crisis. Declining growth, coupled with population increases, resulted in a significant reduction in *per capita* income in Africa through the 1980s. At the same time, Africa's terms of trade were drastically affected by the declining value of the continent's main exports – such as cocoa, coffee and cotton – relative to the cost of imports, leading to a decline in real terms by about a third between 1980 and 1987. In response, African states borrowed heavily, with total African debt climbing from about US$16 billion in 1970, to US$58 billion in 1980, to US$144 billion in 1987. By 1985, foreign debt equalled 43 per cent of Africa's total gross domestic product (GDP), causing a balance of payments crisis. While a number of regimes tried to fend off the crisis through a range of short-term measures, the implementation of structural adjustment programmes guided by the World Bank and International Monetary Fund (IMF) became increasingly unavoidable. While the nature and implementation of these programmes will not be addressed here, recognizing that 'few issues in contemporary African development have been as contentious as the role of these international financial institutions (IFIs) over the past two decades' (Chazan et al., 1999, 334), it is important to emphasize that the vulnerability of the recipient countries gave the IFIs and donor countries tremendous leverage over the policies and priorities of African states.

In reflecting on this period, Clapham (1996, 187) notes that 'whereas the domestic economies of African states were heavily penetrated by external forces which limited the power of the state, African governments were to a very large extent left free to manage politics as they wished.' Domestic human rights records went unchallenged and governance unquestioned by donor states. In the geopolitical context of the Cold War, 'Western states did not want to risk the imposition on Africa of principles of human rights or democracy which would be applicable to their allies as well as to their adversaries, and which would tend to push African leaders into the less demanding arms of the Soviet Union' (Clapham, 1996, 191–2). This rationale led to Western support for regimes with poor human rights and governance records, such as those in Zaire, South Africa, Kenya and Ethiopia.

The end of the Cold War in the late 1980s, however, resulted in a profound and sudden set of changes in Africa. One of the most striking features of this transformation was democratization, with the overwhelming majority of African states committing themselves to some level of democratic reform in the early 1990s. This change was the result of domestic and international pressures which 'made it extremely difficult for [African leaders] to cling to their previous insistence on unfettered sovereignty in the international arena combined with monopoly statehood in the internal one' (Clapham, 1996, 193). For their part, the 'victory' of capitalist and neo-liberal ideology in the Cold War emboldened Western states to seek universal application of, and adherence to, these principles through the formulation of the 'Washington Consensus'. Without the Soviet Union as a counter-balance, African regimes lost one of the main bargaining chips that they 'had been able to use to protect their domestic political hegemony from external attack' (Clapham, 1996, 194). Dependent on Western donor states to provide continued support for their ailing economies, carrying significant debt, and lacking alternatives, African states had little choice but to accept the new terms of their relationship with the West. Given the centrality of political and economic liberalization, compounded by the power imbalance between African states and donor governments and institutions, African states became subject to 'a comprehensive superstructure of international accountability' (Young, 1999, 34–5).

Taken together, these changes in the political and economic landscape in Africa since the mid-1980s have resulted in a number of internal and external constraints on the African state today. Internally, African states have been constrained by the effects of demoncratization and economic liberalization. Externally Africa states face the constraints imposed by the neo-liberal consensus, a lack of policy alternatives and an imbalance of power relations between African states and donor states.

Book outline

These external and internal pressures faced by African states play a predominant role in the formulation of asylum policies. To support this argument, this book has three sections. The first section sets a historical and conceptual context for the book by tracing the history and nature of the crisis of asylum in Africa and efforts to address two of the most often articulated concerns of host states on the continent, namely burden sharing and state security. Section 2 is comprised of three case study chapters, examining how each state has responded to the mass arrival and prolonged presence of key refugee populations since the early 1990s. Section 3 then presents a framework for understanding the politics of asylum in Africa by examining the interplay between factors relating to the presence of refugees, such as the dependability of international assistance and the security implications of refugee movements, and factors unrelated to the presence of refugees, such as democratization, economic liberalization and the sense of vulnerability derived from the peripheral place occupied by African states in the international system.

Chapter 2 traces the history of state response to refugee movements in Africa from the early 1960s, through the wars of national liberation in Southern Africa, post-colonial conflict in independent Africa, and the Cold War, to the emergence of the crisis of asylum in Africa in the 1990s. The chapter examines refugee movements and state responses during this period to illustrate how burden sharing and refugee-related insecurity have been concerns for African host states for many years, and how failures to address these concerns came to be cited by governments as justifications for placing restrictions on asylum from the mid-1990s. The chapter will also draw from the political history of the African state outlined above to argue that broader political factors have also had an impact on the asylum policies of African states.

Chapter 3 critically examines the principle and practice of burden sharing with African states. The chapter begins by defining the principle and outlining its foundations before examining its rising significance in Africa, the challenges of quantifying Africa's refugee burden, and the various mechanisms through which this burden has been shared by other states. By contrasting the African burden sharing experience with the history of burden sharing in other regions, the chapter will argue that African states have been largely unable to alter the level and nature of burden sharing, due partially to the nature of their relationship with the international donor community. While a significant amount of burden sharing with African states does occur, and the presence of refugees may constitute a benefit for host states, the chapter argues that the scope, scale, sustainability and dependability of burden sharing with African states is largely determined by the interests of donor states.

Chapter 4 examines the relationship between refugee movements and security, with a particular focus on Africa. The chapter first highlights the importance of the relationship and outlines the security implications of refugee movements during and after the Cold War. The chapter then considers changing understandings of security since the end of the Cold War and reviews the early scholarly literature on refugees and security. After considering the applicability of this literature to the contemporary security concerns of host states in Africa, the chapter develops an understanding of 'security' appropriate to African states. Finally, the chapter presents a framework for understanding the nature and causes of the refugee-related security concerns of host states in Africa.

Chapters 5, 6 and 7 apply these understandings of burden sharing and security to the cases of Kenya, Tanzania and Guinea. These three countries were selected for this comparative study for a number of reasons. First, they have hosted large and protracted refugee populations from three dominant refugee-producing regions (the Horn of Africa, the Great Lakes region of Central Africa, and the Mano River region of West Africa) and from prominent examples of so-called failed states in Africa (Somalia, Rwanda, Burundi, Liberia and Sierra Leone). Second, these countries hosted the largest refugee populations in Africa at various times during the 1990s. Third, all three states are post-colonial sub-Saharan African states that have acceded to both the 1951 Convention and the 1969 OAU Convention, thereby providing a sufficient conceptual and legal basis for comparison of their asylum policies.

The study is not only comparative between countries, but also over time. As outlined in each case study chapter, each case study considers the state's response to hosting refugees from the arrival of the significant refugee populations to the end of 2007. The Kenya study focuses on the response to the mass arrival of Somali refugees from 1991. The Tanzania study considers the treatment of refugees since the early 1960s, while focusing specifically on the treatment of Burundian refugees in Northwestern Tanzania since 1993. The Guinea chapter examines the case of Liberian and Sierra Leonean refugees who began to arrive in 1990. While it would be problematic to generalize from these cases to the continent of Africa as a whole, such a comparative analysis does illustrate how common political dynamics have led to the formulation of the particular asylum policies of each of these three states.

While the study began with desk research on the themes of the project and individual case studies, the primary source of information for the case study chapters was fieldwork in Kenya, Tanzania and Guinea, in addition to several related visits to UNHCR's Headquarters in Geneva, between 1999 and 2008. During each field visit, interviews were conducted in the capital city and in the refugee-populated areas[3] with representatives of the host government, UNHCR, donor governments, international and national NGOs, civil society and refugee groups. The purpose of the interviews was to understand the interests, perceptions and priorities of key state and non-state actors engaged with the refugee programme, and how these interests changed over time.

Each case study chapter outlines the arrival of a particular refugee population before considering the state response to the initial arrival of that population and subsequent policy changes. In all three cases, concerns relating to burden sharing and security were identified by government representatives as justification for adopting a particular asylum policy. By applying the frameworks developed in Chapters 3 and 4, however, the case studies argue that such concerns do not sufficiently account for the nature of asylum policies adopted by host states. Drawing on the political history of the African state presented above, the case studies argue that the asylum policies of each host state are more fully understood by considering the significance of broader historical and political factors and by understanding the politics of asylum in each case.

Taken together, the case studies argue that Kenya's approach to Somali refugees, Tanzania's approach to Burundian and Rwandan refugees and Guinea's approach to Liberian and Sierra Leonean refugees, while different in substance, are the product of a common logic. While these three states have chosen different strategies, the approach taken is best understood only partially in the context of issues relating to the presence of refugees, such as the increase in numbers, failures of burden sharing and security concerns. More generally, these cases illustrate how states typically interpret the implications of the arrival and protracted presence of refugees according to factors unrelated to the presence of refugees. In Kenya, the presence of Somali refugees was tolerated to placate the donor community, but a history of conflict between the Kenyan state and Somali irredentists led to the securitization of the Somali refugee population and their relegation to the political and geographic periphery of the state. In Tanzania, economic liberalization and democratization have placed pressures on the governing regime, which has used the presence of refugees to its domestic political advantage while seeking to extract additional resources from the donor community. In Guinea, the state has used the presence of refugees to pursue regional priorities and as part of its effort to leverage support from an otherwise restrictive donor community.

Based on this analysis, Chapter 8 develops a framework for understanding the politics of asylum in Africa, highlighting the full range of factors that influence the formulation of asylum policies of African states. The chapter argues that political factors unrelated to the presence of refugees tend to play a predominant role in the asylum policies of states like Kenya, Tanzania and Guinea, and that these states typically incorporate decisions on asylum into their broader political calculus. In this way, the chapter argues that while the presence of refugees may constitute a burden and a security concern in certain circumstances, approaches to such concerns are more often the result of pressures and factors unrelated to the presence of refugees.

Such an approach leads to important lessons not only for the study of asylum in Africa, but also for the wider study of African politics and international relations and the future of the refugee protection regime in Africa. While part of the solution to the challenge of asylum surely lies in addressing concerns relating to numbers, burden sharing and security, part of the solution also lies in engaging in broader political and economic forces that influence a state's asylum policies. African host states do not approach the arrival and prolonged presence of refugees in a historical or political vacuum. If the scholarly understanding of refugees in Africa is to more effectively identify solutions for refugees, it must also adopt such an approach.

2
A History of Asylum in Africa

Migration has been a significant feature of African history for centuries. Forced migration in Africa can be traced back to antiquity, and was a central feature of the consolidation of the Bafour, Ghana, Benin and Lunda empires (Khapoya, 1994). Intercommunal conflict, especially resulting from the *mfecane* in Southern Africa, shifting cultivation and the slave trade also resulted in significant migration both from and within Africa (Zolberg et al., 1989, 290). Colonial policies of forced recruitment and the settler agricultural system also resulted in forced migration. The emergence of the modern refugee phenomenon in Africa may, however, be linked to the anti-colonial struggle and the independence of most African states in the late 1950s and early 1960s for two reasons. First, as argued by Holborn (1975, 825), 'the process of decolonisation brought new and powerful political forces into play and released forces which had been checked or suppressed during the colonial period', resulting in a dramatic increase in the number of refugees in Africa. Second, this increase in the number of refugees occurred in the context of newly independent states, internationally recognized borders and changing relations with the international system. The confluence of these factors not only raised legal questions, but also important political questions.

The goal of this chapter is to trace the major periods of post-independence refugee movements in Africa and outline the response of states. The structure of this chapter builds from Rutinwa's argument that asylum policies in post-independence Africa may be broadly 'classified into two periods' (1999, 1). The first period, from the early 1960s to the 1970s, has been described as a time when African states 'proved remarkably generous in their response to refugee influxes' (Holborn, 1975, 826). Since the 1980s and through the 1990s, however, Rutinwa

(1999, 1) notes 'a marked shift in refugee politics in Africa' with states becoming 'less committed to asylum'. By tracing the trends in refugee movements and asylum policies in Africa from the early 1960s through the 1990s, this chapter outlines the changing response of African states to refugees, and highlights the range of factors that have contributed to the shift towards more restrictive policies.

In contrast with those who argue that the response of African states to refugees in the 1960s and 1970s is best explained in terms of 'traditional hospitality' (Zarjevski, 1988, 102), or who describe the period as a 'golden age' of asylum, when humanitarian concerns superseded political concerns in the formulation of asylum policies (Rutinwa, 1999, 4), this chapter argues that asylum policies have been influenced by political concerns since the emergence of an independent African state system in the early 1960s. In fact, asylum policies have been largely motivated by concerns of domestic politics, national security and international relations. This is not to say that a period of open asylum policies in Africa did not exist, but that it existed for specific political and strategic reasons. As such, the shift to more restrictive asylum policies by African states in the late 1980s was arguably not the result of a new approach to refugees, but the result of the changing political context within which refugee movements occurred.

The chapter concludes by suggesting that we may be entering a new phase of asylum in Africa, where host states are more willing to pursue open asylum policies, leading to the naturalization and local integration of refugees. While it is too early to assess the breadth or depth of these changes, such a shift away from the near-universal restrictive asylum policies of the 1990s suggests that restrictive asylum policies are neither inevitable nor unchangeable, further emphasizing the importance of understanding the context within which asylum policies are formulated. It is only through a more comprehensive understanding of the factors that contributed to restrictive asylum policies that a shift towards more open, solutions-oriented policies may be encouraged.

Post-independence refugee movements: 1960s and 1970s

The first significant refugee movement to result from an African nationalist struggle followed the outbreak of the 1956 Algerian war of independence from France (Loescher, 2001, 97–101; Ruthström-Ruin, 1993; and UNHCR, 2000a, 37–44). During the 1960s and 1970s, however, the overwhelming majority of refugees in Africa were to be found south of the Sahara, and could be broadly divided into two categories. The first category included refugees from wars of national liberation in minority and colonial-governed states. By the early 1970s, 57 per cent of the estimated 1 million refugees in Africa 'originated mainly from the territories still under Portuguese rule, namely Angola, Guinea-Bissau and Mozambique... [and] were living in three neighbouring countries sympathetic to the liberation cause, namely Zaire, Senegal and Tanzania' (Adepoju, 1982, 22). As illustrated by the case of Tanzania in Chapter 6, these refugees, and the liberation movements themselves, were often granted refuge by neighbouring states, both as a gesture of African solidarity and as a means of highlighting the deficiencies of the colonial regimes. As highlighted by Clapham (1996, 209), these early liberation movements in Africa 'acquired a legitimate and even honoured place in the international relations of the continent'.

The second category of refugees was, in the words of Hamrell (1967, 9), the result of 'explosive internal, social and political situations, which existed long before the colonial period but which came to a climax only after independence was reached.' Crises in Zaire, Rwanda, Burundi, Sudan, Ethiopia and Uganda prompted significant refugee movements in the Great Lakes region and in the Horn of Africa, and equally significant challenges for neighbouring states.[1] As argued by Loescher (2001, 114), 'new African governments often viewed refugees as a national security threat because they frequently caused severe interstate tensions.' This was especially true in the case of refugees from Rwanda and Sudan (Cuénod, 1967). Throughout the 1960s and early 1970s, for example, Sudan believed that refugee populations in neighbouring countries provided a base for insurgent groups. In response, the Sudanese military entered border areas in Uganda and Ethiopia, seized refugees, and returned them to Sudan, resulting in a significant strain on relations between Sudan and its neighbours.

While statistics for refugee populations in Africa are problematic,[2] UNHCR estimates that there were just over 1 million refugees in Africa by 1972, as illustrated in Figure 2.1 (below).

The largest refugee populations were in Zaire, which hosted some 478,000 refugees from Angola, Rwanda, Sudan, Burundi and Zambia. Other significant host countries were Uganda, with some 166,000 refugees from Rwanda, Sudan and Zaire, and Tanzania, with some 91,000 refugees from Mozambique, Rwanda, Burundi and Zaire (Holborn, 1975, 835).

Response from African states

The majority of these refugees did not live in camps, but were integrated into local and national economies through the 'zonal

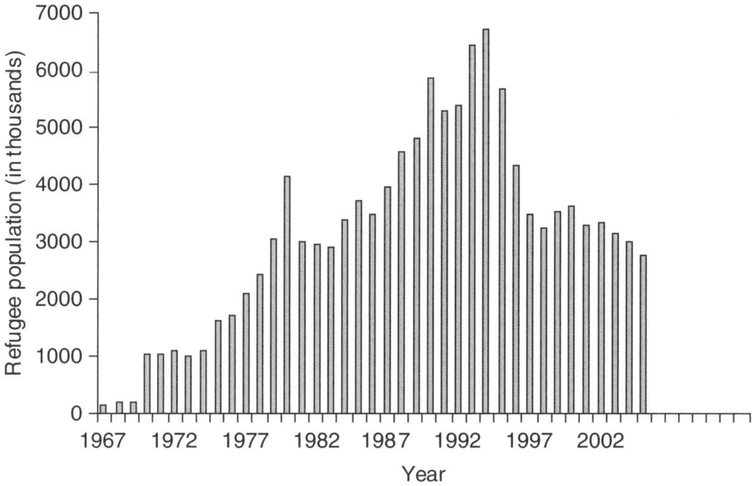

Figure 2.1 Refugee population in Africa (1967–2005) (UNHCR, 2000a; UNHCR, 2007c)

development' approach to refugee settlement (Brooks and El-Ayouty, 1970, 281–91; and Kibreab, 1985, 103–18). As part of the zonal development approach, refugees were allocated land, granted the right to work and encouraged to pursue self-reliance through a range of economic activities.[3] Kibreab (1985, 86) noted that the majority of refugees in Africa were accommodated in such local settlements at the end of the 1970s, with more than 90 per cent of refugees living in settlements in many of the largest asylum countries, including Zaire and Tanzania. While UNHCR and other agencies provided significant support for this approach, with UNHCR spending some two-thirds of its global programme funds in Africa by 1960 (UNHCR, 2000a, 37), credit was mostly given to African states for adopting such open asylum policies. As argued by Kironde (1970, 110), 'zonal development and planning [was] generally accepted [by African states] as the best method of consolidating the economic and social condition of refugee settlements as well as integrating them into the economic and social systems of the country.'

Given the range of concerns relating to the presence of these refugees, it is important to understand why African states adopted such an open response. Many early works on post-independent asylum policy in Africa point to notions of 'traditional hospitality' as a sufficient explanation for the open asylum policies of African states during this period. As argued by Zarjevski (1988, 102):

> Everywhere the fate of refugees is determined by the attitude of the country of reception. In Africa, this attitude has always been influenced by a simple human feeling of brotherly sympathy, and by unshakeable optimism. No persuasion was needed in Africa to make governments grant asylum to refugees who sought it. *Refoulement* at the frontier is the exception rather than the rule, and represents a rare breach of traditional hospitality.

Likewise, Rutinwa (1999, 4) refers to this period as 'the "golden age" of asylum in Africa.' For him (1999, 1), the signing of the 1969 OAU Convention marked the formalization of an 'open door policy' where 'African countries readily admitted all those in search of security and safety'. Rutinwa argues that the expanded refugee definition contained in the 1969 OAU Convention, the Convention's commitment to asylum,[4] provisions for inter-African burden sharing,[5] the granting of a broad range of rights to refugees, including freedom of movement, the right to work and access to education and health services, and, finally, the timely identification of a solution for refugees are hallmarks of the 'golden age' of asylum. While Rutinwa concedes that these provisions were not universally applied, he argues that the codification of these principles demonstrates the degree of African hospitality. A brief review of the process leading to the drafting of the 1969 OAU Convention, however, suggests that, in contrast with the humanitarian considerations implied by notions of 'traditional hospitality', political considerations played a much greater role in the process.

1969 OAU Convention

While most African states became party to the 1951 Convention shortly after gaining their independence, many soon began to 'express increased dissatisfaction that the international refugee instruments did not reflect the realities of the refugee situation in Africa' (Loescher, 2001, 124) and were consequently inadequate to deal with their concerns. In response, African leaders undertook a process to address this gap, while simultaneously responding to concerns surrounding the political and strategic aspects of Africa's early experience with refugees (Amate, 1986; and Rwelamira, 1989).

The origins of the 1969 OAU Convention can be traced to December 1963, when the Liberation Committee of the OAU met in Dar es Salaam to consider the increasing number of refugees resulting from conflicts in independent African countries. The Committee charged two related sub-committees – one covering North and West Africa, the other covering Central, Eastern and Southern Africa – with the task of conducting 'a survey of the refugees and the conditions under which they were living in their countries of asylum' (Amate, 1986, 459). The two sub-committees subsequently submitted a joint report, in which they recommended that 'the OAU should assume direct responsibility for the refugees in Africa, and create a commission under the aegis of the Liberation Committee to look after them' (Amate, 1986, 460). They further recommended that all OAU Member States should be required to contribute to the activities of this new agency, that all international assistance should be channelled through the OAU, and that all able-bodied refugees should be provided with the necessary training to join the armed struggle for independence in their home country.

Before the sub-committees could complete their work, however, the problem of refugees was raised at the OAU Council of Ministers in February 1964 in response to reports that refugees from Rwanda and other independent African states were causing tensions not only within but between other African countries. The Council established its own Commission on Refugee Problems in Africa to 'investigate ways to deal with the political nature of the continent's refugee problems' (Loescher, 2001, 125). In reporting back in July 1964, the Commission reported that 'the movement of refugees from independent African countries into other independent African countries had become a source of friction and, in some cases, of serious dispute between the governments of the countries of asylum and the governments of the countries of origin' (Amate, 1986, 461). In response, the Commission drafted a set of guiding principles that involved action by all African states on the question of refugees. The final steps towards drafting the convention were taken in February 1965, when the Council of Ministers established a committee of legal experts. Although final preparation of the Convention was delayed first by the adoption of the 1967 Protocol, and second by the 1967 *Conference on the Situation of Refugees in Africa*, the OAU Convention was finally signed in 1969.

Alternative explanations for asylum policies

Based on this overview, it may be argued that political concerns played a more significant role in the drafting of the 1969 OAU Convention than notions of 'traditional hospitality'. In fact, a number of authors find the 'traditional hospitality' argument to be problematic.[6] For his part,

Crisp (2000, 5) argues that while the argument 'should not be entirely discounted, it is important to recognize the extent to which the principle and practice of asylum was underpinned by other considerations'. Noting that the majority of refugees in Africa during the 1960s and 1970s were the result of wars of national liberation, Crisp emphasizes how 'the ideologies of pan-Africanism and anti-colonialism remained strong throughout much of the continent' and resulted in open asylum policies. Crisp also argues that substantial international assistance was the essential factor that ensured asylum for refugees fleeing other conflicts in independent African states. He argues that 'an implicit deal was struck' between African states and the international community: that African states would provide the land for refugee settlements, and that donor states would provide the necessary funding. While such assistance from donors did mitigate the impact of the presence of refugees, Crisp adds that such assistance programmes 'provided African states and elites with a welcome source of foreign exchange, employment and commercial opportunities'.

As such, it may be argued that there was a dual imperative for providing asylum to refugees in the 1960s and early 1970s, as illustrated by the case of Tanzania in Chapter 6. Asylum was granted to refugees fleeing wars of national liberation as part of the ideology of pan-Africanism and as a means of highlighting the failures of colonial and minority-ruled territories. Likewise, providing asylum to refugees through the zonal development approach was seen as a means of attracting international assistance to underdeveloped areas of newly independent states. Such an approach, however, was premised on manageable numbers of refugees, sustained international assistance and the ability to insulate the governing regime from the security implications associated with hosting politicized refugee populations. Also significant was the fact that this was the era of 'monopoly statehood' in Africa, as outlined in Chapter 1, where state leaders were able to pursue policies in the absence of domestic or international opposition. As refugee numbers increased, international assistance waned and as security concerns increased, coupled with broader changes in the African political and economic landscape, willingness to host refugees diminished through the 1980s.

Roots of the crisis in asylum: Late 1970s–1980s

The 1970s witnessed two contradictory trends in refugee movements in Africa. On the one hand, it was a time of solutions. In 1972, some 200,000 refugees repatriated to South Sudan, while international engagement helped find solutions for the Ugandan Asians expelled by Idi Amin. The change of regime in Portugal led to the independence of Angola, Mozambique and Guinea-Bissau in 1975 and the subsequent repatriation of some 500,000 refugees. Then, in 1980, significant numbers of refugees repatriated to Zaire, Angola and independent Zimbabwe. As the majority of international assistance remained focused on supporting these operations, however, the number of refugees resulting from other conflicts began to climb in the early 1970s. By 1980, there were over 2 million refugees in Africa (UNHCR, 2000a, 310). As the continent witnessed additional refugee movements, especially from Chad, Ethiopia and Zaire, and as the number of refugees in Africa continued to climb, local solutions, including settlements and zonal development approaches, became more difficult to sustain. By the end of the 1970s, host countries began to argue that refugees had become an 'open-ended burden'. Stein (1987, 51) argues that while this change in perspective was the result of increased refugee numbers and the difficulties of finding quick solutions for refugees, it was largely compounded by the fact that many host countries had 'less sympathy for, and solidarity with, refugees fleeing from their independent neighbour than for those fleeing from imperialism'.

These refugee movements also occurred in a changing international context. As outlined in Chapter 1, many African countries experienced slow economic growth, rapid population growth, balance of payments deficits and a climbing debt burden by the early 1980s, placing additional pressures on host states. At the same time, new refugee movements, especially in Southern Africa and the Horn of Africa, emerged as part of the globalization of the Cold War (Loescher, 2001, 201–46; and Zolberg et al., 1989, 90–120). In contrast with the robust Western response to refugees in other regions, however, there appeared to be little interest in the formulation and implementation of comprehensive solutions for refugee situations in Africa. Unlike the Western response to the Indo–Chinese crisis, as outlined in Chapter 3, there was no political will for the large-scale resettlement of refugees from Africa. Unlike the Western response to the refugee situation in Latin America and the development of the CIREFCA process (UNHCR, 2000a, 136–43), donor governments no longer appeared willing to support large-scale local integration programmes in Africa. Finally, the disengagement of the superpowers from Africa by the end of the 1980s left many of the proxy conflicts unresolved, frustrating repatriation efforts and leaving many refugee populations in limbo. Notwithstanding the large-scale repatriation to Namibia, significant refugee populations from Angola,

Mozambique, Ethiopia, Sudan and elsewhere remained in exile at the end of the 1980s. By 1990, Africa's refugee population was over 5.8 million (UNHCR, 2000a, 310).

The vast majority of these refugees were no longer accommodated in settlements, but in refugee camps. Some, like Loescher (2001, 226), believe that this approach was sought by host states, who, 'concerned about the security risks of hosting refugees from neighbouring countries and about the enormous strains on local economic, political and physical resources, viewed refugee camps as the most convenient way to segregate refugees and to limit their impact on the local community'. This shift was an early indication of changes in the asylum policies of African states. In the context of rising numbers, economic crisis and the politicization of refugee populations, it soon became clear that two of the most important concerns for African states were the question of sharing the burden of hosting large refugee populations for extended periods of time and the security implications of hosting refugees. This chapter now considers how African states and the international community responded to these concerns, and how the failure to address the concerns of African states further contributed to the emergence of restrictive asylum policies by the late 1980s.

Burden sharing: ICARA I and ICARA II

As outlined above, host states generally responded to early refugee populations by implementing zonal development and local settlement schemes. While this approach was initially successful, it proved to be unsustainable over time, and refugee populations became increasingly dependent on international assistance to meet their basic needs. During the 1979 *Conference on the African Refugee Problem*, many states argued that a new approach was necessary if the burdens of African asylum countries were to be more equitably shared (Eriksson et al., 1981). By the early 1980s, it was recognized that donor governments were increasingly reluctant to fund lengthy care and maintenance programmes. At the same time, 'African states stressed the need for greater international burden sharing so that they could better manage the adverse impact of refugees on their economies and environments' (Loescher, 2001, 227).

Using their increased influence in the UN General Assembly (UNGA), African states pushed for additional resources for the assistance of host states in Africa. On 25 November 1980, the UN General Assembly passed Resolution 35/42, which called for an *International Conference on Assistance to Refugees in Africa* to be held the following year. The resolution recognized that Africa had come to host over half the world's refugees, and that the UNGA was 'aware of the consequent social and economic burden placed on African countries of asylum' (UNGA, 1980). Significantly, the resolution also recognized the 'universal collective responsibility to share the urgent and overwhelming burden of the problem of African refugees through effective mobilization of resources to meet the urgent and long-term needs of the refugees and to strengthen the capacity of countries of asylum' (UNGA, 1980).

The Conference, known as ICARA I, had three objectives: to focus world attention on Africa's refugee problem; to mobilize additional resources for the problem; and, finally, to assist host countries through the application of these additional resources. There is some disagreement over the extent to which ICARA I, held in Geneva from 9–10 April 1981, fulfilled its objectives. Stein (1987, 48) argues that the Conference was 'relatively successful in meeting its first two objectives', in that it did focus international attention on the scale of the refugee problem in Africa and mobilized more than US$570 million.[7] In contrast, Stein (1987, 48) argues that it 'fell short of its third objective' as the money pledged was not new money. In fact, most of the money was earmarked for specific programmes, rather than being available for distribution across the continent. As a result, very limited funds were given to countries like Ethiopia, who hosted significant refugee populations but were unpopular with Western donors due to their position within the geopolitics of the Cold War. This level of engagement was, however, justified by many donors on the basis that the requests received were considered to be 'unrealistic and exaggerated', and that in preparation for ICARA I 'old, rejected development projects that had been lying on the shelf were dusted off and given a refugee label, and were submitted for funding' (Stein, 1987, 49).

When the question of assistance to refugees in Africa returned to the agenda of the UN General Assembly in December 1982, it was noted that 'while [ICARA I] succeeded in raising world consciousness about the plight of refugee and returnees in Africa, as well as the problems of asylum countries, the overall results of the Conference in terms of financial and material assistance have fallen short of the expectations of the African countries' (UNGA, 1982). The UN Secretary General, in close cooperation with the OAU and UNHCR, was requested to convene a second *International Conference on Assistance to Refugees in Africa* (ICARA II) in 1984 to review the results of ICARA I, to consider providing 'additional assistance to refugees and returnees in Africa', and 'to consider the impact imposed on the national economies of the African countries concerned and to provide them with required assistance to strengthen their social and economic infrastructure to cope with the burden of dealing with large numbers of refugees and returnees' (UNGA, 1982).

A process of consultation was established through which country reports were prepared for ICARA II, providing a detailed assessment of the assistance needs of refugees and returnees, in addition to the assistance required by host countries to develop the infrastructure necessary to better cope with the refugee burden. While the preparations for ICARA II were impressive, the response from donor countries was not. According to Gorman (1987, 67),

> donor country attitudes toward ICARA II were marked by a lack of enthusiasm and in some cases out-right circumspection. Most donors doubted the motives for the convening of ICARA II. As a rule, they felt – in contrast to the Africans – that ICARA I had been a success, and many were upset with the African criticism of their response to the first conference.

Through ICARA II, it became clear that, notwithstanding the extensive preparative work, there were significant differences between host and donor countries on what burdens were borne by host states and how these should be addressed (Crisp, 2001b, 5). At the same time, it became increasingly clear that it would be the donor states' characterization of Africa's refugee burden that would inform future burden sharing discussions. As this position became entrenched through the 1980s, African states not only felt that their concerns relating to burden sharing were not addressed by the international community, but that they had limited influence over the very terms of the debate.

Security concerns: Attacks on refugee camps and settlements

While the UN General Assembly was attempting to address the burden sharing concerns of African states, UNHCR's Executive Committee was engaged in a second challenge: the question of armed attacks on refugee camps and settlements. While the security implications of refugee movements, especially the presence of armed elements within the refugee population, had been evident in Africa for over a decade (Matthews, 1972; and Hovet, 1970), the question of refugees and stability in Africa was brought into particular focus as a result of specific events in Southern Africa in the late 1970s.

On 4 May 1978, the South African Defence Force (SADF) attacked Kassinga, Angola, killing 600 Namibian refugees. The attack was justified on the grounds that the refugees were actively engaged in an armed struggle against South African control of Namibia. A similar pattern ensued elsewhere in the region as South Africa employed the threat or use of military force to pressure the 'frontline states' of Mozambique, Lesotho, Botswana, Swaziland and Angola into not hosting refugees active in the struggle against white minority rule in Southern Africa (Mtango, 1989; and Molefi, 1984). Other incidents included the January 1981 SADF raid on Maputo, Mozambique, killing 12 South African refugees, the December 1982 SADF attack on Maseru, Lesotho, killing 30 South African refugees and 12 Lesotho nationals and the May 1983 bombing of Matola by the South African air force.

In light of these attacks and similar events elsewhere, UNHCR's Executive Committee decided in October 1981 to examine the need for special measures and procedures to respond to such circumstances. Former High Commissioner for Refugees Felix Schnyder was asked to undertake a review of the situation and make recommendations to the Executive Committee. Schnyder's report, submitted on 15 March 1983, concluded that attacks on refugee camps may 'endanger the national populations of asylum countries and thus lead to the risk of governments of these countries adopting more restrictive attitudes towards asylum seekers' (UNHCR, 1983b, 5). The report proposed a *Draft Declaration on the Prohibition of Military or Armed Attacks against Refugee Camps and Settlements*, containing a range of provisions to ensure the civilian and humanitarian character of camps.

According to Mtango (1989, 98), 'political and strategic considerations prevailed over humanitarian concern' when an earlier version of the *Draft Declaration* was first considered by the Executive Committee in October 1982. As during ICARA II, a split emerged between developing countries, who 'insisted on outright condemnation of armed attacks on refugee camps and settlements', and Western states, especially the US, 'who preferred not to jeopardise the interests of friendly states (Israel and South Africa) who were among the known main culprits' (Mtango, 1989, 98). In the end, the geopolitical interests of the US, who needed South Africa to counter-balance Cuban and Chinese involvement in the Angolan proxy war, trumped the security concerns of African host states (UNHCR, 1983a). As a result, the *Draft Declaration* was finally rejected in 1986.

This prioritization of Western geopolitical concerns over the concerns of African states, coupled with the economic crisis gripping the continent, caused significant concern for host states during the 1980s and resulted in a marked change in their characterization of the presence of refugees. By 1990, African states, through the OAU, claimed that 'the problem of refugees in Africa [had] reached unmanageable proportions' (OAU, 1990, 1). Hosting 5.8 million refugees in increasingly insecure conditions, African states were particularly concerned about the emergence of 'donor fatigue syndrome coupled with declining political will on the part of some of the traditional donors' (OAU, 1990, 3) and the consequent shortfall in UNHCR's Africa programme budget for the first time in four decades. There was a concern that Western states were withdrawing completely from Africa in the dying days of the Cold War. Many of these concerns would be both confirmed and compounded by the events of the 1990s.

The emergence of the crisis: 1990–2003

The 1990s witnessed refugee movements in Africa unprecedented in their scale and complexity. As detailed in the case studies of Kenya, Tanzania and Guinea, conflict in the Horn of Africa, the Great Lakes region and West Africa almost simultaneously resulted in the influx of hundreds of thousands of refugees into neighbouring states. While a resolution of the conflict in Mozambique allowed for the repatriation of some 1.7 million refugees between 1992 and 1996, the proliferation of conflict across the continent saw Africa's refugee population reach 6.7 million in 1994 (UNHCR, 2000a, 310).

Notwithstanding the scale of the problem, it appeared as though Western powers were reluctant to become involved in these crises, especially as their geopolitical interests in Africa were diminished by the end of the Cold War. This lack of Western involvement also contributed to a prolongation of the conflicts that caused these refugee movements (Furley, 1997; Stedman and Lyons, 2004). This response was particularly stark when compared to Western engagement in other regions, as 'the level of international attention and humanitarian assistance to [Africa's] refugees and displaced people was miniscule compared to other high-profile conflicts' (Loescher, 2001, 302), especially in the Balkans. In response, a number of host states across Africa became 'alarmed by the economic, environmental, social, and security costs of hosting mass influxes of refugees' and 'took steps to exclude asylum-seekers from their territory and to ensure the rapid – and in some cases involuntary – repatriation of refugees' (Loescher, 2001, 16). While these concerns were replicated across the continent during the 1990s, their interplay in the context of mass displacement in the Great Lakes region was perhaps the most striking.

Crisis in the Great Lakes region[8]

In the aftermath of civil war and genocide, more than 2 million Rwandan refugees fled to neighbouring countries in 1994. The largest population, some 1.2 million, fled to Eastern Zaire. Many believed that this exodus was 'far from spontaneous' (UNHCR, 2000a, 246), but rather a strategic decision by the Former Government of Rwanda (FGoR) to withdraw a portion of the population of Rwanda to delegitimize the new Tutsi regime, to provide a cover for the political and military activities of the FGoR in exile, and to attract international material assistance. Using the camps as a base and the refugees as a shield, elements of the FGoR and the Hutu militia, the *interahamwe*, launched attacks back into Rwanda throughout 1995, causing significant problems for other refugees, the country of asylum, the country of origin, states in the region and UNHCR (Lischer, 2005, 73–117). At the same time, a number of host states, especially Tanzania, highlighted the range of burdens associated with the arrival and presence of such large refugee populations (OAU and UNHCR, 1998). Most prominent was the negative impact on the environment, physical infrastructure, law and order, social services, food security and local economy in refugee-populated areas.

It soon became evident that the international community was unable or unwilling to address the security implications of the presence of these armed elements. Likewise, the international donor community seemed reluctant to respond to the impact of such massive refugee populations on neighbouring states. Divisions within the international donor community, especially over the question of providing assistance to refugee camps known to contain perpetrators of the genocide, continued through 1995 (Barber, 1997). Meanwhile, UNHCR made 'repeated calls for measures to be taken by the [UN] Security Council to ensure the civilian and humanitarian nature of the refugee camps' (UNHCR, 2000a, 254). In the end, inaction on the part of the international community frustrated efforts to find a solution to either challenge.

By mid-1996, 'the situation in the Great Lakes region was extremely tense' (UNHCR, 2000a, 259). Rwanda was increasingly frustrated with inaction on the part of the international community to separate the armed elements from the refugee population, while host states like Zaire and Tanzania expressed their frustration with the lack of donor engagement to mitigate the burden of hosting large refugee populations. Elsewhere, a *coup d'état* in Burundi on 26 July 1996 brought the Tutsi Buyoya regime to power. In Zaire, violence erupted in South Kivu as elements loyal to Zairian President Mobutu attacked Banyamulenge

Tutsis. In response to the regionalization of the conflict, and in the absence of an effective international response, Rwanda, and to a lesser extend Burundi, began to back Zairian opposition groups as a means of breaking the deadlock in the refugee situation.

In late 1996, the *Alliance des forces démocratiques pour la libération du Zaïre/Congo* (ADFL), led by Laurent Kabila, emerged as the main foreign-backed opposition group in Zaire. Regardless of this group's agenda, it is important to note that 'the refugee camps were the initial target' in the ADFL's march to Kinshasa (UNHCR, 2000a, 263). The first camps attacked were Burundian camps in South Kivu, allegedly used by the *Forces de la démocratie* (FDD) to mount attacks against the Buyoya regime in Bujumbura. Then, in a series of attacks in late October and early November 1996, ADFL forces advanced on Goma and the FoGR-controlled refugee camps. Over the course of the next two weeks, the Rwandan camps in eastern Zaire were overrun by the ADFL. The overwhelming majority of refugees poured back into Rwanda, while thousands more fled deeper into Zaire. After ridding eastern Zaire of the armed elements challenging Rwanda and Burundi, the ADFL turned towards Kinshasa, ousting the regime of Mobutu Sese Seko in May 1997.

These events sent shockwaves throughout Africa. While it was not the first time that a regime in Africa had been overthrown as a result of events stemming from refugee movements,[9] Mobutu was viewed as the 'leading example in Africa of a corrupt but Western-backed dictator' who had been able to cling to power for decades (Clapham, 1996, 203). There was a feeling that if the Mobutu regime could fall as a result of such events, then all regimes in Africa were vulnerable. As detailed in Chapter 6, these events contributed to Tanzania's decision to forcibly expel the Rwandan refugee population on its territory, ending its decades-old tradition of an open asylum policy.

In the aftermath of these events, UNHCR and the OAU co-hosted the *Regional Meeting on Refugee Issues in the Great Lakes* on 8–9 May 1998 in Kampala (OAU and UNHCR, 1998). The meeting was convened at the urgent request of states in the region, many of whom hosted refugees, in order to address issues identified as most pressing by host states and the OAU. It was hoped that the meeting would highlight African concerns relating to the growing refugee problem on the continent. During the meeting, African states identified two issues that needed to be addressed for their confidence as host states to be restored: the security implications of hosting refugees, and the need for increased international assistance to deal with the burdens associated with the mass influx and prolonged presence of refugees.

A wider crisis: Erosion of the quality and quantity of asylum in Africa

Events in the Great Lakes region were, for many, emblematic of a broader crisis of asylum in Africa (AI, 1997b; Crisp, 2000; LCHR, 1995; and Rutinwa, 1999). Many believed that African states, generally, had begun 'to retreat from the fundamental principles of international refugee law' (Rutinwa, 1999, 8), and that African states had shifted from the 'open door' asylum policies of the 1960s and 1970s to a more generally restrictive approach to asylum. Starting in the early 1990s, there was a dramatic rise in examples of *refoulement*, rejection at the frontier, expulsion of refugees and proposals to contain refugees in countries of origin. At the same time, there was a marked decline in standards of protection of refugees by a majority of African states, and a retreat from solutions for refugees other than repatriation.

Rutinwa (1999) and Crisp (2000) were the first to attempt a systematic explanation for this continent-wide shift throughout the 1990s. Both agreed on the overriding significance of the sheer numbers of refugees in Africa, rising from 1 million in the early 1970s to over 6 million in the mid-1990s, as illustrated by Figure 2.1 (above). While this number had dropped to 3.1 million refugees by 2003, this reduction in numbers did not necessarily lead to a simplification of the refugee problem in Africa. 2.3 million (75 per cent) of Africa's refugees in 2003 were trapped in protracted refugee situations (Crisp, 2003a; UNHCR, ExCom, 2004b). These situations, where 'refugees find themselves in a long-standing and intractable state of limbo' (UNHCR, ExCom, 2004b, 1), are found in every region of Africa, and have come to pose significant concerns for refugees, the countries that host them, countries of origin and states in the region (Crisp, 2003a; and Loescher and Milner 2008a). Unlike the 1960s, when most refugees were accommodated in settlements, or the 1990s, when most refugees were in emergency situations, the overwhelming majority of African refugees in 2003 had been contained in Africa's 170 refugee camps for five or more years (Jamal, 2003, 4). As highlighted during meetings between African states and UNHCR in Geneva, finding solutions to these refugee situation was one of the greatest challenges to refugee protection in Africa at the start of the twenty-first century (UNHCR, Africa Bureau, 2001).

Coupled with the protracted nature of many of these refugee situations is declining international support. Crisp (2000, 6) notes that 'donor states can be said to have exacerbated the decline in protection standards in Africa by making it increasingly clear that they are no longer prepared to support long-term refugee assistance efforts.' As detailed in Chapter 3, this diminishing international support for long-term refugee programmes, coupled with a wider recognition of the range of burdens borne by host states, has resulted in the perception by a number of African states that they bear a disproportionate share of the refugee burden.

Crisp and Rutinwa also emphasize changes in the nature of refugee movements and populations in Africa as another set of causes for the rise in restrictive asylum policies. Both highlight the fact that the majority of refugees in contemporary Africa are no longer fleeing wars of national liberation and decolonization, but civil wars taking place in independent countries. As a result, Crisp (2000, 6) believes that 'the new generation of African exiles have not been able to count on the support and solidarity offered to refugees in earlier years.' These changing circumstances, especially in the aftermath of the Rwandan genocide, have resulted in an increased perception of refugees as a security concern for host states, as detailed in Chapter 4, and been increasingly cited by states as a justification for their restrictive asylum policies.

Crucially, however, both Crisp and Rutinwa emphasize the relationship between external factors, including democratization and economic liberalization, and the rise of a more restrictive asylum policy in Africa. Crisp (2000, 8) argues that 'there is growing evidence of a linkage between the process of democratisation on the one hand and the decline in refugee protection standards on the other.' Both emphasize that prior to the 1990s, authoritarian and one-party states in Africa were able to offer asylum to individuals or groups without having to answer to domestic opposition. In contrast, the opening of the political process across Africa has led to 'growing xenophobia in many African countries', often fuelled by the effects of 'austerity programmes imposed by the IMF and World Bank' (Rutinwa, 1999, 1). As structural adjustment programmes frequently required governments to charge citizens user fees for a range of basic services, it has sometimes been resented by the local population that refugees continue to receive these services for free. In the context of democratization, Rutinwa (1999, 2) argues that 'the result has been the adoption of anti-refugee platforms by political parties which result in anti-refugee policies and actions by governments.' Both argue that such factors must consequently be taken into account when considering the asylum policies of African states.

Local integration and the start of a new era?

Against this backdrop, it is important to ask if the trend towards restrictive asylum policies is reversible. As illustrated in this chapter, there was a dramatic shift from open to restrictive asylum policies throughout

Africa between the 1970s and the 1990s. As illustrated by Figure 2.1 (above), this shift was associated with a dramatic increase in Africa's refugee population, in addition to the burden sharing, security and broader political and economic challenges highlighted by Crisp and Rutinwa. While the scale and severity of the new restrictive asylum policies led some, like Rutinwa (1999), to ask if we were witnessing the end of asylum in Africa, recent events suggest that we may be witnessing a very tentative shift towards more open asylum policies in West, Southern and Central Africa. In particular, states like Angola, Guinea, Liberia, Sierra Leone, Tanzania and Zambia have recently expressed their willingness to consider the local integration of a portion of the refugee population on their territory, leading to eventual naturalization. As outlined above, such efforts were the hallmarks of the era of open asylum policies in Africa in the 1960s and 1970s, and a demonstrated return to such an approach in key asylum states like Tanzania might indicate the emergence of a new phase in the history of asylum in Africa. While it is too soon to assess the extent of the shift, or the extent to which recent efforts to promote more open asylum policies will endure, it is important to briefly outline what form these changes might take.

In light of the crisis of asylum in the 1990s, and in response to the adoption of more restrictive asylum policies in Africa and elsewhere, a number of researchers reconsidered the prospects of local integration as a solution for refugees (Crisp, 2004; and Jacobsen, 2001). It was argued that local integration meant more than simply allowing self-reliance and economic activity, but needed to extend to the conferring of permanent legal status, which would negate the need for international protection and refugee status. Jacobsen (2001, 2) noted that while this solution for refugees had been widely pursued in the past, local integration had 'fallen out of political favour, and the term is now a loaded one arousing negative reactions in host governments and donor agencies alike'. This reluctance was likely a result of the same dynamics which resulted in a rise in xenophobia in the context of democratization, as Chapter 8 will argue.

In apparent contradiction to this trend, however, two significant examples of government-supported self-reliance projects were established in Africa between 1998 and 2001 (UNHCR, 2006, 136). In 1998, UNHCR and Uganda established a programme, known as the Ugandan Self-Reliance Strategy, to support both Sudanese refugees and Ugandan IDPs living in Northern Uganda. Likewise, in 2001, UNHCR and Zambia launched the Zambia Initiative to contribute to the food security of Angolan refugee and local Zambian populations in Western Zambia. Notwithstanding a number of concerns raised about these initiatives (Meyer, 2006), they were found to effectively demonstrate 'the role refugees can play as active agents of development, contributing to the economy and society of the host state' (UNHCR, 2006, 136). The success of these initiative, especially their ability to attract additional donor support for both refugees and local populations in host states, has subsequently been used by UNHCR and donor governments as evidence of the benefits of an open approach to asylum, especially during negotiations with more restrictive host states.

The willingness of Uganda and Zambia to allow increased self-reliance for refugees was not, however, necessarily representative of the position of other host states in Africa, or indeed elsewhere in the global South. The resistance of other host states was most clearly demonstrated in 2005, when donor governments encouraged the introduction of a Conclusion on Local Integration at UNHCR's Executive Committee meeting in Geneva. Given the political dynamics of such meetings (Loescher et al., 2008, 76–9), debate on the 2005 Conclusion provided a clear opportunity for host countries in the global South to express their concern that the promotion of local integration by Western donor states was little more than a thinly veiled effort to shift more of the global refugee burden onto some of the poorest states in the international system.

It was therefore something of a surprise that opportunities for local integration have subsequently emerged across Africa. In August 2006, the Director of UNHCR's Africa Bureau hosted a meeting in Geneva with UNHCR's protection and operations divisions to discuss the possibilities of a more comprehensive response to expressions of willingness by a number of African states to consider the local integration of long-standing refugee populations. In particular, the initiative sought to identify solutions for refugees who remained in exile after large-scale repatriation, including populations in Angola, Guinea and Zambia. The result of the meeting was the establishment of a Task Force on Local Integration to provide technical support and sustained political and donor engagement in these key host states.

While the work of this initiative is ongoing (UNHCR, 2007a, 33), and while it is consequently too early to assess its effectiveness, it represents a potentially significant development in Africa and a tentative indication of a shift in asylum policies. The potential for such a shift was further highlighted by Tanzania's announcement in 2008 that it was prepared to naturalize some 218,000 Burundian refugees who had been in exile since 1972, as outlined in Chapter 6, along with local integration initiatives in Sierra Leone and Liberia (UNHCR, 2007b). At this early stage, these developments make two important points. First, asylum policies can change. While asylum policies in Africa became increasingly restrictive in the late 1980s and throughout the 1990s, this is not to say that they cannot change again towards a more open approach. Second, asylum policies do not change of their own accord. As outlined above, a wide range of factors contributed to the shift from open to restrictive asylum policies in Africa, and similar factors may contribute to the formulation and implementation of more open asylum policies in the future. If more open asylum policies are to be encouraged, it is important to learn the lessons of history and develop a more comprehensive understanding of the complex set of factors that affect the asylum policies of African states.

Conclusion

This chapter has traced the history of refugee movements in Africa from the early 1960s to the end of the 1990s and highlighted the changes in African asylum policies. In the 1960s and early 1970s, solidarity with liberation movements and the desire to attract international assistance motivated newly independent African states to adopt a 'zonal development' approach to refugee settlement. This approach proved untenable in the late 1970s and early 1980s as refugee numbers increased and as the economic crisis gripped Africa. The globalization of the Cold War and emergence of proxy wars in Southern Africa and the Horn of Africa politicized the refugee problem, leading not only to security concerns for host states, but frustrating efforts to find solutions. The international donor community, however, seemed unwilling or unable to address these concerns, as illustrated by the outcomes of the ICARA process and the *Draft Declaration* on attacks on refugee camps.

These concerns were compounded in the early 1990s by the end of the Cold War and the proliferation and regionalization of conflict in Africa. The emergence of so-called failed states in Somalia and Liberia not only produced significant refugee flows, but proved difficult to resolve throughout the 1990s, leading to protracted refugee situations. Likewise, the aftermath of conflict and genocide in the Great Lakes brought home with particular force the potential negative impact of hosting large refugee populations, especially following the fall of the Mobutu regime. More generally, the 1990s witnessed an erosion of refugee protection principles in Africa. While the scale and protracted nature of the continent's refugee situations, coupled with concerns about burden sharing and security, clearly contributed to the adoption of restrictive asylum policies in the late 1990s, pressures such as democratization and economic liberalization also played a crucial role.

Given recent developments and the possibility of local integration in a number of African host states, subsequent chapters provide a more comprehensive understanding of the range of factors that explain the nature of asylum policies adopted by countries of asylum in Africa. The following two chapters will critically consider the concepts of burden sharing and the relationship between refugee movements and security in Africa, before the relative importance of these and other factors are considered in the cases of Kenya, Tanzania and Guinea.

3

The Principle and Practice of Burden Sharing with Africa

Burden sharing, in the context of refugees, is the principle through which the diverse costs of granting asylum assumed by the host state are more equitably divided among a greater number of states. In recent years, there has been a perceived lack of global burden sharing, which has been cited by many states, especially in the global South, as a justification for placing limits on the asylum they offer to refugees. Given these restrictions, the fact that the majority of the world's refugees are in some of the world's poorest countries, and the growing tendency of Southern host states to identify adequate burden sharing as a precondition for hosting refugees, burden sharing has become one of the most crucial challenges for international refugee protection. This is especially true in the case of Africa.

Given the importance of this challenge, this chapter examines the principle and practice of international burden sharing with African states and develops a more critical understanding of the concept of burden sharing appropriate to the study of asylum in Africa. By identifying the various mechanisms through which Africa's refugee burden has been shared, this chapter argues that a significant level of burden sharing with African states does, in fact, take place. Crucially, however, the scope and scale of these burden sharing activities are largely based on the interests of donor states, with the priorities and demands of African states influencing the practice of burden sharing in only very limited ways. This limited influence, in turn, can partially be explained by the nature of the relationship between African states and the international donor community and the strategies employed by African host states.

This emphasis on global burden sharing efforts with African states is not intended to suggest that inter-African burden sharing does not occur.

There have, in fact, been a limited number of examples of inter-African burden sharing, such as Tanzania's decision to resettle Rwandan refugees from Zaire in the 1960s. More recently, Benin and Burkina Faso had short-lived resettlement programmes in 2000–02 (Sperl and Bradisteanu, 2004). Given the very limited scale of these activities, however, this chapter concentrates on burden sharing activities by Western donor states with African host states, which has historically been a much more significant area of activity.

The chapter begins by outlining the principle of burden sharing before considering a range of factors that have contributed to the perceived significance of the burden sharing debate in Africa in recent years. Section 2 considers how the refugee burden has been measured, before considering the ways in which the presence of refugees could constitute both a burden and a benefit to host states and refugee-populated areas. The chapter then examines the various ways in which donor states have shared Africa's *financial* and *physical* refugee burden. Based on this disaggregated understanding of burden sharing, section 4 considers the renewed debate on burden sharing to highlight the limited ways in which African states have been able to influence burden sharing discussions. The history of burden sharing in Africa will then be contrasted with examples of burden sharing with South-East Asia and Macedonia to consider what factors have led to successful burden sharing in other regions.

The goal of this chapter is to develop a more critical and disaggregated understanding of burden sharing. This understanding will emphasize the need to consider which state interests determine the scope, scale, sustainability and dependability of financial and physical burden sharing, while also considering the potential ways in which the presence of refugees may constitute a benefit for the host state and refugee-populated area. By applying this disaggregated understanding of burden sharing to the cases of Kenya, Tanzania and Guinea, subsequent chapters will consider the extent to which the characterization of refugees as a burden by host states is influenced by broader political factors unrelated to the presence of refugees, while also considering the extent to which the presence of refugees may constitute a benefit to host states and communities. Given that the perception of refugees as a burden has played a considerable role in justifying more restrictive asylum policies, a more disaggregated understanding of the burdens and benefits associated with the presence of refugees could have important implications for discussions on the future of asylum in Africa.

The principle and significance of burden sharing in Africa

The principle of burden sharing, also referred to as international solidarity or responsibility sharing, has been expressed in a wide range of statements since the founding of the modern international refugee regime in the early 1950s. As expressed in the Preamble of the 1951 Convention, 'the grant of asylum may place unduly heavy burdens on certain countries, and ... a satisfactory solution ... cannot therefore be achieved without international cooperation.' Similar statements have been repeated in numerous UN General Assembly resolutions and in a significant number of Conclusions of UNHCR's Executive Committee over the past 25 years (Hurwitz, 2002, 170–1). More recently, the importance of the principle has also been highlighted by the Global Consultations on International Protection (2000–01), the subsequent Agenda for Protection and the Convention Plus initiative (Loescher et al., 2008, 61–6). While illustrating the desirability of burden sharing, however, these statements do not constitute binding obligations on states and international law, by custom or treaty, does not include a duty on states to engage in burden sharing (Hurwitz, 2002, 191–3).

While burden sharing is not a binding obligation, it is important to understand the link between burden sharing and *non-refoulement*, defined by article 33(1) of the 1951 Convention as the prohibition on expelling or returning a refugee 'in any manner whatsoever to the frontiers of territories where his life or freedom would be threatened'. Unlike burden sharing, this prohibition is binding not only on states party to the 1951 Convention but has also become a principle of customary international law, and is consequently binding on all states in the international system (Goodwin-Gill, 1996, 16–71; and Hathaway, 1991, 24–7). As such, states are generally understood to have a duty to offer, at minimum, temporary protection to refugees entering their territory. The responsibility to host refugees consequently falls primarily on those states neighbouring the refugee-producing country, with most states consequently hosting refugees due to an 'accident of geography' (Hathaway and Neve, 1997, 141). As a result, there is an uneven distribution of refugees in the world, which results in some countries and regions hosting a disproportionate share of the world's refugees, while others are less affected.

To address this unequal distribution, it has been argued that there is an international collective responsibility to uphold the principle of *non-refoulement* through burden sharing. According to Fonteyne (1983, 175), 'burden sharing, certainly in cases of large-scale refugee movements, is a virtual *sine qua non* for the effective operation of a comprehensive *non-refoulement* policy.' Some have argued that in recognizing this implicit link, the drafters of the 1951 Convention understood that 'if the burden became too much to bear, countries of asylum may be forced not to respect the principle of *non-refoulement*' (Kibreab, 1991, 31). As illustrated by recent cases in Africa and elsewhere, host states are more likely to engage in *refoulement* when they believe that they have been abandoned by the international community, suggesting that the link between *non-refoulement* and burden sharing has been under increasing strain in recent years.

A number of factors have added to this strain. First, African states believe that they host a disproportionate share of the world's refugees. In 2006, African states hosted more than 11 million (32 per cent) of the estimated 34 million persons of concern to UNHCR,[1] compared to Western European and North American states who together hosted some 2.8 million (eight per cent) (UNHCR, 2007a, 12). In fact, as illustrated by Table 3.1, Africa has hosted roughly a third of the global refugee population since 1964.

This pattern of distribution gives rise to concerns about the impact of refugees on poorer states, an issue that gained prominence in Africa in the mid-1990s. Following the 1994–96 Rwandan refugee crisis and in response to concerns raised by host states in the region, an assessment of the impact of refugees on host countries has subsequently been presented every year to UNHCR's Executive Committee. These assessments have generally argued that 'from the moment of arrival, refugees compete with the local citizens for scarce resources such as land, water, housing, food and medical services', and that 'over time, their presence leads to more substantial demands on natural resources, education and

Table 3.1 Refugee populations: Africa and Global (1954–2004) (UNHCR, 2000a; and UNHCR, 2007c)

Year	Africa	Global	%
1954	5,400	1,749,500	0.3
1964	1,269,600	3,873,600	33
1974	1,108,600	2,460,600	45
1984	3,408,100	10,685,400	32
1994	6,752,200	15,291,400	44
2004	2,863,400	9,593,000	30

health facilities, energy, transportation, social services and employment' (UNHCR, ExCom, 1997, 1). Such concerns are compounded by the increasingly protracted nature of many refugee situations and the fact that refugees tend to be hosted in more marginal and impoverished areas of the host state. As solutions remain elusive, and as the needs of both refugees and the local population remain unaddressed, host governments come to perceive the hosting of refugees as an unending burden.

These concerns are further exacerbated by the reluctance of donor states to fund protracted assistance programmes, arguing that 'programmes which have already been in existence for a number of years...should be brought to an end as rapidly as possible' (Crisp, 2000, 7). This argument stands in stark contrast with the willingness of donor states to provide assistance to refugees in regions that are seen to be more politically relevant. For example, in 1999, at the height of the Kosovo crisis, it was reported that donors contributed about US$0.11 per refugee per day in Africa, compared to an average of US$1.23 per refugee per day in the Balkans (Vidal, 1999). Likewise, substantial donor support was received for potential refugee movements in the weeks preceding the US-led invasion of Iraq in 2003, while programmes across Africa were simultaneously forced to make budget cuts (interviews, Geneva, 2004).

Measuring Africa's refugee burden

The combined effect of these various pressures has given added significance to the burden sharing debate in Africa in recent years. There is, however, no consensus on how to measure or quantify Africa's refugee burden. In fact, this question has long been a challenge for scholars and practitioners. For example, the technical teams preparing submissions for ICARA II in the early 1980s found that while the assumption that the presence of large refugee populations in poor host states results in a burden was 'widely held' it was 'almost impossible to verify with hard data' (Gorman, 1987, 30).

In an effort to address this problem, a number of indicators have been used since ICARA II to facilitate comparison of the *relative* burden borne by various countries: the total number of refugees in a host country, the number of refugees relative to the national population (refugees *per capita*), and the number of refugees relative to the wealth of the country (refugees *per capita* GDP). While some efforts have been made to refine these measures, they are still generally seen to be the most effective way of ranking countries according to the scale of their refugee burden (UNHCR, 2007c, 73–6). According to these measures, countries in regions of refugee origin bear the greatest refugee burden. For example, when the measure of refugees *per capita* GDP in 2005 is used, the countries with the largest refugee burdens, in declining order, were the DRC (Democratic Republic of the Congo (formerly Zaire)), Pakistan, Tanzania, Ethiopia and Uganda (UNHCR, 2007c, 75).

Such measures, however, provide a highly simplified representation of the refugee burden in any one country. In particular, these figures do not indicate how the presence of large refugee populations may have a differentiated impact on different parts of a host country, nor do they reveal the extent to which the presence of refugees is distributed evenly across a country or concentrated in particular areas. In addition, such quantitative measures do not reveal if the presence of refugees constitutes a burden or a benefit for the host state or local population. As argued by Kibreab (1991, 56), 'a review of the literature on refugee impact on national, regional and local economies and social infrastructure reveals two discernable views. One view looks on refugees as a problem or as a burden on the economies and societies of the host countries, while the other looks on refugees as representing an opportunity for social progress and improved welfare.' For this reason, a more disaggregated understanding of the impact of refugees on host states and communities is required, including an assessment of both the negative and positive impact that the presence of refugees may have.

The benefits relating to the presence of refugees

While recognizing that the presence of refugees may have a *negative impact* on host states, as outlined above, a number of authors have argued that the presence of refugees and refugee assistance programmes can also have a *positive impact* on the development of host communities and host states (Chambers, 1986; Jacobsen, 2005; Jacobsen, 2002; Kibreab, 1985; and Landau, 2003). While accepting that 'the massive influx of refugees in an underdeveloped African country…represents a heavy burden', early research on refugees in Africa also found that 'the presence of refugees can turn from a burden to a stimulus leading to an economic growth and development' (Kibreab, 1985, 119). Such benefits may be experienced either by the local population or by the host state, and should be considered as part of a more comprehensive understanding of the nature of Africa's refugee burden.

In the 1980s, Chambers (1986) and Kibreab (1985, 119–29) both argued that the arrival of refugees in rural areas could lead to regional development as refugees could be settled on underutilized land and contribute to the local economy through increased agricultural production. As noted by Chambers (1986, 250), 'much of the local welcome to rural refugees can be attributed to benefits from the cheap labor they provide.' While arguing that poorer, wage-dependent members of a host community could be adversely affected by the arrival of refugees, Chambers (1986, 245) concludes that 'in rural refugee-affected areas, the better-off and more visible hosts usually gain from the presence of refugees and from refugee programs.' Building on these ideas, Gorman (1986; and 1993) subsequently advanced the notion of refugee aid and development, arguing that a closer linkage between refugee assistance programmes and national development plans would increase benefits for both refugees and local populations.

More recently, Jacobsen (2005; and 2002) has shed additional light on the level of economic activity undertaken by refugees and the political economy of refugee-populated areas. Like Kibreab, Jacobsen (2002, 577) recognizes that while refugees may impose a range of burdens on host countries, they also 'embody a significant flow of resources in the form of international humanitarian assistance, economic assets and human capital'. She notes that the protracted nature of most refugee situations in Africa means that refugee-related resources are available for extended periods, and may be used to attract development assets to regions that remained otherwise underdeveloped. More generally, she argues that the presence of refugees, even with the associated burdens, can contribute to the process of African statebuilding by compelling the state to enhance its control over border areas, or, in the words of Herbst (2000, 1), to more effectively 'broadcast power' to the periphery of the state.

There are, in fact, three ways that the presence of refugees can have a positive economic impact on the refugee-populated area. First, as a result of the presence of a large refugee programme, additional services, facilities and opportunities may be available to the local population. Refugee programmes create local employment as a wide range of positions need to be filled by international agencies and NGOs. There may also be benefits to the local population as humanitarian agencies invest in more reliable transportation and communication networks, especially by building more permanent roads and bridges. Second, many refugee operations include specific programmes to benefit the local population, both to alleviate local burdens and to foster better relations with the local population. In this way, local water sources, schools and hospitals may be rehabilitated. It should, however, be emphasized that given the precarious nature of funding to refugee programmes in

Africa, such activities may be the first to be cut in the event of budget shortfalls. Finally, in situations where refugees are allowed to engage in wage-earning employment, they may significantly contribute to agricultural production and the local economy. As illustrated by the cases of Kenya, Tanzania and Guinea, many of these three forms of benefits are present in contemporary African states.

Ways of sharing the refugee burden: Financial and physical burden sharing

Just as it is important to disaggregate the impact of refugees, it is also important to disaggregate the practice and forms of burden sharing with African states in recent years. There are essentially two ways in which third countries can share the refugee burden of the country of first asylum. First, states may engage in *financial burden sharing* by providing financial assistance to host countries and international agencies to help them provide for refugees *in situ*. Second, states may engage in *physical burden sharing*, by physically relocating refugees to their territory, either through temporary relocation or permanent resettlement. Any consideration of burden sharing in Africa should include an examination of both these mechanisms as financial and physical burden sharing are the two sides of the burden sharing coin (Hurwitz, 2002, 174–87; Hans and Suhrke, 1997; and Acharya and Dewitt, 1997).

Financial burden sharing

There are a number of ways in which donor states may engage in financial burden sharing with countries of first asylum. Financial and material assistance may be provided bilaterally or be channelled through multilateral avenues, such as the World Bank or UNHCR. Material and in-kind assistance may also be channelled through agencies such as the World Food Programme (WFP). This section focuses on the practice of multilateral financial burden sharing through UNHCR, which is taken to be a useful barometer of donor engagement in financial burden sharing more generally. In fact, given that UNHCR has received billions of dollars in voluntary contributions for its work in the past decade, it may be concluded that substantial financial burden sharing does, in fact, take place. This section will examine the scale and dependability of financial contributions to UNHCR, the gap between programme needs and funding, and the practice of financial burden sharing as a means of considering the state of financial burden sharing with African host states.

Any consideration of the state of financial burden sharing should be mindful of the politics of UNHCR's relations with donor countries (Loescher et al., 2008, 91–7). According to Chapter III(20) of UNHCR's Statute, 'no expenditure other than administrative expenditures relating to the functioning of the Office of the High Commissioner shall be borne on the budget of the United Nations and all other expenditures relating to the activities of the High Commissioner shall be financed by voluntary contributions.' As a result, and given the dramatic increase in the organization's operational activities over the past 50 years, contributions from the United Nations Regular Budget now account for less than three per cent of UNHCR's Annual Budget.[2] UNHCR is consequently almost entirely dependent on voluntary contributions to carry out its programmes.

UNHCR's dependence on voluntary contributions is compounded by the fact that a limited number of donor states are responsible for the majority of contributions to UNHCR. Between 1995 and 2005, ten donors accounted for more than 86 per cent of contributions to UNHCR, as illustrated by Figure 3.1.

Moreover, just three donors were responsible for over 50 per cent of all contributions to UNHCR during the same period: the US, the European Commission and Japan.

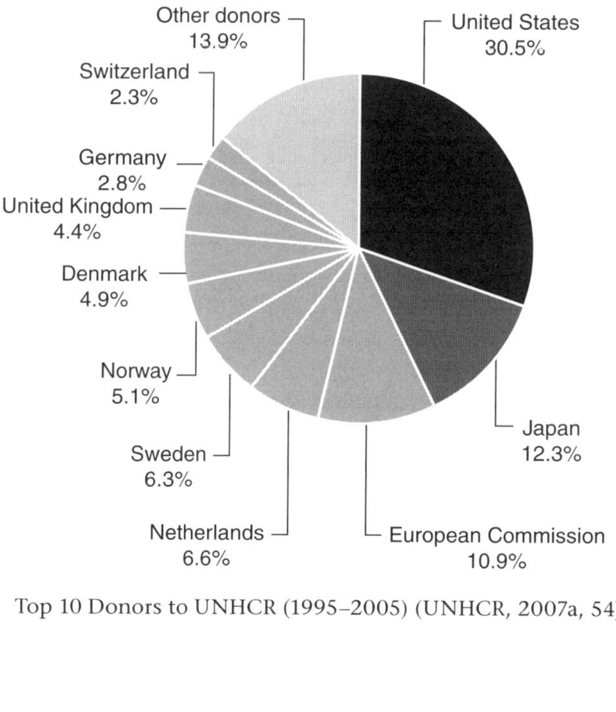

Figure 3.1 Top 10 Donors to UNHCR (1995–2005) (UNHCR, 2007a, 54)

These donors exercise additional control over UNHCR by 'earmarking' their contributions.[3] In 2006, 100 per cent of contributions to UNHCR from the US, the European Commission and Japan were earmarked (UNHCR, 2007a, 82–90). Overall, only 20 per cent of all funding to UNHCR in 2006 was unrestricted, while 52 per cent was earmarked at a regional, sub-regional, or country level, and 28 per cent was earmarked for certain themes (UNHCR, 2007a, 57). Through earmarking of voluntary contributions, donors exercise considerable influence over the work of UNHCR by specifying how their contributions may be used. As a result, programmes considered to be important by key donors receive substantial support, while those deemed less important receive less support. In their study of donor behaviour and humanitarian financing, for example, Smillie and Minear (2003) found that the foreign and domestic policy concerns of donor states are more important determinants of contributions to agencies such as UNHCR than humanitarian considerations.

Since the mid-1990s, donor preference resulted in a regional disparity in funding to UNHCR, with Africa being the clear loser. As argued by Loescher (2001, 335), during the late 1990s, 'while the international community focused attention and resources on the crisis in Kosovo and East Timor, conflict and displacement in Africa were virtually ignored ... donor governments continued to give vastly disproportionate amounts of aid to a few well-known crises and trivial amounts of aid to dozens of other hidden humanitarian emergencies.' Likewise, in August 1999, it was reported that UNHCR had received little more than half of its request for refugee programmes in sub-Saharan Africa. In 2002, another funding crisis loomed as a shortfall of some US$100 million was predicted in contributions to UNHCR's budget. Similar challenges led UNHCR to cut 20 per cent from all programmes in 2006.

At first glance, however, UNHCR's budget does not appear to support this argument of a donor bias against Africa. In 2006, UNHCR's total budget for programmes in sub-Saharan Africa was some US$670 million, more than 47 per cent of UNHCR's global budget of almost US$1.4 billion (UNHCR, 2007a, 62). Given that Africa hosted only 32 per cent of persons of concern to UNHCR in 2006, it may be argued that Africa received a disproportionate share of financial burden sharing. It is, however, important to understand how these funds were earmarked by donors. Over 75 per cent of voluntary contributions to UNHCR's Africa programme in 2006 were earmarked for high-profile operations such as the Chad/Darfur border and repatriations in Liberia and Sudan, leaving less for protracted refugee situations elsewhere on the continent. It may, therefore, be argued that while significant funds have been contributed to refugee programmes in Africa, these funds have been allocated more according to the interests and preferences of donors. Donor preference and the practice of earmarking have meant that significant funds have been allocated to certain high-profile emergencies and repatriations, while other programmes and regions receive little support. Also, given that this pattern has been repeated over a number of years, it may be concluded that neither host states nor UNHCR has been able to alter these preferences and that the interests of donors have prevailed over those of African host states.

Physical burden sharing

The second form of burden sharing is physical burden sharing, either through permanent resettlement to a third country or through temporary relocation. Given the limited practice of temporary relocation, especially in the African context, this section focuses on third country resettlement, defined as 'the making available in a third country, on a voluntary basis, permanent residence to a refugee who is in another country, in a manner where the resettled person enjoys ... rights similar to nationals' (UNHCR, ExCom, 2003c, 6). While no country is under a legal obligation to resettle refugees, refugee resettlement has increasingly been recognized as 'a tangible expression of international solidarity' that allows states to 'help share each other's burdens' (UNHCR, Global Consultations, 2002, 5). While there have been significant developments in recent years in the area of international resettlement policy – namely on the strategic use of resettlement (UNHCR, ExCom, 2003c), the functions of resettlement (UNHCR, Global Consultations, 2002) and the role of resettlement in comprehensive solutions (UNHCR, High Commissioner's Forum, 2004a) – this section focuses on resettlement as a burden sharing mechanism. In particular, it examines the practice of physical burden sharing through the resettlement of refugees from African host states.

Resettlement has long been a feature of the international response to refugee crises. During the Cold War, Western governments, led by the United States, used resettlement not only as a tool of protection for those in need, but also as a means of highlighting the failures of communist regimes. In this way, large-scale resettlement tended to be focused on particular groups of refugees and driven by the foreign policy of Western states (Loescher and Scanlan, 1986). While the end of the Cold War removed many of these foreign policy motivations, domestic pressures, especially in the United States, sustained global resettlement programmes, and made resettlement activities more geographically diverse. According to UNHCR, these shifts resulted in 'significant and positive changes for Africa' (Elizondo, 2001, 2). Through UNHCR, 7776 refugees were resettled from African countries of first asylum in 1995. That number had increased to 14,319 refugees by 2006, representing almost half of the 29,560 resettled refugees assisted by UNHCR that year (UNHCR, Resettlement Section, 2007, 255). While this represents a small fraction of the total number of refugees in the region, it does indicate increased donor interest in one form of burden sharing with Africa.

As with financial burden sharing, many resettlement countries earmark their resettlement offers to specific regions. In this way, seven resettlement countries made specific quotas available for the resettlement of refugees from Africa in 2003,[4] as outlined in Table 3.2 (below).

It is important to note that as UNHCR reported in 2003 that 57,836 refugees in Africa were in need of resettlement on protection grounds (UNHCR, Resettlement Section, 2003c), the quotas in Table 3.2 indicate that resettlement countries expressed a willingness to resettle roughly half of those refugees in Africa identified as being in need of resettlement.

As also indicated by Table 3.2, the US is the largest resettlement country. In fact, the US has resettled more refugees in the past decade than all other countries in the world combined. Between 1975 and 2003, the US resettled over 2.5 million refugees (USA, 2003). While only 135,081 of these refugees were from Africa, pressure from US-based NGOs, including Refugee Council USA, has led to a gradual increase in the resettlement quota from Africa. This quota increased from 7000 refugees per year from Africa in 1998, representing 8 per cent of the US Resettlement

Table 3.2 Geographic resettlement quotas (2003–04) (UNHCR, Resettlement Section, 2003c)

Country	Africa	Global	% for Africa
Australia	1,700	4,000	42.5
Canada	2,100	7,500	28
Denmark	110	500	22
Finland	130	750	17.3
Norway	300	1,630	18
Sweden	125	770	16
US	20,000	70,000	28.5
Total	24,465	85,150	28.73

Program (USRP), to 20,000 refugees per year from Africa in 2003, representing 28 per cent of the programme.

Another motivation for this increase arguably arose from the aftermath of the two month suspension of the USRP following the terrorist attacks on New York and Washington on 11 September 2001. When the programme was reactivated in November 2001, increased security requirements for resettled refugees and travel restrictions on US government officials frustrated resettlement activities in traditional programme areas, especially the Middle East and Southwest Asia. Given domestic pressures to maintain a large resettlement programme, the US government turned its attention to large and identified groups of refugees in need of resettlement from Africa. As argued by Noll and van Selm (2003, 10), the identification of large groups of refugees is 'important to a program facing significant domestic pressure to maintain certain numbers', which has led to 'gradually greater emphasis on Africa as a major producer of refugees, as it once did to emphasis on the Middle East'. As with the interests of donors that affect the scope and scale of financial burden sharing, it is important to emphasize that the increase in resettlement activities in Africa was motivated more by the interests of resettlement countries, like the US, not in response to the nature of the refugee burden articulated by host states in Africa.

Also significant is that while resettlement opportunities from Africa have been increasing marginally in recent years, UNHCR's capacity to identify refugees for resettlement in the region remains low. UNHCR cases have first priority under the USRP, and could theoretically fill the entire quota, but limited processing capacity in UNHCR offices in Africa means that it is unable to submit a significant number of resettlement cases to the US. In fact, UNHCR believes that it only has the capacity to process resettlement applications for 18,850 (68 per cent) of the 27,670 refugees identified as being in need of priority resettlement from countries of first asylum in Africa (UNHCR, Resettlement Section, 2007, 243). While UNHCR has made significant effort since 2000 to increase its resettlement capacity in Africa, its overall capacity remains strikingly low, and the burden sharing benefits of resettlement in Africa have consequently yet to be fully realized.

The renewed debate on burden sharing

Given the link between burden sharing and *non-refoulement*, as outlined above, coupled with a perceived lack of dependability in burden sharing, scholars of refugee law have long debated ways of formulating more structured burden sharing mechanisms (Fonteyne, 1983; Grahl-Madsen, 1980; Grahl-Madsen, 1983; and Weiner, 1995). At the core of early proposals was a common understanding that 'collective action would strengthen protection for refugees by reducing inequities among recipient states' (Suhrke, 1998, 2). The emergence of the 'crisis in asylum' in the mid-1990s gave added momentum to the burden sharing debate, and prompted some, like Hathaway (1997), to reconsider the structures of the global refugee regime to make burden sharing more dependable.

Hathaway's proposals followed the six-year *Towards the Reformulation of International Refugee Law* project, based at the Centre for Refugee Studies (CRS) at York University in Toronto, Canada. At the core of the Reformulation Project's findings was a proposal for a mechanism to ensure the dependability of burden sharing based on four principles (Hathaway, 1997). First, it argued that refugee protection should actively seek solutions in line with state interests. It also argued that refugee law should adopt a more 'robust' concept of temporary protection according to the logic that 'if the protection of refugees is ... respectful of human dignity, it need not be permanent' (Hathaway, 1997, xxiii). The Project also emphasized that there is no need to assume that every state will play an identical role, and outlined how state interests could be more effectively addressed if they were allowed to play a 'common but differentiated responsibility' for refugees (CRS, 1996). Finally, it argued that the institutions of the international refugee regime need to be 'retooled' to 'promote and coordinate a process of collectivized responsibility' (Hathaway, 1997, xxiv), thereby ensuring confidence amongst states that a more systematized and coordinated approach to burden sharing would result in a more dependable response. The Reformulation Project concluded that burden sharing would be more effectively administered if it took place in the context of pre-negotiated responsibilities within 'interest-convergence groups'.

While the proposals were quickly criticized for being unethical, unworkable and contrary to the principles of international refugee law (Anker et al., 1998), it is also important to understand how states responded to these concepts during the 1998 meeting of UNHCR's Executive Committee, where 'International Solidarity and Burden Sharing in all its Aspects' was adopted as the annual theme (UNHCR, ExCom, 1998a). The Chairman's summary of the debate recognized that the theme was challenging 'even though international solidarity and burden sharing are not new concepts' (UNHCR, ExCom, 1998c, 25). There was widespread support for the concept of burden sharing, but not for the systemization of a burden sharing system or for the introduction of obligations in addition to those of the 1951 Convention. There was endorsement for increased 'institutional collaboration at the operational, advocacy and fundraising levels', but 'less support for global mechanisms' (UNHCR, ExCom, 1998c, 25). Clearly, there was little state interest in the type of mechanisms proposed by the Reformulation Project.

It is also interesting to contrast statements made during the debate by Tanzania, one of the largest host states in Africa, and the US, the largest donor and resettlement country. The US delegation encouraged all participants, especially host states in the global South, to not characterize refugees only as a burden, arguing that 'many countries – East and West, North and South – have benefited from the intellectual and economic contributions of individual refugees' (USA, 1998). The US also argued that burden sharing must be focused on solutions, reflecting the donors' reluctance to keep funding long-term refugee programmes, and that the donor community 'should be seen as more than just the handful of nations who contribute the bulk of the cash and commodities to UNHCR'.

In contrast, the Tanzanian delegation noted that 'countries of asylum are to a large extent left to bear the brunt of the burden of hosting the refugees they admit onto their territories' (Tanzania, 1998). In the absence of a global mechanism to apportion responsibility for refugees, Tanzania argued that 'whatever resources that are made available to the countries of asylum remains a matter of charity, left to the discretion of individual [donor] states.' The delegation pointed to the need to address the wide range of burdens faced by host states, assist the local population in refugee-populated areas in addition to refugees, and ensure that burden sharing is sustainable, arguing that 'all the sympathy and support evaporates once there is less publicity given to the crisis.' Crucially, Tanzania noted that 'the recipient countries who bear the brunt of the burden of hosting refugees do not have much say in determining the extent to which they should be assisted by the international community.' These contrasting statements illustrate that differences between host states and donor states, evident during the ICARA process, remained in Africa at the end of the 1990s, and suggest that host states remained unable to significantly influence the terms of the burden sharing debate.

This inability of host states to influence the burden sharing debate has been further highlighted through discussions on proposals from European governments to increase engagement in regions of refugee origin as a substitute for providing asylum in Europe (Betts and Milner, 2006; Oxfam, 2005; and Loescher and Milner, 2003). Oxfam (2005, ii) highlights how, in recent years, 'EU (European Union) member states and institutions have presented an array of initiatives with one common theme: instead of receiving asylum seekers on EU territory, they propose to deal with them abroad.' Such proposals have led to a renewed 'protection in regions of origin debate', and proposals by the UK, the Netherlands and Denmark to develop 'extra-territorial' approaches to protection, where refugees would be prevented from seeking asylum in Europe, but would instead be contained in 'regional protection zones' and resettled to Europe on a limited quota basis (Betts, 2005b, 13–17).

Although such approaches would 'turn the notion of international solidarity on its head' by 'shifting the refugee burden away from richer, more stable countries and placing more of it on poor and unstable countries that already host the overwhelming majority of the world's refugees' (Loescher and Milner, 2003, 603–4), it is striking how the proposals have been presented in terms of burden sharing initiatives. While there may be positive aspects to some of the proposals, including 'financial and technical assistance to refugee-hosting countries ... to provide better legal, physical, and material protection to refugees', there is a more general concern of their being used as 'a means of migration management, reducing the numbers of secondary movements to the EU and creating the conditions for the return of asylum seekers from Europe' to states in the region of refugee origin (Oxfam, 2005, iv). While the investment of additional resources for refugee protection in regions of refugee origin is a potentially important development, it should not come at the cost of undermining the global refugee protection regime by shifting additional burdens onto poor states in regions of refugee origin who already host the vast majority of the world's refugees.

To what extent can African states counter these 'burden shifting' proposals? In addition to the concern expressed by the Tanzanian delegation in 1998 that African host states 'do not have much say in determining the *extent to which* they should be assisted by the international community' (Tanzania, 1998, emphasis added), it could be added that they have limited say in the *ways in which* they should be assisted by the international community. To highlight this dynamic, this chapter now turns to a brief consideration of historical examples of 'successful' burden sharing.

Historical examples of burden sharing

Given the shortcomings in burden sharing articulated by African states, it is important to ask why African states have not been able to exert greater pressure on donor governments to extract more reliable and appropriate levels of burden sharing, especially given the importance of the link between *non-refoulement* and burden sharing. Given the absence of an international legal obligation to engage in burden sharing with host countries, it is also important to consider those situations where international cooperation has successfully resulted in the sharing of the costs of granting asylum more equitably among a greater number of states. In light of the limited results of the ICARA process, as outlined in Chapter 2, this section briefly considers examples of burden sharing with South-East Asia and Macedonia to consider what factors have led to successful burden sharing in other regions.

Refugees from Indochina

The consolidation of communist South-East Asian regimes in 1975 resulted in an estimated 3 million people fleeing Vietnam, Cambodia and Laos in the following two decades (Bari, 1992; Robinson, 1998, UNHCR, 2000a). Most fled in small boats, and many died in shipwrecks or were targeted by pirates. Humanitarianism, coupled with the geopolitical interests of the United States, motivated Western states to recognize the 'boat people' as refugees *prima facie* and to resettle them. More than 550,000 Indo-Chinese sought asylum in South-East Asia between 1975 and 1979, of which 200,000 were resettled. As arrivals continued to exceed resettlement quotas, however, regional states declared in June 1979 that they had 'reached the limit of their endurance and decided that they would not accept new arrivals' (UNHCR, 2000a, 83).

This reluctance, and reports of regional states pushing boats carrying asylum seekers away from their shores, led to the *International Conference on Indo-Chinese Refugees* in July 1979. States agreed that worldwide resettlement quotas would be doubled, that the boat people would be recognized as refugees *prima facie*, that illegal departures would be prevented, and that regional processing centres would be established. The result was a formalized *quid pro quo*; burden sharing through resettlement to Western states in exchange for assurances of *non-refoulement* and first asylum in the region. The immediate results were positive: resettlement increased, 'push-backs' ended and arrival rates fell dramatically as heavy penalties were imposed on clandestine departures. By 1988, however, the number of asylum seekers began to rise dramatically as promises of resettlement resulted in a pull factor. Believing that these new arrivals no longer warranted automatic refugee status, Western countries introduced selective criteria and reduced resettlement quotas. In response, regional asylum countries returned to earlier policies of preventing arrivals, including push-backs.

In light of this new reality, the UN General Assembly called for a *Second International Conference on Indo-Chinese Refugees*. The Conference, convened in June 1989, adopted the Comprehensive Plan of Action for Indo–Chinese Refugees (CPA), which contained a number of mechanisms through which the countries of origin, countries of first asylum and resettlement countries would cooperate to resolve the refugee crisis in Southeast Asia (UNGA, 1988). The CPA is seen to have generally achieved its objectives of reducing the number of clandestine departures and finding extra-regional durable solutions for recognized refugees. In 1989, roughly 70,000 Vietnamese sought asylum in South-East Asia. By 1992, this number had fallen to 41. At the same time, over 1,950,000 refugees had been resettled by the end of the CPA in 1995 – 1,250,000 to the United States alone. On this basis, and notwithstanding a number of criticisms (Bari, 1992), the CPA is seen by many as a success, and a dramatic example of the possibilities of burden sharing arrangements to address refugee crises.

Suhrke (1998, 11) highlights how the strategic interest of the US in the region was a key precondition to the success of the CPA. US interests in the CPA were rooted in its regional strategic interests, domestic public pressure, a sense of responsibility for the victims of the wars in Indochina relating to the Vietnam War, and its desire to support non-communist allies in the region who were facing a heavy refugee burden. Responding to these interests, Suhrke argues, the US played a crucial leadership function by ensuring that the issues remained high on the policy agenda and that key actors remained engaged. As such, the CPA demonstrates that there is potential for burden sharing by a wide range of actors where key states recognize that they have political, economic and strategic interests in a particular region or refugee situation (CRS, 1996, 12–4). Some have argued, however, that as the CPA was undertaken during the Cold War, its relevance to contemporary discussions of burden sharing and comprehensive solutions is limited. To counter this argument, it is useful to consider how similar motivations factored into the international response to the Kosovo refugee crisis.

The Kosovo refugee crisis

The end of the Balkan wars in the mid-1990s did not lead to peace in the province of Kosovo (Barutciski and Suhrke, 2001; Suhrke et al., 2000). By the late 1990s, clashes between the Kosovo Liberation Army (KLA) and Serbian forces had led to the internal displacement of some

175,000 persons. Anxious to avoid another Balkan war, NATO (North Atlantic Treaty Organization) members pressed for UN Security Council Resolution 1199 of September 1998 and the deployment of observers from the Organization for Security and Cooperation in Europe (OSCE) to the region. While this deployment resulted in a temporary lull in the conflict, hostilities continued in January 1999. Following the collapse of peace talks on 19 March, NATO launched a series of air strikes on 24 March 1999.

The NATO air campaign triggered an escalation in the conflict on the ground as fighting between the KLA and Serbian security forces intensified. According to UNHCR (2000a, 234), thousands of Kosovar Albanians were killed and over 800,000 fled or were expelled from Kosovo. Within nine weeks of the start of the NATO air campaign, an estimated 444,600 refugees fled to Albania, 344,500 to the Yugoslav Republic of Macedonia, and some 69,900 to Montenegro (Suhrke et al., 2000, 6). While Albania was generally willing to accept ethnic Albanian refugees, Macedonia, concerned about pre-existing tensions with its own ethnic Albanian minority, refused to allow the Kosovar refugees to enter its territory. In the absence of international commitments to share Macedonia's refugee burden, Macedonia declared that it could not uphold its obligation to *non-refoulement* and closed its borders.

In the first week of April 1999, some 65,000 Kosovar Albanian refugees were left stranded at the Blace border crossing into Macedonia, leading to concerted international efforts to 'unblock Blace' (Suhrke et al., 2000, 36–9). Similar to the international response to the refugee crisis in South-East Asia, negotiations led to a *quid pro quo*: Macedonia agreed to allow the refugees to enter its territory on a temporary basis, to allow for either their evacuation to third countries or their transfer to Albania. In addition, Macedonia received an emergency credit of US$40 million from the World Bank.

Two programmes were devised to share Macedonia's physical refugee burden. The first was the Humanitarian Evacuation Programme (HEP), which resulted in the emergency resettlement, on either a permanent or temporary basis, of some 92,000 refugees to 29 different host countries (UNHCR, 2000a, 239). According to Barutciski and Suhrke (2001, 101), while there were numerous problems in its implementation, 'overall, HEP contributed positively to the protection of the refugees by alleviating the burden on a reluctant host state that feared destabilization.' A more controversial burden sharing mechanism was the Humanitarian Transfer Programme (HTP), through which Albania and Turkey agreed to receive tens of thousands of refugees directly from the Macedonian border. By mid-May 1999, however, only 208 refugees had been transferred to Albania under the programme.

Barutciski and Suhrke (2001, 101) argue that 'the combination of strategic and humanitarian concerns ensured that the Kosovo refugee crisis received extraordinary attention from the powerful Western states' which 'rapidly resulted in a solution based on burden sharing.' Having initiated the bombing campaign without UN Security Council approval, NATO members felt vulnerable to criticism if a humanitarian catastrophe resulted. At the same time, the refugee movement was one of the largest in modern European history. In the aftermath of the Bosnian refugee crisis in the early 1990s, European states were anxious to manage the Kosovo refugee crisis more proactively.

Lessons for burden sharing with Africa

The similarities between the responses to the Indochina and Kosovo crises hold important lessons for burden sharing with Africa. In both cases, countries of first asylum leveraged substantial burden sharing commitments from Western donor states by violating, or threatening to violate, the principle of *non-refoulement*. At the same time, Western states had specific strategic and foreign policy reasons for engaging in both refugee emergencies and for providing substantial burden sharing. Finally, in both cases, the primary means of sharing the burden of countries of first asylum was through physical burden sharing.

Given the asymmetrical relationship between African states and the international donor community, it may be argued that African states are not in a position to leverage the same concessions from donor states as did either Macedonia or South-East Asian states. This is likely for two reasons. First, African states do not have the same political significance of either South-East Asia or Macedonia, especially since the end of the Cold War (Clapham, 1996; and Somerville, 1999). Second, given the dependence of African states on donor countries and lending institutions, as detailed in Chapter 1, it may be argued that African states cannot jeopardize their broader economic relations with the West by threatening to violate the principle of *non-refoulement*. In this way, it may be argued that the nature of burden sharing in Africa may be at least partially explained by the peripheral place that African states occupy in the international system and the limited influence that African states can exert over the international donor community. This link will be examined in subsequent chapters to consider the importance of including such political dynamics in future considerations of burden sharing with Africa, and the potential benefits of setting the debate on burden sharing in Africa within the broader context of Africa's peripheral place within the international system.

It is also important to note that instead of seeking to build on the potential benefits of refugees, African states have tended to focus on the negative impact of refuges on host populations and regions. Over the past 25 years, African states have consistently advocated for compensation from the international community to address these negative impacts (Gorman, 1987, 113; and UNHCR, Africa Bureau, 2001). More generally, African states have highlighted these burdens at the local, national and regional level as a means of advocating for a dramatic increase in levels of financial burden sharing from donor states, and have made little, if any, reference to increased physical burden sharing. In contrast, donor states have, since ICARA, been reluctant to approach burden sharing as a means of compensating states for hosting refugees, and have earmarked financial burden sharing for areas and programmes they deem to be more important. Subsequent chapters will also consider this dynamic, especially given the difficulties inherent in quantifying the refugee burden, to consider the extent to which the characterization of refugees as a burden by host states is influenced by broader political factors unrelated to the presence of refugees.

Conclusion

This chapter has critically examined the principle and practice of burden sharing with African host states. It has argued that while a substantial amount of burden sharing does take place, the practice of burden sharing in Africa has been donor-driven, with the interests of donor states largely determining the scale and nature of burden sharing with African host states. In contrast with other examples of burden sharing, such as the CPA and the Kosovo crisis, African states have not been successful in leveraging substantial burden sharing from donor states. Notwithstanding the problematic task of quantifying a host state's refugee burden, this chapter has also argued for a more disaggregated understanding of burden sharing, including both a consideration of financial and physical burden sharing and a more general recognition of both the benefits and burdens associated with the presence of refugees.

A more disaggregated notion of burden sharing further highlights the significance of a number of concepts that need to be included in the analysis of cases like Kenya, Tanzania and Guinea. In particular, it is important to consider the *scope* of burden sharing by examining the range of burdens that are shared and the various forms of burden sharing, both financial and physical. It is also important to examine the *scale* of burden sharing, namely the quantity of burden sharing with a given host state relative to other states in the region, and the *sustainability* of burden sharing over time, especially as the refugee situation becomes protracted. Finally, the dominant role played by the interests of donor states emphasizes the need to consider what factors will affect the *dependability* of burden sharing. At the same time, the case studies will consider another question raised by this chapter: how can the *benefits* of hosting refugees be understood in relation to the refugee burden?

These concepts will form the basis for examining the burden sharing concerns of Kenya, Tanzania and Guinea in subsequent chapters. Chapter 8 will then revisit this understanding of burden sharing and consider its effectiveness in disaggregating the burden sharing concerns of these host states, while considering the role that broader political factors play in the identification of refugees as exclusively a burden. Before considering these questions in the case studies, the next chapter considers the relationship between refugee movements and security in Africa.

4
Host State Security and Refugee Movements in Africa

While it is widely understood that refugees flee their homes and seek asylum in another country because they are *victims* of insecurity, can refugee movements and the prolonged presence of refugees *cause* security concerns for host states? Host states, in both the global North and South, now cite a wide range of security concerns as a justification for placing limits on the asylum they offer. Host states in Africa have been among the most vocal about the security implications of hosting refugees, especially since the fall of the Mobutu regime in 1996. African states have argued that the arrival of refugees is associated with sources of insecurity ranging from armed elements in refugee camps, the spill-over of conflict, and even the spread of disease. But these concerns are not new. During the Cold War, refugee movements were closely associated with a range of security concerns as so-called refugee warriors played a significant role in proxy conflicts throughout the Third World. Since the end of the Cold War, however, responses to the security implications of refugee movements have changed. While refugee movements as a *consequence* of insecurity may be evident, these changing dynamics highlight the importance of also considering if and how refugee movements may be a *cause* of state insecurity.

Given the delicate balance between state security and the protection of refugees, the changing context within which this balance occurs, and the potentially significant implications of this balance for refugees themselves, it is important to develop a more critical and rigorous understanding of the relationship between refugee movements and host state security. Such an understanding will not only allow for a more nuanced understanding of the legitimate security concerns associated with the movement of refugees, but also more clearly reveal how states may 'scapegoat' refugees and invoke security as a justification for undertaking certain restrictive policies. To this end, the goal of this chapter is to critically examine refugee movements as a cause of state insecurity, especially in Africa. The chapter argues that while the language of security may be abused, and while refugees themselves often continue to experience insecurity while in exile, the hosting of refugees may result in a number of security concerns for African host states and governing regimes. Building on previous work (Milner 2000; Loescher and Milner, 2005; and Loescher and Milner, 2008a), this chapter outlines how these concerns may be divided into *direct security concerns* – resulting from the presence of armed elements within the refugee population, the spillover of violence and the proliferation of small arms within the host country – and *indirect security concerns* – resulting from increased crime and insecurity within the refugee-populated area, grievances against refugees by the local population, and changes in the domestic political opportunity structure arising from the arrival and prolonged presence of refugees.

While many of these concerns are not new, the vulnerabilities of many states in Africa, coupled with the changing nature of conflict and donor engagement in Africa, now lead a number of African states and regimes to portray refugee movements as threats to their security. In response, many have adopted more restrictive asylum policies. This chapter argues that a critical understanding of security appropriate to the state in Africa is required to more fully understand this dynamic. By outlining a conceptualization of security appropriate to contemporary African states, which also considers the range of direct and indirect security concerns perceived by the host state and governing regime, this chapter will consider the extent to which the characterization of refugees as a security concern by host states is influenced by broader political factors unrelated to the presence of refugees.

This chapter begins by highlighting the significance of the relationship between refugees and security and its link to the principle of *non-refoulement* before outlining the security implications of refugee movements during and after the Cold War. The chapter then considers changing understandings of security since the end of the Cold War and reviews the early scholarly literature on refugees and security. After considering the applicability of this literature to the security concerns of host states in Africa, the final section of this chapter develops an understanding of security appropriate to Africa. By assessing the role that vulnerabilities play in the perception of a phenomenon as a security concern by African states and regimes, the final section then develops a framework for understanding the security concerns that may arise as a result of the mass arrival and prolonged presence of refugees.

The significance of security concerns for refugee protection

Refugee movements had security implications for states throughout the twentieth century. The influx of refugees from Russia and the Balkans as a result of World War I exacerbated tensions between European states, prompting the League of Nations to take steps to ensure that the refugee situation was effectively managed (Loescher, 2001, 22–8; and Skran, 1995). Likewise, the United Nations created a number of refugee organizations, including UNHCR, and oversaw the drafting of the 1951 Convention in response to the threat posed to the fragile European state system by the displacement of some 12 million persons at the end of World War II (Loescher et al., 2008, 6–16; and Goodwin-Gill, 1996, 139). As a result of this context, the drafters of the 1951 Convention were significantly influenced by security concerns, and consequently ensured that such concerns were reflected in the functioning of the Convention.

Indeed, Article 33(2) of the 1951 Convention specifies that the benefit of *non-refoulement* may *not* be claimed by '...a refugee whom there are reasonable grounds for regarding as a danger to the security of the country in which he is, or who, having been convicted by a final judgement of a particularly serious crime, constitutes a danger to the community of that country'. Likewise, Article 1(F) of the 1951 Convention *excludes* from refugee status 'any person with respect to whom there are serious reasons for considering' that s/he had 'committed a crime against peace, a war crime, or a crime against humanity', had 'committed a serious non-political crime', or had been 'found guilty of acts contrary to the purposes of the United Nations'. In this way, it is important to begin any consideration of the relationship between refugee movements and security by understanding that the identification of refugees as a threat to the host state's security may allow that state to legitimately derogate from its obligation to *non-refoulement*. In other words, international law recognizes that the security of the host state takes precedent over the protection of refugees.

Such considerations highlight the importance of the issue, and the need for a precise understanding of the relationship so as to not precipitate a further erosion of international refugee protection. It has been argued that states may find instrumental value in portraying refugees as a security concern, thereby justifying restrictions that would be politically popular but not otherwise legally defensible (Huysmans, 2000). In this sense, Chimni (1998b, 287–90) cautions that 'a broadened concept of security allows states to trump the obligation to respect the principle of *non-refoulement*', which, he adds, is precisely why vague definitions of security are so 'attractive to states'. To address these concerns, but mindful of the fact that refugee movements have resulted in legitimate security concerns for states, Weiner (1993, 9) calls for an 'analytical stance that, on the one hand, does not dismiss fears, and, on the other, does not regard all anxieties over immigration and refugees as a justification for exclusion'. The objective of this chapter is to outline such an approach appropriate to the context of Africa.

Refugee movements and security during and after the Cold War

While refugee movements frequently raised security concerns for states during the Cold War, they were largely approached as part of the geopolitics of the East–West struggle (Loescher, 2001, 201–46). In addition to resettling refugees, Western powers provided support to so-called refugee warriors (Zolberg et al., 1989, 275–8). These organized elements of exiled communities, typically intermingled with a refugee population and based in a country of asylum, were engaged in a wide range of armed campaigns against their countries of origin. During the 1970s and 1980s, examples of refugee warrior communities could be found among Afghan *mujahidden* in Pakistan, the *Khmers Rouges* in Thailand, and the Nicaraguan *Contras* in Latin America. As part of the Cold War logic of international security, these groups received Western military and political support, as they 'symbolized for the West the popular rejection of communist governments and served to legitimate the resistance movements' (Loescher, 2001, 11).

Similar groups were also present in Africa (Jacobsen, 1993; and Matthews, 1972). Some groups, like those associated with proxy wars in the Horn of Africa and in Southern Africa, received Western support as part of the logic of the Cold War. Others were linked to wars of national liberation, especially in Southern Africa. A third group of refugee warriors existed in Africa during this period, but were associated with neither proxy wars nor wars of national liberation. These groups, like the Rwandan exiles from the 1960s who formed the basis of the Rwandan Patriotic Front (RPF) (Prunier, 1998; and van der Meeren, 1996), raised a number of concerns for African states, as highlighted by the process leading to the drafting of the 1969 OAU Convention.

All regions of Africa were affected by refugee warrior communities between the 1960s and the end of the Cold War. Concerns about security dominated the treatment of refugee populations in the Horn of Africa, especially given the interplay between refugee populations in, and conflicts between, Ethiopia, Sudan and Somalia in the 1970s and 1980s (Bariagaber, 1999). In Central Africa, UNHCR notes that 'the failure to address the problems of the Rwandan refugees in the 1960s contributed substantially to the cataclysmic violence of the 1990s' (UNHCR, 2000a, 49). In addition to the problem of attacks on refugee camps and settlements in Southern Africa in the late 1970s, the militarization of the refugee population perpetuated the Angolan civil war long after independence in 1975 (Zolberg et al., 1989, 91–4). In West Africa, Guinea's decision to host Cabral's liberation movement resulted in the Portuguese attack on Conakry, as described in Chapter 7. During this period, however, a number of African states were willing to host these populations for political reasons. Liberation movements were frequently hosted as an expression of solidarity with the anti-colonial struggle, while armed exiled communities from independent African states were also hosted as an extension of the host country's interests in the conflict in the country of origin.

The end of the Cold War did not diminish the relevance of refugee warriors, especially in Africa. UNHCR now recognizes that refugee movements often consist of 'mixed movements of populations' which include not only refugees, but also 'armed elements seeking sanctuary in neighbouring countries' (UNHCR, Global Consultations, 2001a, 1). In many cases, refugee warriors use refugee camps as a base for mobilizing against the country of origin, potentially regionalizing conflict (Lischer, 2005, 1–43). The actions of refugee warriors often lead to a breakdown of law and order in camps, and violate the rights of refugees, especially through forced recruitment, physical and sexual violence, and intimidation. Moreover, they frustrate attempts at identifying durable solutions and result in a general hostility towards refugees. Given the changing nature of conflict in Africa, and especially after the fall of the Mobutu regime, most African states appear less willing to host armed elements.

More generally, states in Africa have come to perceive a much wider range of security concerns to be associated with refugee movements since the end of the Cold War. This perception stems not only from the withdrawal of superpower support for regional conflicts on the continent, but also from a heightened sense of vulnerability on the part of many African regimes. Juma (2002, 2) argues that this heightened sense of vulnerability, coupled with the lack of differentiation between refugees and those who should be excluded from refugee status, has contributed to a 'tendency...to collectively criminalize refugees and view them within a security prism'. At the same time, the range of security issues perceived by African states has multiplied, with environmental degradation, rising poverty, the spread of HIV/AIDS, the proliferation of small arms, the spread of crime, and conflict between local groups – all concerns claimed to be associated with refugee movements – addressed as national security concerns. In the context of the external and internal pressures now experienced by African states, many feel limited in their ability to respond. As a result of these pressures, 'refugee protection is increasingly subsumed under the imperatives of security and strategic priorities of hosting states' (Juma, 2002, 23). As argued later in this chapter, a number of these concerns have been exacerbated as a result of US concerns about insecurity and state fragility in Africa since 2001.

Changing notions of refugee movements and security

This proliferation in the perceived sources of insecurity has not been limited to African states. Indeed, the end of the Cold War resulted in a broad revisiting of the nature of security by states and academics alike, with a more diffuse range of issues being identified as security concerns. This process, described by some as a period of 'issue-widening' (Buzan et al., 1998; Ullman, 1983; and Matthews, 1989), grew out of a frustration with the narrow Cold War understanding of security. For Buzan et al. (1998, 2), 'this dissatisfaction was stimulated first by the rise of the economic and environmental agendas in international relations during the 1970s and 1980s and later by the rise in concerns with identity issues and transnational crime in the 1990s.' Part of this period of 'issue-widening' was the emergence of a distinct literature on refugee movements and security. As argued by Gibney (2002, 40), 'the defusing of the major security threat of the post-War period – the threat of nuclear annihilation – provided academics, governments and military officials with a strong incentive to concentrate their energies on a range of new (and hitherto distinctly second rate) security concerns. The "threats" posed by asylum seekers and refugees were simply one of a number of new non-state threats to be formulated in this period.'

Early literature on refugees and security

Loescher (1992) and Weiner (1993) were the first two authors to comprehensively examine the question of refugee movements and state security at the end of the Cold War.[1] Their work made seminal contributions to this area of research by raising the issue of forced migration as both a potential consequence and cause of insecurity, developing a basic typology of migration flows and their related security concerns, and charting a cross-regional framework for future research in the area. Both authors illustrate the importance of the issue by emphasizing the 'high-politics' aspects of international migration. For Loescher (1992, 3), 'refugee exoduses are commanding the attention of high-level policy-makers not only for humanitarian reasons and because of the increasing numbers involved, but also because of the serious consequences that mass displacements have for national stability, international security and the emerging new world order.' Likewise, Weiner (1993, 1) argues that 'migration and refugee issues, no longer the sole concern of ministers of labor and immigration, are now matters of high international politics, engaging the attention of heads of state, cabinets, and key ministries involved in defence, internal security, and external relations.'

At the core of Loescher's work is the argument that, in light of the end of the Cold War, South–South refugee movements would come to present the West with significant security challenges. Loescher (1992, 41) draws on a range of historical examples to outline how 'refugee movements can both create or exacerbate conflict between neighbouring states and challenge the integrity of the host state.' These implications are argued to be particularly acute 'in conflicts involving the spill-over of turmoil across national borders' while 'the activities and ambitions of refugees themselves, as well as those of the governments of asylum and of the guerrilla movements in both sending and receiving states, are additional significant factors in the prolongation and complexity of refugee problems' (Loescher, 1992, 41). Fundamentally, Loescher (1992, 5) argues that 'it is no longer sufficient to discuss the subject of refugees within a narrow national context or as a strictly humanitarian problem requiring humanitarian solutions. Too often, refugees are perceived as a matter for international charity organizations, and not as a political or security problem. Yet refugee problems are in fact intensely political: mass migrations create domestic instability, generate interstate tension and threaten international security.'

While Loescher's argument is rooted in the tradition of international relations, Weiner seeks to locate the question of host state security within the migration literature. In particular, Weiner argues that a 'security/stability' framework should be considered when examining international migration, in addition to a purely economic view. Such a framework, he argues, 'complements rather than replaces an economic analysis by focusing upon the role of states in both creating and responding to international migration' (Weiner, 1993, 5). Weiner's argument is based on a framework of five broad categories or instances in which 'refugees or migrants may be perceived as a threat to the country that produces the emigrants, to the country that receives them, or to the relations between the sending and receiving states' (Weiner, 1993, 11): when the migrants are actively opposed to the regime in the country of origin, and this opposition, and actions motivated by this opposition, becomes a source of tension between the sending and receiving states; when, directly and indirectly, those migrants may come to be seen as a security or political concern for the host state, either through armed campaigns against the host country or through criminal activities of foreign elements within a host state; when the issue of immigrants as threats to the culture of a host community is addressed, before turning to the threats resulting from the social and economic pressures associated with migration; and finally, when 'the host society uses immigrants as an instrument of threat against the country of origin' (Weiner, 1993, 19–21).

Both works have made a significant contribution to the study of the relationship between refugee movements and security concerns, especially as the frameworks they introduced remain the dominant models for understanding the security implications of refugee movements, particularly in the global South. There are, however, two important limitations to these early works. First, neither work incorporates a critical conceptualization of 'security' appropriate to the study of refugee movements. Second, the nature of the security implications of refugee movements portrayed in these works focuses disproportionately on the 'high politics' concerns of states at the expense of 'low politics' concerns. While both works refer to concerns surrounding host community receptivity and questions of ethnic affinity, it is significant to note that domestic, 'low politics', security concerns have proven to be more pervasive and preoccupying for host states, especially in Africa, as outlined below.

It is also important to note how limited the literature has remained in this area following the early work of Loescher and Weiner. As noted by Morris and Stedman (2008, 69), 'despite a few exceptional attempts to bridge the gap between the study of refugees and the study of international security and conflict management, there remains a deep chasm between these two topics.'[2] They argue that 'refugee movements are all too often seen only as a by-product of conflict, with limited attention paid to the various ways they may cause conflict, prolong conflict, or frustrate efforts to resolve conflicts' (Morris and Stedman, 2008, 82). The need to address this gap in the literature is only heightened given the range of security concerns raised by states in justifying restrictive asylum policies.

Understanding security

The development of a more appropriate understanding of the relationship between refugee movements and security should begin with a more critical understanding of the concept of security. Given the relationship between security and *non-refoulement*, however, particular attention must be paid to the scope of the understanding of security employed in relation to refugee movements. In fact, conceptualizations of 'security' should be mindful of the fact that 'the invocation of security has been the key to legitimizing the use of force, but more generally it has opened the way for the state to mobilize, or to take special powers, to handle existential threats. Traditionally, by saying "security", a state representative declares an emergency condition, thus claiming the right to use whatever means are necessary to block a threatening development' (Buzan et al., 1998, 21).

It is essential to highlight this tension: while a clear notion of security is central to dependable refugee protection, given its link to *non-refoulement*, a fluid notion of security is of greater instrumental value to governing regimes, especially vulnerable regimes such as those in Africa. Notwithstanding the dangers of a fluid definition, however, Buzan (1991) argues that security is an 'essentially contested concept' and therefore cannot be effectively defined. Instead of providing a precise definition, argues Buzan, essentially contested concepts 'delineate an area of concern' and that they therefore 'require theoretical analysis in order to identify the boundaries of their application, the contradictions which occur within them and the significance for them of new developments' (Buzan, 1991, 8).

Understanding security since the end of the Cold War

Following Buzan's caution, this chapter does not seek to define 'security'. Instead, its aim is to develop a framework for analysing the security implications of refugee movements for states in Africa. Such a framework should be premised on an understanding of 'security' appropriate for the Third World, generally, and Africa, specifically. In this context, Ayoob (1995) argues that any application of security to the Third World must begin with an understanding of the conditions and histories of Third World states and a critical consideration of the applicability of traditional Cold War notions of security, which, he argues, were dominated by 'two major assumptions: one, that most threats to a state's security arise from outside its borders and two, that these threats are primarily, if not exclusively, military in nature and require a military response' (Ayoob, 1995, 5). He argues that such a historically constructed and Western notion of security simply does not fit with the reality of states in the global South. Indeed, Ayoob outlines how 'despite the rhetoric of many Third World leaders, the sense of insecurity from which [Third World states] suffer emanates largely from within their own borders rather than outside' (Ayoob, 1995, 7).

The questionable relevance of traditional conceptions of security is illustrated by the changing nature of conflict in the global South. The end of the Cold War brought significant changes in the nature of conflict on the periphery of the international system, with a marked proliferation in the number of conflicts and a shift in their focus. In fact, of the 96 armed conflicts recorded between 1989 and 1996, 91 were intra-state, nearly all in the Third World (Stedman and Lyons, 2004). To this must be added an understanding of the regionalization of conflict, with intra-state conflicts in the Third World having the demonstrated ability to engulf whole regions and become 'inter-state conflicts because of the spill-over effect into neighbouring, often similarly domestically insecure, states' (Ayoob, 1995, 7). Within this context, Ayoob argues that the security concerns of Third World states and their particular predicament can be characterized by a shared weakness and vulnerability. The state's primary objective, therefore, becomes the reduction of the deep sense of insecurity from which Third World states and regimes suffer, both domestically and internationally.

This understanding of Third World security provides an important foundation for understanding the possible security implications of refugee movements. While stressing the central importance of the political realm of the state when defining security, Ayoob does not discount the possibility that the political realm cannot be affected by other factors. In fact, Ayoob argues that 'although it retains its primacy in the definition of security, the political realm must be informed by other realms of human activity. However ... when developments in other realms – ranging from the economic to the ecological – threaten to have immediate political consequences or are perceived as being able to threaten state boundaries, political institutions or governing regimes, these other variables must be taken into account as part of a state's security calculus' (Ayoob, 1995, 8). In this sense, refugee movements may constitute a security concern for a host state if they have the demonstrated ability to 'affect the survivability of state boundaries, state institutions, or governing elites or weaken the capacity of states and regimes to act effectively in the realm of both domestic and international politics' (Ayoob, 1995, 9).

It is, however, also important to stress how this sense of insecurity has been intensified by the rise of so-called 'failed', 'fragile' or 'collapsed' states since the end of the Cold War (Rotberg, 2004; and Zartman, 1995). This is especially true in Africa, which was home to 'eight of the world's ten most failing states' in 2007 (Williams, 2007, 1021). While the support of superpowers made state collapse a near impossibility during the Cold War, all regions of Africa contain post-Cold War examples of either failed or failing states, with particular examples to be found during the 1990s in the Horn of Africa, the Great Lakes region and West Africa. As argued by Young (1999, 24), 'until Charles Taylor's band of insurgents sparked a chain reaction of disintegration in Liberia in 1989, and the ouster of Muhammad Siad Barre from Somalia in 1991 triggered a power struggle in which warlords and their clan militia demolished the institutional superstructure of the state, state collapse had never been seriously contemplated as a likely scenario by analysts of African politics.' As illustrated by these examples, however, state collapse became a very real prospect in the 1990s, with the mass outflow of refugees being but one manifestation of the phenomenon.

The prospect of state failure, coupled with the geopolitics of the US-led 'war on terror' since 11 September 2001, has also arguably had a significant impact on the context of security discourse in Africa (Carmody, 2005; Kraxberger, 2005; and Williams, 2007). As argued by Kraxberger (2005, 48), 'the attack of 11 September 2001 and the rise of militant transnational Islamism has prompted American foreign-policy elites to reassess Africa', leading to the point where 'much of the American foreign-policy establishment now views Africa's failing or failed states as real or potential breeding grounds for terrorists.' In particular, Kraxberger (2005, 59) outlines how US security planners have come to pay increasing attention to the weakness of many states in Africa and their limited ability to control their borders, especially focusing on the movement of 'people, weapons and finance', believing that 'if Africa's borders can be tightened up ... terrorists will find it more difficult to operate on the continent.' This dynamic has had a particular impact on the securitization of refugees in Africa, as illustrated by the case of Kenya in Chapter 5.

Security in Africa: State versus regime versus individual security

While this understanding of security is an important point of departure, it is also important to note that the ability of many states and regimes in Africa to 'act effectively in the realm of both domestic and international politics' has been affected by a number of external and internal constraints, as outlined in Chapter 1. Internally, states and regimes have been constrained by the effects of democratization and economic liberalization. Externally, they are constrained by the power imbalance between African states and the donor community. Along with the historical constraints identified by Ayoob, these new constraints, which have coalesced since the early 1990s, have increased the sense of vulnerability experienced by many states and regimes in Africa. As argued by Clapham (1996), these constraints have increased concerns about the survival of a number of African states and regimes. Given that these concerns over state survival have only been heightened by growing evidence of state fragility in Africa, as outlined above, the significance of such constraints needs to be reflected in any framework that considers the security implications of refugee movements in the context of modern Africa.

Such considerations, however, also raise the important question of whose security is at stake – the state's or the governing regime's? This is especially relevant given Buzan's caution that 'the weaker a state is, the more ambiguous the concept of national security becomes in relation to it. To use the term in relation to a weak state, as if such a state represented the same type of object as a strong state, simply paves the way for the wholesale importation of national security imperatives into the domestic arena, with all the dangers of legitimized violence that this implies. The security of governments becomes confused with the security of states, and factional interests are provided with a legitimacy which they do not merit' (Buzan, 1991, 102).

While the fall of the Mobutu regime appears to counter Suhrke's assertion that refugee movements 'rarely represent a threat that even a small and weak state cannot handle on its own by applying some military force' (1998, 6), it is important to ask to what extent refugee movements, coupled with the constraints placed on African states, tend to have greater security implications for governing regimes rather than states. To this end, to what extent is 'state survival' rather than 'regime survival' at the core of the security calculus of African states? Notwithstanding increased concerns about state fragility in Africa, Jackson (1992, 89) argues that while 'African states are externally secure, there is in many of them a persistent and widespread – in some a horrendous – problem of internal security' (Jackson, 1992, 90). Many of these internal security concerns challenge the survival of the regime, not the state.

Similarly, it is important to assess the balance between individual and state security. In some instances the state and governing regime have become one of the greatest sources of insecurity for citizens. In fact, Williams (2007, 1023) argues that 'Africa's people have long been the victims of a powerful and warped version of regime security'. Such an understanding, and a desire to escape this condition, has given rise to the notion of 'human security'. Such an approach takes the individual as the focus and emphasizes two characteristics of security: safety from chronic threats such as disease and repression, and protection from sudden and hurtful disruptions in the pattern of daily life (UNDP, 1994, 22). For its part, UNHCR argues for a 'human security' approach when considering the relationship between refugees and security, emphasizing that 'forced displacement of people is a clear indication that the web of rights and obligations which links the citizen to the state has broken down' (UNHCR, 1997a, 12–13).[3]

Notwithstanding the potential utility of the human security approach to advancing wider debates on security in Africa (Williams, 2007), this book takes the state and the governing regime as the referent objects in its consideration of security. Such an approach is necessary largely because the primary objective of this work is to understand the factors that have motivated the actions of host states, including security concerns. While a human security approach highlights the significant implications of refugee movements and restrictions on asylum for individual refugees, it does not explain how refugee movements can cause insecurity at a local, national or regional level, and therefore does not address the security concerns of host states and consequently their asylum policies. This is not to say that a human security approach is not potentially useful, only to say that it is not the appropriate approach for the purposes of this book.

The importance of taking the host state and governing regime as the referent object, however, is further highlighted by the importance of the state in the granting of asylum. The granting of asylum is tied to access to a territory where the individual fleeing persecution may benefit from international protection to compensate for the lost national protection of the country of origin. While local communities play a significant role in extending this protection, especially in the initial stages of mass influx situations, and while the porousness of borders in Africa makes the prevention of such mass influxes difficult for many states, over time it is the state that determines asylum policies. At the same time, and given that 'one of the primary roles of the state is to provide peace and security for its citizens within the national territorial boundaries as well as to ensure their protection against threats from outside' (Maluwa, 1995, 694), states may be said to have a security imperative. Given this imperative, states are likely to choose security over asylum. As illustrated by the limitations on *non-refoulement* contained in the 1951 Convention, security is a priority for states; the granting of asylum is not. For this reason High Commissioner for Refugees Sadako Ogata argued in the aftermath of the crisis in the Great Lakes region that there was a clear need to 'reconcile refugee protection principles with the legitimate security concerns of states', not the other way around (UNHCR, 1998a, 2).

Understanding refugee movements and security in Africa

Notwithstanding limitations in this area of research, as noted by Morris and Stedman (2008), a number of authors have, in recent years, re-examined the links between refugee movements and security in light of developments in the global South, in general, and Africa, in particular (see: Jacobsen, 2000; Lischer, 2005; and Maluwa, 1995). These works make important contributions to our understanding of the security implications of refugee movements in Africa. For example, Jacobsen breaks down the division between high-politics and low-politics by outlining how refugee movements result in two types of threats: military threats and non-military threats. She argues that 'military threats occur when camps or refugees are directly attacked by being shelled or subjected to raids by rebel forces or regular (government) forces of the host or sending state', while 'non-military threats refer to the violence, crime and intimidation that occurs in the [refugee-populated area], usually in camps, resulting from the absence or breakdown of law and order, or simply as a result of poor planning or policy' (Jacobsen, 2000, 5).

Although Jacobsen's framework is focused on the security concerns of refugees, not on refugee movements as a security concern for the state, her framework makes three important contributions to the development of a framework for understanding the potential security implications of refugee movements in Africa. First, it highlights the need to separate security concerns into broad types, each with different causes and therefore calling for different responses. Second, it points to the importance of disaggregating the state when considering security concerns.

The threats identified by Jacobsen are limited to refugee-populated areas, typically on the periphery of the state. This distinction suggests that different threats and concerns may be experienced and perceived in other parts of the host state. Third, it emphasizes the importance of considering the broader political and security context of the refugee-populated area when considering the specific security implications of refugee movements (Jacobsen, 2000, 13–17). Such broader considerations include the historical background to the influx, domestic political and economic factors at play in the host state, regional political forces and the interests of donors and relief organizations.

Similar to Jacobsen's concern with military threats for host states, the focus of Lischer's work is to understand how refugee crises can cause violent conflict, a more specific category than insecurity. She argues that such conflict is better explained by 'the political context of the crisis', such as the 'origins of the refugee crisis, the policy of the receiving state and the influence of external state and non-state actors', rather than socio-economic aspects of the refugee population (Lischer, 2005, 10). Central to Lischer's work is the argument that the militarization of refugee populations is not inevitable. To this end, she presents a disaggregated understanding of various types of refugee populations to argue which populations are more likely to become militarized and why. Lischer argues that in instances where refugee populations exist as part of a strategy of an exiled political organization and instances where host governments are either unwilling or unable to prevent militarization, refugee populations are very likely to be engaged in violent conflict. In contrast, in instances where refugees have fled generalized violence, and where the host state is both willing and able to exercise its responsibilities towards the security of the refugee population, the potential for violence is very low (Lischer, 2005, 18–43).

It is, however, also important to consider whether individuals engaged in these types of violence would be excluded from refugee status. In particular, the 1951 Convention and the 1969 OAU Convention both *exclude* from refugee status individuals engaged in attacks against the host or sending state. In fact, it is important to differentiate between security concerns arising from individuals or elements within the refugee population as distinct from those arising from refugees themselves. As highlighted by Juma (2002), failure to distinguish between refugees and foreign nationals engaged in activities that would exclude them from refugee status frequently leads to an unnecessary securitization of the refugee population as a whole. Likewise, Nowrojee (2000) argues that this lack of differentiation may be a deliberate strategy on the part of the host state to facilitate the securitization of the entire refugee population for political purposes.

In contrast with Lischer and Jacobsen, whose works draw from examples in the global South more generally, Maluwa (1995) roots his consideration of the security implications of refugee movements exclusively in an African context. Taking the state as his referent object, Maluwa highlights how changing notions of security since the end of the Cold War have led a number of states in Southern Africa to perceive the presence of refugees as a security concern in various ways. Maluwa emphasizes that refugee movements may result in both high-politics and low-politics security concerns for states. For example, while the militarization of refugee populations and the presence of armed elements within the refugee population may 'exacerbate and influence relations between states in many ways', Maluwa notes that it is equally important to consider how the presence of refugees can 'exacerbate domestic political tensions' (Maluwa, 1995, 656–7). Maluwa cautions, however, that 'feelings of resentment and suspicion' towards refugees may be fanned by unrelated political and economic forces, and may lead to a point where 'poverty, unemployment, scarcity of resources, and even crime and disease, are suddenly attributed to the presence of these refugees' (Maluwa, 1995, 657). Such considerations illustrate that the range of security concerns that have come to be associated with the presence of refugees extend far beyond military threats and the question of refugee warriors.

Building from these works and the understanding of security presented above, the security concerns of host states in Africa may be divided into direct and indirect security concerns (Milner, 2000; Loescher and Milner, 2005; and Loescher and Milner, 2008a). *Direct security concerns* address the high-politics concerns of states, and stem from the presence of armed elements within the refugee population, the spillover of violence and the potential regionalization of conflict. In contrast, *indirect security concerns* address the low-politics concerns of states, and arise when the presence of refugees exacerbates previously existing intercommunal tensions in the host state, shifts the balance of power between communities, or causes grievances among local populations. Differentiating security concerns in this way not only highlights the security implications of neighbouring a refugee-producing state, as opposed to the hosting of refugees, but also helps identify the legitimate security concerns of the host state, as opposed to instances where the host state securitizes the presence of refugees for broader political reasons. This section now presents the key elements of this framework, which will then be applied to the cases of Kenya, Tanzania and Guinea. The framework will then be reconsidered in Chapter 8 to illustrate how the security concerns of states can usefully be disaggregated in this way, but also how broader political factors often play an important role in the construction of refugees as a security concern.

Direct security concerns

The direct security concerns faced by the host state, posed by the spill-over of conflict and the presence of 'refugee warriors', is by far the strongest link between refugee movements and insecurity. Here, there are no intervening variables between refugee movements and insecurity, as elements associated with the refugee movement are actively engaged in armed campaigns typically, but not exclusively, against the country of origin. Such campaigns have the potential of regionalizing the conflict and dragging the host state into what was previously an intra-state conflict. As highlighted by Dowty and Loescher (1996, 49), the presence of armed elements in contentious border regions makes their presence especially salient as 'raids and guerrilla activity across the border may drag the host state into an existing conflict and, in fact, this may be the deliberate strategy of the armed exile group.'

The security implications of such activities for host states are real. They may include cross-border attacks on refugee-populated areas, the proliferation of small arms within the host state and the expropriation of humanitarian resources by armed groups. In such situations, armed groups hide behind the humanitarian character of refugee camps and settlements, use these camps as an opportunity to recruit among the disaffected displaced populations and draw upon humanitarian aid, including food, medical assistance and other support mechanisms, to support armed campaigns. Such activities may be perceived by host states as infringements on their sovereignty, especially given the varying control many host states have over their border regions. Direct security concerns can also lead to serious bilateral and regional diplomatic tensions, as illustrated with the case of Tanzania in Chapter 6, can violate core principles of international refugee law, and, at their most extreme, constitute threats to international peace and security.

Indirect security concerns

Refugee movements may also result in indirect security concerns, which are more difficult to identify but potentially just as significant as direct concerns. This is a key concept that has been largely overlooked in both academic and policy considerations of the security implications of refugee movements. In these cases, refugees alone are a necessary but not a sufficient cause of host state insecurity. It is not refugees that are the source of insecurity, but the context within which they exist that contributes to their securitization. Indirect concerns may arise when the presence of refugees exacerbates previously existing intercommunal tensions in the host country, shifts the balance of power between communities, or causes grievances among local populations. Local and national grievances are particularly heightened when refugees compete with local populations for scarce resources, jobs and social services, including health care, education and housing. Refugees are sometimes seen as a privileged group in terms of services and welfare provisions, or as the cause of low wages in the local economy and inflation in local markets. Refugees are also frequently scapegoats for a breakdown in law and order, both in refugee-populated areas and in urban centres.

Indirect security concerns are largely affected by shifts in the political opportunity structure and by an increase in grievances towards refugees. 'Political opportunity' can be understood as the 'consistent dimensions of the political environment that provide incentives for people to undertake collective action by affecting their expectations for success or failure' (Tarrow, 1994, 85). According to this understanding, when groups hold an advantage in the area of resources, alignments, elite support and potential allies, they will act against the holders of power, based on the belief that their likelihood of success has been increased (Tarrow, 1994, 81–8). Two key features of political opportunity structures must be emphasized. First, they are relative, with a group's opportunity measured in relation to competing groups. Therefore, political opportunity can be seen as a zero-sum game, where a gain in resources or allies by one side represents a relative loss for another. Second, political opportunity structures change. Groups are motivated to act when the balance is perceived to be in their favour.

This notion relates to the security concerns of host states in two ways. First, Loescher (1992, 42) has argued that 'in countries which are divided into antagonistic racial, ethnic, religious or other groupings, a major influx can place precariously balanced multi-ethnic societies under great strain and may even threaten the political balance of power.' Indeed, such concerns are specifically linked to the understanding that the presence of refugees has been demonstrated to accelerate 'existing internal conflicts in the host country' (Weiner, 1993, 16). While such concerns were central to Macedonia's decision to close its border to the arrival of Kosovar Albanian refugees, as outlined in Chapter 3, it is also important to consider how they apply in the African context.

Second, and especially in the context of democratization, understandings of political opportunity structure illustrate how competition arising from such constraints limits the space within which the state can make policy decisions. Rutinwa (1999, 2) notes that the rise in xenophobia against refugees and foreigners in Africa has 'emerged at a time when most of Africa is democratizing and governments are compelled to take into account public opinion in formulating various policies.' Indeed, just as 'government leaders found themselves facing more and more pressures to restrict entry' as 'asylum became part of the cut and thrust of domestic politics' in Western Europe in the 1980s (Gibney, 2001, 7), 'the rise of multiparty democracy in Africa...has arguably diminished the autonomy of state elites in determining the security agenda' (Gibney, 2002, 40).

It is, however, important to note that recent work on democratization, especially in Africa, has not problematized the process and its consequences for a state's social and humanitarian policy. The literature on democratization in Africa generally sees democracy as having only positive benefits, and prioritizes its expansion and consolidation as quickly as possible (Ambrose, 1995; Bratton and van de Walle, 1997; Conteh-Morgan, 1997; Gyimah-Boadi, 2004; and Hyslop, 1999). In contrast, the case of asylum policies would appear to indicate that democratization does not bring exclusively positive results, and may have a negative impact on refugee protection, as discussed in Chapter 8.

Notions of political opportunity structures also help explain the dynamics of internal competition between the core and periphery of a state, and how the presence of refugee camps typically on the periphery of a state influences this dynamic. The presence of large numbers of refugees on the periphery of a state may give that region significance that it did not previously posses. This is particularly true when the political geography of the African state is considered. Herbst (2000, 3) argues that 'states are only viable if they are able to control the territory defined by their borders' and that such control is 'assured by developing an infrastructure to broadcast power and by gaining the loyalty of citizens'. As African states have concentrated power in economic centres and often have very limited control over the periphery of the state, the presence of large refugee populations in these 'hinterlands', combined with the large presence of international relief agencies, may come to constitute a serious concern for the governing regime.

These dynamics may combine with more traditionally understood direct security concerns in potentially significant ways. Herbst (2000, 255) argues that, 'unlike the situation in the 1960s where the government had all the guns', recent movements on the periphery of the state have demonstrated the ability to 'procure weapons on the international market, especially after Central European countries began to dump their stocks when the Cold War came to an end'. This fact, combined with examples of organized and effective armed opposition groups being formed in the border regions of several African states in the 1990s, clearly adds to an understanding of why African states are increasingly concerned about the security implications of large, insecure refugee camps and settlements in their hinterland, as illustrated by the case of Guinea in Chapter 7. This gives rise to concerns about the 'politics of the border' (Clapham, 1996, 215–22), and the need to consider the dynamics between areas of the state in the formulation of asylum policies.

Somewhat paradoxically, however, most states have kept refugee camps and settlements on the periphery of the state, possibly in an attempt to minimize the impact that refugees can have on the opportunity structure at the economic and political core of the state. As Crisp (2003a, 6) has observed, 'one of the most evident characteristics of Africa's protracted refugee situations is that they are usually to be found in peripheral border areas of asylum countries: places which are insecure, where the climate and conditions are harsh, which are not a high priority for the central government and for development actors, and which are consequently very poor.' As such, it is important to consider why refugee camps are located where they are, and the extent to which political factors contributed to their establishment in such remote locations. These dynamics are particularly evident in the case of Kenya, as argued in Chapter 5.

Another important characteristic of refugee camps highlighted by Crisp (2003a, 13–17) is the prevalence of concerns relating to material and psychological deprivation among refugees who inhabit them. In many states in Africa, refugees are required to remain in refugee camps and are prohibited from engaging in economic activity outside the camp, making them fully dependent on international assistance to meet their basic needs. When this assistance is interrupted or reduced, refugees may turn to alternative coping mechanisms. These coping mechanisms may range from leaving the camp illegally, which would result in a statistical increase in crime rates, to theft of local food crops, prostitution and banditry. These are many of the non-military threats identified by Jacobsen that are associated with the interplay between asylum policies and levels of international assistance to encamped refugees. Such concerns have been most notable in the case of Tanzania, as outlined in Chapter 6.

Crucially, however, not all refugees are perceived as threats. The question of which refugees are seen as threats, and why, may be partially explained by understanding whether they are perceived as members of the local political community or as outsiders. As Maluwa (1995, 672) argues, 'unwanted migrants and refugees may cause...intercommunal tensions within a receiving state' due to either antagonistic ethnic, cultural, religious or linguistic forces within the host population or where refugees are seen as being in competition for scarce resources. In this sense, the importance of affinity and shared group identity cannot be overstated. If a host community perceives the incoming refugee as 'one of us', then positive and generous conceptions of distributive justice will apply. The empirical evidence is overwhelming. As Loescher (1992, 42) argues, during the 1980s, 'the remarkable receptivity provided to millions of Afghans in Pakistan and Iran, to ethnic kin from Bulgaria in Turkey, to Ethiopians in the Sudan, to Ogadeni Ethiopians in Somalia, to southern Sudanese in Uganda, to Issaq Somali in Djibouti and to Mozambicans in Malawi has been facilitated by the ethnic and linguistic characteristics they share with their hosts.'

Conversely, if the refugees are seen as members of an 'out-group', they are likely to receive a hostile reception. In cases where there is a division along ethnic, linguistic or religious lines, 'a major population influx can place precariously balanced multi-ethnic societies under great strain and may even threaten the political balance of power' (Loescher, 1992, 42). Indeed, even UNHCR's Executive Committee recognized in 1997 that refugees, 'as an out-group, can be blamed for all untoward activities'. As Chapter 8 will argue in more detail, the increasing perception of refugees as an 'out-group' has been reinforced by economic liberalization and democratization in two ways. First, economic liberalization and the imposition of structural adjustment programmes now means that the local population must pay user fees for services that refugees continue to receive for free within refugee camps. Second, democratization has reinforced boundaries between nationals and foreigners in many African countries, which has contributed to an erosion of solidarity with refugees and contributed to the introduction of more restrictive asylum policies.

Such considerations also illustrate the importance of the 'scapegoat strategy' employed by many regimes in Africa as a means of ensuring their survival. Job (1992, 29) notes that a common security strategy of regimes in weak states is to 'focus upon external enemies...to try to create a common national concern and mobilize support around the state (i.e., regime) and its efforts against this threat'. Such a strategy is often deployed when the regime is under pressure and seeks to either divert attention from its inability to respond to popular demands or to rally the support of the population by emphasizing a common objective against an outside group. In this way, Crisp (2003, 4) highlights that 'politicians have an interest in mobilizing electoral support on the basis of xenophobic and anti-refugee sentiments', especially in the context of the range of internal and external pressures faced by African states. As the following case studies will show, Kenya, Tanzania and Guinea have all employed the tactic of scapegoating refugees in response to such pressures.

Conclusion

The scapegoating of refugees and the identification of *bone fide* refugees as security concerns, thereby justifying exclusion, has led a number of commentators to express concern about the linking of refugees and insecurity in academic research. For example, Chimni (1998b, 284) argues that the recent attention paid to the links between refugee movements and security by researchers and policy-makers 'presents a disturbing trend'. While Chimni concedes that refugee flows may have security implications for host states and for the international community, he emphasizes that 'it is one thing to address the legitimate security concerns and another to define and articulate humanitarian interests in the matrix of an elastic concept of security eminently manipulable by states' (Chimni, 1998b, 286). These concerns should remain at the core of our understanding on the relationship between refugee movements and security.

Mindful of these concerns, this chapter has critically examined notions of security as they apply to the relationship between refugee movements and security in Africa. It has argued that refugee movements had security implications for states, both in Africa and elsewhere, throughout the twentieth century. While refugees may be scapegoated for political reasons and the language of security abused, this chapter has argued that refugee movements may result in legitimate security concerns for host states in Africa. Based on an examination of the notion of 'security' relevant to Africa and of past literature on refugees and security, this chapter proposed a framework for understanding the security concerns of states as either direct or indirect security concerns. This framework differentiates between the security concerns caused by refugees as opposed to other elements within or associated with the refugee population. At the same time, this framework helps distinguish the various causes of insecurity experienced at different levels of the state, and highlights the linkages between the securitization of refugees and the rise in internal and external constraints on the state in Africa, especially arising from economic liberalization, democratization and declining donor engagement in protracted refugee situations.

The following sections of this book consider the understandings of burden sharing and security presented in Chapters 3 and 4 in the context of three major African asylum countries. The cases of Kenya, Tanzania and Guinea will be used not only to examine the utility of these frameworks, but to highlight the full range of issues that affect a state's asylum policies. The lessons drawn from these cases will lead to a more comprehensive understanding of the politics of asylum in Africa, as detailed in Chapter 8.

5
Kenya

Kenya's asylum policy was profoundly affected by the arrival of over 400,000 refugees from Somalia in 1991 and 1992. After initially trying to prevent their arrival, Kenya opened its borders and allowed hundreds of thousands of refugees to enter its territory, a move that won praise from the international donor community for the regime of President Daniel arap Moi. At the same time, however, Kenya placed significant restrictions on the quality of asylum it extended to refugees. Claiming that the sheer number of new arrivals had caused the collapse of Kenya's previously open asylum policy, the government ceased to conduct individual status determination interviews for new asylum seekers. Refugee affairs were transferred almost exclusively to UNHCR, who became responsible for the establishment and running of camps in government-designated areas. Finally, Kenya imposed restrictions on access to employment and freedom of movement for refugees, stipulating that refugees live in designated camps.

Kenya has been widely criticized for adopting and maintaining a restrictive asylum policy, especially by the human rights community (Verdirame, 1999). While it is important to highlight the shortcomings of Kenya's approach, it is also important to understand *why* Kenya has acted the way it has, especially in the face of such international criticism. Why did Kenya adopt this dual policy of abdication and containment in the early 1990s, and why has the policy been largely continued, notwithstanding the stabilization of the refugee population since 1995? This chapter argues that while the protracted nature of the refugee situation, diminishing donor support and a multiplicity of security concerns have been highlighted by the government to justify its continued policy of containment, and while there may be very tentative signs of a shift in Kenya's policy (Kagwanja and Juma, 2008), additional factors have also played a significant role in the formulation and continuation of Kenya's policy towards Somali refugees. In particular, historical factors, including memories of the *shifta* wars and the securitization of Kenyan politics by the Moi regime after the attempted *coup* in 1982, resulted in the construction of all Somalis, both Kenyan and Somalian,[1] as threats. Domestic and international factors, including the suspension of aid to Kenya in 1991, externally-imposed democratization and Kenya's role in the US-led 'war on terror' since 11 September 2001, have further served to limit the space within which Kenyan asylum policies for Somali refugees have been formulated. By illustrating how these historical, domestic and international factors, unrelated to the presence of refugees, have played a significant role in Kenya's response to Somali refugees, this goal of this chapter is to illustrate how Kenya's asylum policy is best understood when examined from a broader political perspective.

Although Kenya hosts refugees from more than ten countries,[2] this chapter focuses primarily on the question of Somali refugees in Kenya. While reference is made to other nationalities, this chapter concentrates on the Somali refugee population for three reasons. First, the Somali population remains the largest refugee group in Kenya. Second, the arrival of Somali refugees precipitated the change in Kenyan policy in 1991–92. Third, many Kenyan policy-makers continue to see the Somali refugees as the most problematic refugee population in Kenya. Interviews with UN and NGO representatives in Nairobi suggested that Somali refugees have consistently been the refugee population of greatest concern for Kenya, and consequently an understanding of Kenya's approach to Somali refugees could provide important insight into the Kenyan approach to refugees more generally (interviews, Nairobi, 2001 and 2004). The chapter begins by briefly considering Kenya's asylum policy prior to 1991 before outlining the scale of the Somali refugee emergency in 1991–93, Kenya's policy response, and the government's justification for adopting and maintaining its policy of abdication and containment. After critically examining the elements of this justification, the chapter concludes by examining broader historical, domestic and international factors that have played a predominant role in shaping Kenya's asylum policy for more than 15 years.

Kenya's asylum policy prior to 1991

Almost every country in East Africa witnessed some period of civil conflict in the second half of the twentieth century, which, in turn, produced large numbers of refugees. In particular, conflict, violence and revolution in the Sudan, Uganda and Ethiopia from the 1960s to the late 1980s resulted in significant numbers of refugees fleeing to neighbouring countries. Countries of origin became countries of asylum, as the web of displacement became entangled in regional and global alliances, which, in turn, fuelled the cycle of violence.

Kenya shares borders with all three of these states, but was largely isolated from the refugee flows that accompanied these conflicts. It was not until 1987 that the number of refugees in Kenya exceeded 10,000 (UNHCR, 2000a, 311–10). The majority of these refugees were from Uganda, many of whom brought skills as doctors and teachers that contributed to Kenya's development and relative prosperity. This contribution, in turn, 'tempered hostility against asylum seekers' (Kagwanja, 2002, 98). Recognizing the benefits of hosting refugees, Kenya pursued an open asylum policy. Individual status was granted by a government agency, and refugees enjoyed freedom of movement, access to employment markets, and the benefits of many of the social rights detailed in the 1951 Convention. While the priority in this period was to socially and economically integrate refugees as quickly as possible, there was no formalized refugee policy or national refugee legislation. Prior to 1991, Kenya's open refugee policy operated on a largely *ad hoc* basis.

The Somali emergency and system collapse: 1989–93

This approach changed dramatically with the arrival of the first Somali refugees in the late 1980s and early 1990s. From 1989 until the fall of the Barre regime, the Kenyan military maintained a large presence at the border and off the Kenyan coast to prevent the arrival of Somali refugees. With the exception of former government officials and military officials associated with the Barre regime, who were granted asylum in Nairobi, thousands of Somalis were prevented from entering Kenya, through forcible return at the border and by 'push-backs' of boats carrying Somalis. The situation changed dramatically in early 1991 with the fall of the Barre regime and a significant increase in the number of Somalis seeking refuge in Kenya. In March 1991, there were an estimated 16,000 refugees in Kenya. That number rose to 39,000 by July, and to 92,200 by December 1991. The rate of arrival continued to climb the following year, as the refugee population in Kenya reached an estimated 246,000 in May 1992 and peaked at 427,278 by the end of 1992. The refugee population in Kenya had grown by more than 400,000 in just two years.

Kenya's *ad hoc* refugee system was overwhelmed, and President Moi appealed to the international community to come to Kenya's aid.

He lifted the state of emergency in the North Eastern Province[3] and requested UNHCR to respond to the refugee crisis. It was clear that a new approach was required and that 'UNHCR and international NGOs were needed... since the large numbers of arrivals far outstripped the government's ability' to respond (Parker, 2002, 34). Seven new refugee camps were opened in 1992, stretching from Mandera and El-Wak in the extreme north-east corner of Kenya to Utange and Hatimy, practically suburbs of Mombasa, Kenya's second largest city and an important port on the Indian Ocean. Refugees were transferred to the camps, and the government transferred responsibility for camp management to UNHCR.

As UNHCR later reported, however, its capacity in Kenya was not immediately able to fully respond to the scale of the challenge: 'UNHCR's staff in Kenya was small at the time, and geared toward addressing the protection needs of a relatively small, urban caseload... Support, in terms of human resources and material, was often slow in coming. When it did arrive, it was frequently inadequate' (UNHCR, Inspection and Evaluation Service, 1996, 6). As a result, death and malnutrition rates among the refugee population soared through 1992, while cross-border raids by Somali elements posed a significant security threat to refugees and aid workers. Death rates reached 100 a day per 100,000 refugees, five times higher than 'normal' levels. Malnutrition rates were recorded as high as 54 per cent among refugee children in some camps, reported to be 'one of the worst results in years anywhere in Africa' (USCR, 1993, 63).

In an attempt to reduce the extremely high levels of morbidity and mortality in the camps, UNHCR introduced a range of programmes in 1992 to respond to the needs of vulnerable populations. To support these activities, UNHCR issued an appeal for an additional US$37.5 million in donor support on 15 May 1992. Within the first month, donors pledged US$14.7 million, of which US$8.5 million was from the US. Finally, in June 1993, UNHCR declared that the emergency was over. The number of arrivals had fallen dramatically, and UNHCR had succeeded in consolidating those refugees remaining in Kenya into ten refugee camps and, working with almost thirty implementing partners, had begun to shift from an emergency operation to a 'care and maintenance' programme.

The stabilization in the number of refugees was not, however, mirrored in the stabilization of their security. Bandits, collectively referred to as *shiftas,* continued to attack refugees and relief workers seemingly at will, targeting the camps in search of food and money. Refugee women and girls were especially victims of insecurity, with a significant increase in cases of rape and sexual abuse (Crisp, 1999a; UNHCR, Inspection and Evaluation Service, 1996). For many, it was clear that the violence in Southern Somalia had spilled over into Kenya. Human rights organizations reported that former Somali government soldiers and other armed groups routinely staged raids into North Eastern Kenya and then 'retreated over the border, eluding capture by Kenyan security forces' (HRW, 1995, 37). Accordingly, the location of the refugee camps, just a few miles from the Kenya–Somali border, significantly compromised the security of refugees (UNHCR, Central Evaluation Section, 1994, 2).

Kenya's post-1991 asylum policy: Abdication and containment

Kenya's response to these events was striking. Instead of increasing its presence in the border areas in response to these violations of its sovereignty, or moving the camps away from the border to reduce threats to its national security, Kenya pursued a new refugee policy centred on two principles: 'abdication' of responsibility for refugees to UNHCR (Kagwanja, 2002, 102) and the containment of the refugee population on the periphery of the state. While the government generally kept its borders open to new arrivals, both during the 1991–93 emergency and subsequently, it placed increasing limits on the quality of asylum it offers to these refugees by insisting on their containment in isolated camps. In stark contrast to the government's approach prior to 1991, which actively promoted the integration of refugees, these two priorities continued to drive refugee policy in Kenya, certainly until the election of a new government in 2002 and the passage of the 2006 Refugee Act.

The first feature of Kenya's post-1991 approach was the abdication of responsibility for refugees from the government to UNHCR. Notwithstanding the principle that the primary responsibility for refugees lies with the host state, 'a deliberate choice was made by Kenyan government officials in the 1990s to largely cede refugee affairs to UNHCR' (Helton, 2002, 161). In the words of one senior Kenyan government official as recently as 2004, the state bureaucracy believed that refugees were 'the UNHCR's responsibility, not ours' (interview, Nairobi, 2004). As a result, UNHCR assumed a wide range of responsibilities that would normally have fallen under the authority of the host country, including refugee status determination and the administration of refugee camps.

In considering whether this abdication of responsibility was by accident or design, it is important to note that the Moi regime had drafted national refugee legislation in 1990, which would have formalized its *ad hoc* approach to refugees, but did not take steps to have it pass through Parliament following the influx of Somali refugees. The draft legislation included proposals for appointing a refugees coordinator and establishing a Committee on Refugee Status and a National Council on Refugees, and detailed on the rights and duties of those recognized as refugees by the Committee (Kenya, 1990). While the Bill would have provided the legal basis for government responsibility for refugee affairs, it was not brought before Parliament by the Moi regime.

In contrast, the National Rainbow Coalition (NARC), led by Mwai Kibaki, made refugee legislation a priority shortly after its election in late 2002. As part of the new government's effort to re-engage the international donor community, a draft Refugee Bill, based largely on the 1990 Refugee Bill, was introduced in 2003 and finally passed in 2006 (Kenya, 2007). Although passage of the legislation took some three years, and resulted in particularly heated debate, as outlined below, refugee advocates welcomed the 2006 Refugee Act as an important step forward in Kenya's management of the refugee populations on its territory (RCK, 2006). In particular, the 2006 Refugee Act includes provisions for the establishment of a Department of Refugee Affairs, which would assume responsibility 'for all administrative matters concerning refugees in Kenya' and would 'in that capacity, co-ordinate activities and programmes relating to refugees' (Kenya, 2007, 6). UNHCR hopes that the establishment of the Department will allow it to 'shift its focus from directly protecting and assisting refugees to a more advisory function' (UNHCR, 2007b, 147). While it is too soon to assess Kenya's ability and willingness to fully implement sections of the 2006 Refugee Act relating to the management and coordination of the refugee programme, it may be an early indication of potential shift in one aspect of Kenya's refugee policy (Kagwanja and Juma, 2008, 225–6).

The second element of Kenya's post-1991 refugee policy has been containment. Since 1991, Kenyan policy has been to contain refugees in camps, located in isolated and insecure border regions. According to the Refugee Consortium of Kenya (RCK), 'the government implements a refugee encampment policy' whereby refugees 'are obliged to reside in a camp while awaiting a durable solution' (RCK, 2003a, 17). Refugees must reside in camps to qualify for assistance, and those refugees found outside the camps are classified as illegal aliens and subject to deportation.[4] Unlike the policy of abdication, the 2006 Refugee Act does not contain provisions to reverse this policy. This stands in contrast to its pre-1991 policy of allowing freedom of movement for refugees to facilitate their self-sufficiency and local integration.

While encampment has been one of the hallmarks of Kenya's approach to refugees, it is also important to consider where these camps are located. Since the stabilization of the refugee population in 1995, the government has sought to situate the refugee 'problem' as far as possible from the political core of the state and to insulate the regime from the presence of refugees. This has been accomplished by closing refugee camps close to urban areas in the mid-1990s, especially Nairobi and Mombasa (UNHCR Kenya, 1998), and relocating refugees to camps in the border areas, on the political and physical periphery of the state. To reinforce this encampment policy, the police have conducted regular raids in urban areas to apprehend refugees residing there illegally since at least 1996 (Parker, 2002; and Kagwanja and Juma, 2008, 224–5). The clear objective of these operations has been to keep refugees out of cities, especially Nairobi.

Justifications for the new approach

Since 1993, Kenya has consistently highlighted three justifications for its approach to refugees. First, the government has claimed that the sheer magnitude of the refugee influx in the early 1990s overwhelmed its refugee procedures, and that the numbers remain too high to reverse its encampment policy. Second, many government sources point to a lack of burden sharing as a justification for keeping refugees in camps, stating the presence of refugees has placed a strain on the environment and public services, that it has carried a significant refugee burden for too long, and that a solution to the refugee problem should therefore be found outside Kenya. Finally, the government has blamed the presence of refugees for a rise in crime and insecurity, both in refugee-populated areas and in urban areas, in addition to the proliferation of small arms in Kenya.

It is striking how these three concerns have been consistently upheld by the government over the span of a decade. In January 1993, for example, the Kenyan government asked UNHCR to repatriate all refugees, arguing that 'the number of refugees in Kenya has not only seriously compromised the security of this country, but greatly outstretched the infrastructure and medical services' (cited in Carver, 1994, 53). Many of these concerns were echoed by the Minister of State for the Office of the Vice President when she addressed the Kenyan Parliament on 20 November 2003, arguing that 'the influx of refugees in the early 1990s has had its adverse effects on the economy and security of this country. It has also had an effect on the environment...The proliferation of small arms may be indirectly linked to the presence of these aliens in our country' (Parliament of Kenya, 2003, 3981). While these are only two of hundreds of statements made by the government relating to refugees in Kenya, they illustrate how these justifications have been upheld both by the Moi government (pre-2002) and the NARC government (post-2002). Over time and governments, the scale and protracted nature of the refugee presence in Kenya, coupled with the security concerns of the state and burdens associated with the hosting of refugees, have been highlighted by Kenya to justify its restrictive, camp-based, asylum policy. Given the consistency of this argument, it is now important to critically examine these justifications to ask to what extent they can fully explain Kenya's asylum policy.

Examining the elements of the justification

Numbers

The sheer number of refugees arriving in Kenya at the height of the 1991–93 emergency was unprecedented in Kenya's history. As outlined above, the refugee population in Kenya increased by more than 400,000 between 1991 and 1992. As Figure 5.1 illustrates, however, the number of refugees in Kenya fell below 250,000 by 1995, and has remained relatively stable ever since.

Given that the refugee population has been stable for more than ten years, between 225,000 and 250,000, it is important to ask how the number of refugees in Kenya may continue to be used to justify a

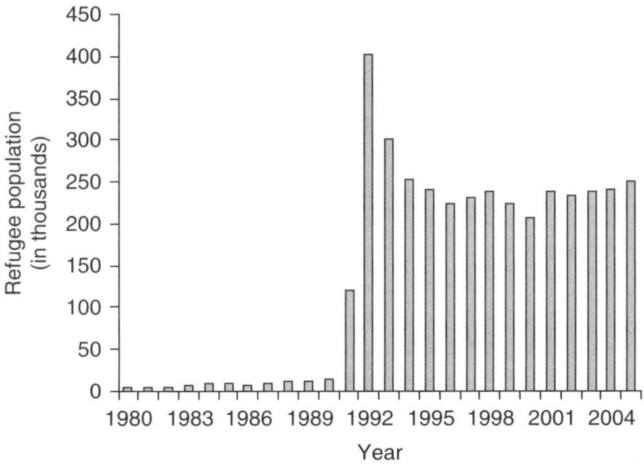

Figure 5.1 Refugee population in Kenya (1980–2005) (UNHCR, 2000a; UNHCR, 2007c)

restrictive asylum policy. The stability of the refugee population has not been viewed positively by Kenya nor as an opportunity to move to a more solutions-oriented approach. Instead, it has been viewed with great concern, and demonstrates that the Somali refugee situation in Kenya is a protracted refugee situation. As a result, the ongoing concern about numbers revolves not only around the size of the refugee population, but the seemingly unending nature of their stay and the limited prospect of solutions. The protracted and seemingly never-ending nature of the Somali refugee situation, coupled with the protracted nature of the conflict in Somalia, has given rise to a view within the government that Kenya has hosted too many refugees, for too long, and with no prospect of a solution in the foreseeable future.

Burden sharing

Compounded by the protracted nature of the refugee situation, there is a generally held view that the hosting of refugees is a burden, both on the refugee-populated area and the country as a whole. The scale of the burden was frequently highlighted by Members of Parliament during the debate on the Refugee Bill in 2003, claiming that the presence of refugees has had a negative impact on the local environment, security, markets, infrastructure and local services (Parliament of Kenya, 2003). But to what extent has the prolonged presence of refugees constituted only a burden for Kenya, and to what extent has the international community shared this burden?

It is generally held that there was a great deal of financial burden sharing with Kenya during the refugee emergency of the early 1990s, but that support subsequently waned. In fact, the refugee programme in Kenya has faced significant funding crises since the late 1990s, as 'international aid on behalf of Somali (and other) refugees in Kenya [has been] small and shrinking' (ECRE and USCR, 2003, 75). This has resulted in dramatic and recurring shortfalls in funding to UNHCR's Kenya programme, leading to a number of cuts to education, shelter, sanitation and protection activities in the Dadaab camps. In 2007, for example, UNHCR reported that the capacity of its Kenya programme 'to attain – and in some sectors to maintain – minimum standards of protection and assistance to refugees was severely curtailed by the 20 per cent cut in the budget at the start of the year' (UNHCR, 2007a, 242). Likewise, in 2004, UNHCR reported that 'a 10 per cent gap between identified needs and the available budget caused the services delivered to refugees to be below the established minimum standards' (UNHCR,

2004b, 193). As a result, the primary objective for UNHCR activities in Kenya in recent years has been to 'maintain minimum standards of emergency humanitarian assistance whilst ensuring that refugees have access to essential services' (UNHCR, 2004b, 191). It should be emphasized that UNHCR was still striving to provide emergency humanitarian assistance more than a decade after it declared the emergency to be 'over'.

In addition to difficulties related to sharing the financial burden, the sharing of Kenya's physical burden through the resettlement of refugees to third countries has also posed significant challenges in recent years. Resettlement was an important component of the international response to the 1991–93 refugee crisis. In October 1993, UNHCR reported that 5972 refugees had already been accepted for resettlement. Of these, 3657 were resettled to the US, of which 2751 (75 per cent) were Somali. While these numbers may seem limited, they are significant when compared to global resettlement activities out of Africa in the early 1990s. During this period, resettlement out of Kenya accounted for over 75 per cent of resettlement out of Africa. Between 1991 and 1998, almost 35,000 refugees were resettled to third countries from Kenya (UNHCR Kenya, 1998), an average of 5000 refugees a year. This trend continued as 'more refugees were resettled from Kenya in 2000 than from any other country in Africa' (ECRE and USCR, 2003, 77).

The scale of resettlement activities in Kenya was, however, dramatically affected by a corruption scandal in 2001. In January 2002, the UN Office of Internal Oversight Services (UNOIOS) reported how 'a "criminal enterprise" allegedly infiltrated the refugee status determination and resettlement process in Nairobi in the late 1990s to force bribes from people seeking resettlement to third countries' (UNHCR, 2002e). According to the UNOIOS report, the investigation resulted in the arrest of three UNHCR staff members, two members of an affiliated NGO, and four others (UNSG, 2001). The investigation also led to a suspension both in the processing of active resettlement files and in the identification of new resettlement cases, pending review and the full implementation of the conclusions of the report (ECRE and USCR, 2003, 77). Resettlement activities resumed in 2003 after new safeguards were introduced to the process. By 2006, UNHCR reported that it had submitted applications for the resettlement of 4292 refugees from Kenya, representing an important return to previous levels of resettlement activities (UNHCR Resettlement Section, 2007, 49).

The benefits of hosting refugees

While there have been a number of shortcomings in donor support for the protracted presence of refugees in Kenya, especially in sharing the financial burden, it is also important to recognize the extent to which their presence has brought benefits, especially to refugee-populated areas. Some researchers have argued that 'there is no doubt that the establishment of infrastructure and social amenities' by NGOs and UNHCR 'can be valuable for economic development and benefit both refugees and indigenous populations' (Pérous de Montclos and Kagwanja, 2000, 206). Others argue that 'in a back-handed and perhaps ironic way, the refugee camps in Kenya's North Eastern Province have stimulated economic and social development in the form of jobs and the increased availability of commodities, primary education and medical services which are offered in the camps' (Hyndman and Nylund, 1998, 28). Likewise, a UNHCR evaluation found that 'the presence of refugees is both an economic asset to the local Somali community, as well as a source of competition for scarce resources. However, of the two, the resources provided by the presence of UNHCR and its implementing partners to the area – in terms of employment and commercial opportunities, healthcare, services, the digging and maintenance of boreholes among other things – largely outweigh the costs to the local population' (UNHCR, EPAU, 2001, 20).

In more anecdotal terms, many of the UN and NGO staff who have served in Dadaab since the early 1990s explain that, as a result of the refugee programme, the town of Dadaab has been transformed.[5] They explain that the population increased five-fold – from an estimated 3000 inhabitants in 1993 to approximately 15,000 inhabitants in 2004 – newspapers now arrive from Nairobi on the day of publication, the variety of goods available in the market has increased dramatically, the roads have improved, and employment opportunities for the local population have transformed a previously underdeveloped and largely ignored corner of Kenya. As the ultimate indication of Dadaab's development, *SafariCom*, Kenya's largest mobile telephone network, extended coverage to the region in February 2004. Such an investment in the region, unimaginable 15 years ago, is attributed largely to the presence of the refugee programme.

In addition, specific programmes have been implemented to support the local population. A significant component of the refugee programme in Dadaab is the Local Assistance Project (LAP), managed by CARE Kenya.[6] This programme grew out of a realization in the mid-1990s that the gap in livelihoods between refugees and the local population was large, growing and a significant source of conflict between the two groups. As a result, CARE, UNHCR's largest implementing partner in Dadaab, proposed that their programme in Dadaab should include both local and refugee assistance as a means of reducing grievances within the local population and demonstrating the tangible benefits of hosting refugees. Between 1994 and 2004, CARE projects benefiting the local population in and around Dadaab totalled over US$13 million. Investments have been made in local educational, water, and health care projects. Training programmes and apprenticeships are offered to the local population to gain qualification as auto-mechanics, administrators, community health care workers and in the maintenance of water and sanitation infrastructure, including boreholes and latrines. The largest collaborative project was the construction of a laboratory and library for the Dadaab Secondary School in 2000–02.

UNHCR also runs a number of programmes designed to support the local community and authorities in Dadaab. In addition to providing monthly monetary incentives, equipment and transportation to the local police, UNHCR has constructed 14-room barracks in each of the camps and in Dadaab town, an 80-room administrative block for the District Office – complete with water and electricity, canteen and compound fencing. UNHCR has invested more than US$440,000 since 1995 to rehabilitate and improve roads and airstrips in the Dadaab region. Since 1992, it has constructed and maintained almost 30 water boreholes for the local population, installed water and electricity to the Dadaab Primary School, rehabilitated livestock boreholes, and provided water tanks for the local population. UNHCR has also provided free medical care to the local population since 1992. Finally, UNHCR has been involved in a range of environmental projects, contributing over US$4 million to environmental rehabilitation projects.

While these are significant investments in an otherwise impoverished region of Kenya, it is important to note that it is the burdens of hosting refugees and the shortfalls in donor assistance that are highlighted at a national level in Kenya, not the benefits. There is a view that Kenyan officials in Nairobi characterize the presence of refugees exclusively as a burden as a way of advocating for greater support from the donor community. While there is evidence that the presence of refugees in Kenya has caused burdens on the host state and host community, and that burden sharing with Kenya has been problematic in recent years, it should also be stressed that, as a result of the refugee programme, the protracted presence of refugees in Dadaab has contributed to local development.

Direct and indirect security concerns

Finally, Kenyan officials have cited the perceived security implications of hosting Somali refugees as another justification for adopting a restrictive refugee policy. In addition to the scale and nature of the insecurity in and around the refugee camps in Dadaab in the mid-1990s, as outlined above, issues of small arms proliferation and terrorism have come to be blamed on Somali refugees, and cited as a justification for their containment. As this section will argue, however, the nature and causes of security and insecurity relating to the presence of refugees are rooted largely in the perception of the Somali refugee population, and less on evidence of the presence of refugees as a *cause* of insecurity in Kenya. In contrast, failures of burden sharing have resulted in a number of indirect security concerns, especially around the Dadaab camps.

The most significant security concerns perceived to be caused by the presence of Somali refugees relate to the flow of small arms into Kenya and the threat of terrorism. These concerns are exacerbated by Kenya's long and porous border with Somalia which facilitates 'the uncontrolled flow of arms ... but also the spill-over effects of the conflicts themselves' (IRIN, 2003a). As a result of these perceived threats, the Somali refugee population has been collectively viewed as a security concern by the Kenyan state, thereby reinforcing the encampment policy. Likewise, there is an increasing view among officials in Nairobi that the Dadaab camps may be harbouring Islamic terrorist elements. For example, Kenya took the exceptional step in early 2007 of closing its border with Somalia to prevent the arrival of additional Somali asylum seekers. This move, which was later reversed, was justified on the grounds that the group of refugees attempting to cross into Kenya contained elements of the Union of Islamic Courts who were fleeing the advance of Ethiopian troops (UNHCR, 2007d).

There is no doubt that Kenya has faced a number of significant security concerns in recent years. In early August 1998, for example, over 250 people were killed and some 5000 injured when the US Embassy in central Nairobi was attacked by a car bomb (Rake, 2004, 552). Likewise, on 28 November 2002, coordinated attacks took place in Mombasa. Almost simultaneously, three suicide bombers attacked the Paradise Hotel, killing 16, while two surface-to-air missiles narrowly missed their target of an Israeli charter plane during take-off from the Mombasa airport. Both attacks were blamed on Somali-based Islamic organizations with links to the al-Qaeda network. Shortly after the Mombasa attack, it was reported that US intelligence sources believed that a group known as al-Ittihad al-Islamiya, 'a prominent militant group in the Horn of

Africa with links to Osama bin Laden's al-Qaeda network' (BBC, 2002a), was responsible.

Investigations into the activities of al-Ittihad al-Islamiya eventually led to the Dadaab refugee camps. Investigators believed that Kenya's long porous border with Somalia and the presence of large refugee camps in a remote corner of the country provided the ideal cover for the operations of a terrorist organization, while the disaffected and desperate camp population provided a fertile base for recruitment (Harman, 2002). They also believed that there was a direct link between al-Ittihad al-Islamiya and the al-Haramain Islamic Foundation, which provided some religious training in the camps. In March 2002, the US Treasury Department blocked the funds of the Somalia branch of al-Haramain, claiming that it was linked to al-Ittihad al-Islamiya and that 'over the past few years, al-Haramain Somalia has funnelled money to al-Ittihad al-Islamiya by disguising funds as if they were intended for orphanage projects or Islamic school and mosque construction' (USA, 2002). As a result, a connection, albeit tenuous, was drawn between the terrorist attacks on Kenya and the presence of refugees.

Likewise, a connection has been drawn between the presence of refugees and the flow of small arms into Kenya. While precise figures on small arms in general are 'sketchy at best' (Knickerbocker, 2002), it has been argued that small arms originating from Somalia and Sudan are widely available in Kenya. An increase in the supply of small arms has consequently resulted in a significant fall in their price. As reported by IRIN (2003a), an AK-47 assault rifle cost 60 head of cattle in northern Kenya in the 1960s, but 'today the same rifle costs as little as the price of a chicken.' During interviews in 2001 and 2004, several Kenyan government officials expressed concern that refugees were at least partially responsible for the proliferation of small arms in Northern Kenya and in urban areas. For her part, Austin has argued that the link is much clearer, and that the Dadaab camps were 'used for sheltering the weapons, facilitating the arms deals, and for security transport' (Austin, 2002, 3).

While there is no doubt that the small arms problem and the consequences of terrorism are legitimate concerns for the Kenyan state, and that many of these concerns do originate in Somalia, it is important to consider to what extent they are *caused* by the presence of refugees, or to what extent the link is the result of a public perception that views elements associated with Somalia or Somalis as *prima facie* a cause of insecurity. For example, Adelman and Abdi (2003) argue that there is no proof of the link between refugees and either terrorism or the proliferation of small arms, but there is a strong public perception that the two are linked. They argue that media reporting on the issues, especially after the Mombasa attacks, 'has influenced public perception at the national and international levels, reinforcing the allegations that the Somali refugees in Dadaab are criminals, thus reducing sympathy Kenyans and others have for the plight of the Dadaab refugees' (Adelman and Abdi, 2003, 60–1). While this raises important questions about the range of factors that contribute to this perception, as the final section of this chapter will outline, it is also important to consider more indirect security concerns relating to the protracted presence of the Somali refugees, including conflict between refugees and the local population resulting from competition over scarce resources and levels of banditry and violent crime in and around the camps.

The Dadaab camps are located in a semi-arid region of Kenya with a long history of competition over scarce resources. Indeed, 'conflict over resources between a number of local Ogadeni clans was a feature of the area prior to the arrival of the refugees' (UNHCR EPAU, 2001, 19). These delicate clan relations were challenged, and the potential for conflict increased, with the arrival of the refugees from a number of other clans and sub-clans who 'brought to the area and the refugee camps a history of clan rivalries from Somalia' (UNHCR EPAU, 2001, 19). Adding to these dynamics, Crisp (1999a) found that this mixture of rival clans and sub-clans with the increasingly scarce resources was a significant cause of insecurity in and around the camps. In addition, he found that 'in Dadaab, the distinction between "refugees" and the "local population" is in many ways a fuzzy one, as most of the people living in and around the three camps share a common language and culture, and belong to clans which straddle the border between Kenya and Somalia' (Crisp, 1999a, 12).

Recent evidence, however, would seem to suggest that the solidarity between refugees and the local population has diminished. As argued by Veney (2007), the process of democratization in Kenya, however frail, has contributed to a hardening of the lines between refugees and Kenyan nationals. One consequence has been an increase in grievances felt by the local population towards the refugees, exacerbated by local politicians who, for electoral gain, perpetuate a view that refugees receive a privileged treatment over the local population (RCK, 2003a, 17). When combined with the chronic and acute resources scarcity characteristic of the area around Dadaab, it is easy to see how this perception of refugees receiving more than 'their fair share' can provoke conflict.

Coupled with the tremendous levels of physical insecurity experienced by refugees during the 1990s, the rising grievances of the local population and the increase in conflict between the host community and refugees became significant concerns for local authorities and UNHCR. A series of programmes were designed and implemented in the late 1990s, with the primary objective of reducing levels of physical insecurity for refugees, but with the secondary objective of addressing local grievances and the perception of refugees as a local security concern (Crisp, 1999a). The most significant programmes to be introduced were: the 'security package', designed to reinforce the capacity of the Kenyan police to enforce law and order in and around the refugee camps by providing them with additional equipment, facilities, and incentives; the mobile court programme, designed to enhance access to the judicial process for victims of crime in Dadaab by facilitating the sitting of the district court in Dadaab; and, third, the Firewood Project, designed to reduce levels of sexual violence against refugee girls and women during firewood collection by directly providing 30 per cent of their firewood needs.

The most significant benefit credited to these projects has been a ten-fold reduction in levels of violent crime in and around the Dadaab camps since 1998. As illustrated by Figure 5.2, the total instances of violent crime fell from 300 in 1998 to 36 in 2003, with instances of rape, murder and armed robbery also falling proportionally.

Given these developments, many NGO workers now believe that Dadaab, once infamous for its violence, is now safer than Nairobi and the safest region in the North East Province.[7] Accordingly, many in Dadaab believe that the protracted presence of refugees, and the associated presence of international agencies, has made Dadaab safer than it was prior to the arrival of the refugees. In short, and somewhat paradoxically, the presence of refugees has been good for local security.

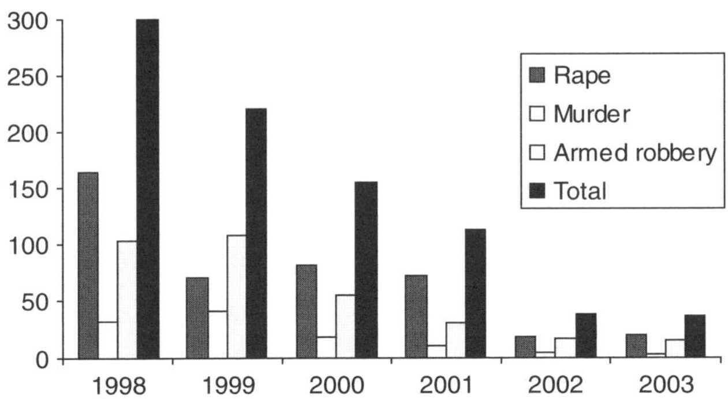

Figure 5.2 Instances of violent crime in Dadaab refugee camps (1998–2003) (UNHCR Dadaab, 2002. 2003 data collected during fieldwork in 2004.)

Security of what? Perceptions of security at the core and periphery

This discussion of the security concerns relating to the presence of refugees suggests different perceptions of refugee-related insecurity at different levels of the state. In Nairobi, there is a view that refugees remain a significant cause of insecurity, associated with the proliferation of small arms and links to terrorism. There is also a perception in the capital that levels of violent crime in and around the camps, especially banditry, remain at pre-1998 levels. It is felt that refugees are a real security threat, and consequently need to be contained on the periphery of the state. In the refugee-populated area, however, there is a different view. Interviews in Dadaab in 2004 found that local government officials have a more nuanced view of the security implications of the presence of refugees. While acknowledging security concerns related to their presence, especially pertaining to competition over scarce resources and banditry resulting from local grievances, there is also a recognition that the situation has improved since 1998. There is also a view that targeted interventions, such as the Firewood Project and Local Assistance Projects, can play a significant role in mitigating that sense of grievance and addressing indirect security concerns.

There are also important difference in understandings of the source of the threat between the core and periphery of the Kenyan state. In Nairobi, there is an apparent lack of differentiation between Kenyan Somalis, Somalian Somalis, and Somali refugees. Compounded by the lack of legal status for refugees (Hyndman and Nylund, 1998), and fuelled by a strong association between Somalis and criminality, especially in the wake of the terror attacks on Nairobi and Mombasa, this lack of differentiation has led to the securitization of all Somalis. As a result, all Somali refugees are seen to be a threat, thereby justifying actions to contain that threat. In contrast, the differentiation between Kenyan Somali and Somali refugee in Dadaab, where 98 per cent of the local population are Kenyan Somalis, appears to be growing, and the division between local Somali and refugee becoming more significant. As a result, there is greater differentiation between the two groups and a more precise understanding of the sources of insecurity.

Taking a broader view

The important role that perception plays in the identification of the prolonged presence of Somali refugees as a threat to the Kenyan state suggests that factors beyond numbers, burdens and security concerns have motivated the government in Nairobi to first adopt and then maintain its restrictive refugee policy. In an effort to better explain the motivations of the Kenyan government in this area, this section considers a number of broader historical and political factors, unrelated to the presence of refugees, that have defined the political space within which the Kenyan government, and specifically the Moi regime, has formulated its response to the protracted presence of Somali refugees in Kenya.

Historical factors

A significant colonial inheritance for post-independence Kenya has been a conflictual relationship between the government in Nairobi and the North Eastern Province of Kenya, formerly the Northern Frontier District. The region has seen a long history of underdevelopment and repression of its ethnic-Somali inhabitants, driven by fears of irredentism and threats to the territorial integrity of modern Kenya (Drysdale, 1964; Lewis, 1963; Samatar, 1984; and Turton, 1972). It is these practices, rooted in colonialism, and the subsequent history, which not only preclude the integration of Somali refugees in Kenya, but result in Somali refugees being viewed as a threat by the Kenyan state.

The pastoral Somalis were one of many groups to be separated by European colonial borders during the 'scramble for Africa'. The Somali people were divided into five parts at the Berlin Conference of 1884: French Somalia (now Djibouti), British Somaliland, Italian Somaliland, Ogaden (now part of Ethiopia) and the Northern Frontier District (NFD) of British East Africa (now the North Eastern Province of Kenya). As argued by Turton (1972), early evidence of political activity by Somalis in each of these territories was motivated by a desire for Somali unification under a single state. Indeed, by 1951, the Somali National League had emerged as an organized movement in British East Africa. Their objectives included the unification of the Somali people and territories (Lewis, 1963, 149). Such irredentist ambitions and anti-colonial sentiments of the Somali pastoralists in the NFD won them no favours with the British administration. The colonial powers maintained the NFD as a closed district, restricting entry and exit from the region. In addition, the region was politically and administratively isolated, with negligible development or investment occurring during the colonial period.

By the early 1960s, however, the cause of the Somalis in the NFD was taken up in the Somali National Assembly, which passed a motion in 1961 in support of the integration of the NFD into the Somali Republic (Lewis, 1963, 155). This was consistent with the broader priorities of the new republic. Reunification was such a driving force in early Somali politics that it was represented in the Somali flag: the five points of the white star on the Somali flag represent the five 'Somali territories' – including most of northern Kenya (Lewis, 1963 ; and Samatar, 1984). Somalia was also the only country in the region that did not sign the OAU Charter, which, at its core, agreed to maintain the national borders drawn by the colonial powers. Finally, the 1960 Somali constitution 'gave Somali citizenship to all the Somali living outside the country, entitling them to the same rights as those living inside' (Pérouse de Montclos, 2001, 298).

The future of NFD was a point of contention in the run-up to Kenyan independence in 1963 (Orwa, 1989, 232). Prior to final negotiations with the Kenyan nationalists, a commission of enquiry was sent to determine if the estimated 200,000 Somali of the NFD wished to remain within an independent Kenya or be ceded to Somalia. The commission found that 'the vast majority of the Somali of the Province desired secession and union with the Republic' (Lewis, 1963, 158). Despite these findings, secession was not granted. Instead, the North Eastern Province (NEP) was created within an independent Kenya, with an almost exclusively Somali population. In response, violence erupted across the NEP as groups of rebels attacked outposts of the newly-independent Kenyan government. By December 1963, the scale of the violence was such that the Kenyan government declared a state of emergency in the region, just 13 days after achieving independence. The state of emergency retained the colonial prohibition on travel in and out of the area, but also included broader powers of detention without charge and significant restrictions on the pastoral communities. This state of emergency remained in effect until 1991, when it was lifted by Moi to allow UNHCR and other humanitarian agencies to respond to the mass arrival of Somali refugees.

What followed, between 1963 and 1967, is commonly referred to as the *shifta* war.[8] Somalis in the NEP waged a guerrilla campaign of secession for almost four years, allegedly supported and supplied by the Somali government in Mogadishu. In response, the newly-independent government of Jomo Kenyatta, 'afraid of an invasion by Somalia' (Pérouse de Montclos, 2001, 299) and determined to preserve the territorial integrity of the Kenya state, 'spent US$70 million in unplanned for military expenditure between 1964 and 1967 in a war of attrition with the *shiftas*' (Orwa, 1989, 232). During this period, the Kenyan army 'grew from about 6500 at independence to 16,000 in 1967' (Orwa, 1989, 232). By 1967, the *shifta* movement had been defeated, and Kenya and Somalia signed a non-aggression and cooperation agreement in Arusha in October 1967.

Concerns over the threat of Somali expansion, however, remained a significant foreign policy concern for the regime in Nairobi, especially after the *coup* in Mogadishu that brought Siad Barre to power in 1969. In particular, Barre's commitment to the restoration of a Greater Somalia, demonstrated by his invasion of the Ogaden region of Ethiopia in 1977, reinforced the view in Nairobi that the greatest threat to the Kenyan state was the irredentist sentiments remaining with the population of the NEP. As a result, police and army presence mounted, the Somali population was collectively viewed as a threat to national security, and increasingly draconian measures were taken against the Kenyan Somali population.

These concerns were compounded by the attempted *coup* against President Moi in August 1982, when a section of the Kenyan Air Force attempted to take control while Moi was out of the country. The *coup* failed, and led to an estimated 3000 arrests and the disbanding of the Air Force. A much greater consequence, however, was the securitization of all aspects of domestic affairs in Kenya. As argued by Widner (1992), the *coup* demonstrated to Moi that he was on a 'political island' surrounded by Kikuyu supporters of Kenyatta. In response, he implemented radical polices to ensure the rise of members of his Kalenjin ethnic group to support his Presidency. More generally, there was a total change to state security after the *coup* as the President became profoundly concerned about the vulnerability of his regime. He responded by implementing measures to protect his regime which led to the mass violation of human rights.

In addition to the repression of social and political rights at the core of the Kenya state,[9] the securitization of Kenyan politics led to an escalation of security activities in the NEP. Kenyan security forces carried out a number of campaigns to eliminate any remaining *shifta* elements in the early 1980s. The largest of these campaigns occurred in Wajir in February 1984, when 5000 men were arrested on suspicion of being *shiftas* (Africa Watch, 1991, 273–7). They were reportedly taken to the local airstrip, forced to strip naked, and lie on the burning-hot tarmac. Those who refused were shot, while the rest were denied food and water for several days. Many were beaten, while others were reportedly burned alive. In the end, an estimated 2000 were believed to have been killed. There was no opposition to these activities in the Kenyan Parliament. On the contrary, in response to the policy of repression of Somalis in the NEP, the Minister of Internal Security was reported in the daily press to have said 'the only good Somali is a dead one' (Africa Watch, 1991, 273).

National security continued to justify a series of actions against the Somali community through the 1980s, right up to the arrival of the Somali refugees in the early 1990s. In 1988, the securitization of Somalis in Kenya was extended to the public campaign against poaching, when 'the government called the poaching crisis a "security problem" and blamed it on ethnic Somalis, with no clear distinction between the participation of illegal Somali nationals and Kenya's own ethnic Somali population' (Africa Watch, 1991, 289–90). All Somalis were portrayed as a threat, and their repression was justified on grounds of national security. It is in this context that the government's restrictive response to the mass arrival of thousands of Somali refugees can best be understood.

Domestic factors

While such historical factors help explain the securitization of Somali refugees, a number of other factors shed light on the Moi regime's response to the initial arrival of Somali refugees and the policy responses that followed. It should be noted that when the Somali crisis erupted in 1991, the Moi regime was facing a number of simultaneous crises. In November 1991, the international community suspended aid to Kenya, citing the need for democratization and improved human rights. Kenya's economy was heavily dependent on aid (Orwa, 1989, 226), and the Moi regime had little choice but to comply. In late 1991, the Kenyan ruling party, KANU (Kenya African National Union), revised the Constitution and legalized political parties. As a further concession to donors, the first multiparty elections were scheduled for late 1992 (Throup and Hornsby, 1998). At the same time as these reforms, violence erupted in the Western and Rift Valley Provinces, as Kalenjin youths displaced Kikuyu farmers from their land. While it was later argued that the 'land clashes' were state sponsored, and intended to disrupt opposition strongholds in the run-up to the elections (Nowrojee and Manby, 1993), the result was nonetheless the internal displacement of an estimated 300,000 Kenyans. Responding to this displacement posed a significant challenge to the Moi regime (Kenya, 1992).

In the midst of these events, and sustained pressure from the donor community, the challenges posed by the arrival of over 400,000 Somali refugees was almost a blessing in disguise. With the combined pressure of the land clashes and democratization, the arrival of refugees allowed the Moi regime to show the international community that it was upholding human rights by allowing the refugees to enter its territory. Indeed, the generous quantity of asylum afforded by the Moi regime in 1991 and 1992 won praise from the donor community, and resulted in the release of urgently-needed assistance to Kenya (Hyndman and Nylund, 1998, 24).

While an arguable lack of alternatives resulted in a generous quantity of asylum, security concerns relating to the influx of Somalis led to the policy of containing the refugees in the NEP. It has been argued that 'the North of Kenya is a peripheral region, a space of relegation where, since colonial times, opponents have been sent' (Pérouse de Montclos, 1998, 168, author's translation). It is an arid and sparse region, where the government has invested little since independence and which, in turn, has contributed little or nothing to the national economy. Finally, it has been 'placed on the periphery of a very centralized state' to the extent that 'the province lacks autonomous power to allow its local elites to manage local affairs without the supervision of the government in Nairobi' (Pérous de Montclos, 2001, 297). It is, in fact, geographically, economically and politically far from the core of power in Nairobi, and therefore a suitable place to contain a perceived threat.

Moreover, the process of democratization since 1992 has witnessed the entrenchment of anti-refugee sentiments and stigmatization of the Somali community within Kenyan politics. As argued by the Refugee Consortium of Kenya (RCK):

> Experience has shown that in the run-up to elections many politicians will not hesitate to manipulate the refugee situation as an electioneering gimmick. Members of Parliament have been known to distort facts and stereotypes and vilify refugees as the sole source of increased crime and insecurity, proliferation of illegal arms and scarcity of resources. They have even been known to point to humanitarian assistance to refugees in the camps as evidence that refugees allegedly enjoy a better lifestyle than the locals. Blaming refugees detracts attention from their own responsibilities towards their constituents. (RCK, 2003a, 17–18)

Others have argued that refugees have become 'caught in the cross-fire' in the context of 'increased domestic fragility and instability' as ruling parties find themselves under increasing pressure from opposition groups and as 'competition for political space increases' (Juma, 2002, 7). These dynamics have been displayed with particular force since the first change of government in Kenya's post-colonial history in December 2002. These pressures have combined with other international factors to place increased restrictions on the political space within which refugee policy may be formulated.

International factors

As a victim of two significant terrorist attacks in recent years, and neighbour to a 'failed state' seen as a possible base for international terrorist networks (Menkhaus, 2004), Kenya has become a key partner in the US-led 'war on terror'. As argued by Juma (2002), the willingness of East African states generally to jump on the anti-terror bandwagon is partially motivated by their very real concerns about terrorism, but also by their desire to negotiate benefits from abroad to help them cope with challenges at home. Juma (2002, 6) argues that 'undergoing political transitions to democracy and faced with poverty and fiscal difficulties, East African governments have readily embraced the global coalition against terrorism in the hope that Western countries will support incumbent regimes and intervene favourably with the international financial institutions.' In the case of Kenya, it has been argued that Moi's eagerness to support the war on terror after 11 September 2001 was partly an attempt to gain support from the US for the KANU regime ahead of the December 2002 elections, in exchange for access rights to Kenyan territory for US anti-terror activities in the region (Barkan and Cooke, 2001).

An important aspect of the rise of terrorism on the Kenyan agenda has been a further retrenchment of anti-Somali sentiments, especially in Nairobi, and increased justifications for restrictions on Somali refugees. It has been reported that the Kenyan police used the November 2002 terror attacks in Mombasa to justify a crackdown on refugees in Nairobi (HRW, 2002a). This link has been reinforced by concerns regarding the role of Islam in recent politics in Kenya, the radicalization of the Kenyan coast, the alleged links between al-Qaeda and the Dadaab camps, and the rise in xenophobic sentiments. Compounded by 'suspicion and resistance to radical Islamic ideology among sections of refugees', states like Kenya approach the question of Somali refugees motivated by a desire to 'stave off militant nationalism and irredentism, which are inspired and often supported by global pan-Islamic groups' (Juma, 2002, 10). As a result, refugee advocates in Kenya see the 'war on terror' as a convenient cover for a long awaited 'war on refugees' (RCK, 2003b).

It is, however, important to emphasize that while international engagement has allowed Kenya to justify restrictions on refugees in the name of the 'war on terror', continued international engagement continues to limit the extent to which Kenya can act with a free hand on refugee issues. There is a view among some officials in Nairobi that it is not possible for Kenya to approach the question of refugees without considering the foreign policy implications. Specifically, there is a view that if the government mishandles the question of refugees, it will have a negative impact on relations not only with its neighbours, but more crucially on its relations with donor countries, upon whom it is dependent.

Conclusion

This chapter has examined Kenya's response to the mass arrival and prolonged presence of Somali refugees. It has argued that Kenya's decision to adopt a dual policy of 'abdication and containment' was due initially to the scale of the influx and its desire to seek concessions from an otherwise restrictive donor community. Over time, however, Kenya has justified the continuation of this policy by pointing to the scale of the refugee population, its impact on refugee-populated areas, declining donor engagement to share Kenya's refugee burden, and a range of direct and indirect security concerns. While findings from Dadaab highlight the significance of a number of these concerns, this chapter has argued that a number of other historical, domestic and international factors have contributed to Kenya's asylum policies. In particular, the history of the *shifta* wars and the vulnerability of the Moi regime, compounded by the suspension of international aid to Kenya in November 1991, led Kenya to grant asylum to the Somali refugees on the condition that they be contained on the periphery of the state. While the presence of refugees has resulted in a number of benefits for the local population, the perceived vulnerability of the regime in Nairobi, notwithstanding the election of the NARC government and the passage of the 2006 Refugee Bill, has largely led to a continuation of the policy of 'abdication and containment'.

6
Tanzania

Soon after achieving independence in 1962, Tanzania established a reputation as one of the most hospitable countries of asylum in Africa, if not the world. Through the 1960s and 1970s, it hosted tens of thousands of refugees fleeing both wars of national liberation in Southern Africa and post-colonial conflict and repression in neighbouring states. Tanzania provided refugees with land, and refugees were encouraged to achieve self-sufficiency, with many entering the country's workforce. This reputation changed dramatically in the context of renewed conflict and genocide in the Great Lakes region of Central Africa. Tanzania received hundreds of thousands of refugees from Burundi and Rwanda in 1993 and 1994. In response, and in advance of the country's first multiparty Presidential elections, Tanzania ended its long-standing 'open-door' asylum policy by closing its border with Burundi in March 1995 and by expelling the overwhelming majority of Rwandan refugees from its territory in December 1996.

The expulsion of Rwandan refugees did not, however, lead to a return to Tanzania's previously open asylum traditions. Instead, the decade that followed witnessed the formulation and implementation of a series of increasingly restrictive asylum policies. The combined effect of these policies are seen to have made conditions in the camps hosting Burundian refugees so unbearable that many refugees felt compelled to repatriate to Burundi, notwithstanding the prevailing insecurity there. More generally, these restrictions prevented refugees from engaging in economic activity, leading some to turn to illegal coping mechanisms in response to declining donor assistance to UNHCR's Tanzania programme. Such activities further reinforced Tanzania's sense of vulnerability, leading to a greater application of restrictive measures.

This chapter examines Tanzania's response to the arrival and continued presence of refugees in light of the country's tradition of asylum in the 1960s and 1970s, the Great Lakes crisis of the mid-1990s, and the treatment of Burundian refugees in the decade following the forced return of Rwandan refugees. The chapter argues that the treatment of refugees in Tanzania, from independence to present, has been determined by a range of political and economic considerations, and that restrictions on asylum are not the result of a new logic, but the result of changes largely unrelated to the presence of refugees. Indeed, the logic behind Tanzania's refugee policy has, since independence, remained rooted in economic, political, strategic and ideological considerations. By tracing the history of refugees in Tanzania in light of the country's political and economic challenges, this chapter will argue that, in addition to the changing scale and nature of refugee movements in the last 45 years, the changes in Tanzania's approach to refugees are best understood as a result of the pressures of economic collapse in the 1980s and democratization in the 1990s, the changing 'idea' of the Tanzanian state since Nyerere, and the changing relationship between Tanzania and donor countries.

Understanding these dynamics is particularly important given recent developments in Tanzania's refugee policy. In February 2008, UNHCR announced that Tanzania had agreed to consider the naturalization of some 218,000 Burundian refugees who have been settled in Tanzania since 1972, and requested some US$34 million from donors to support the initiative (UNHCR, 2008a). While it is too soon to assess the effectiveness of this programme,[1] especially in light of efforts to locally integrate Rwandan refugees in the early 1980s (Gasarasi, 1990), this development does suggest that restrictive asylum policies are potentially reversible. Any effort to encourage a more open approach to asylum in Tanzania should, however, be fully informed by the factors that led to the initial adoption of a more restrictive policy in the late 1980s. Without learning these lessons of history, and without addressing the factors that contributed to the shift, Tanzania's asylum policy could easily shift again, and prospects of a return to the open asylum policies of the 1960s become even remote. To this end, this chapter begins by consider what factors underpinned Tanzania's open approach to asylum under its first President, Julius Nyerere.

Asylum policies under Nyerere: 1962–85

Tanzania had been hosting forced migrants long before obtaining independence (Chaulia, 2003, 148–54). In particular, thousands of Africans fled coerced colonial labour in Portuguese Mozambique as early as 1899 and high population density in Ruanda-Urundi from the 1920s. Tanzania's experience with refugees, however, became more complex in the early days of independence. By the end of 1966, Tanzania was hosting thousands of Tutsi refugees from Rwanda and a similar number of refugees fleeing the war of national liberation in Portuguese Mozambique (Zolberg et al., 1989, 45–9). Thus began Tanzania's hosting of two separate types of refugees: those fleeing conflict in neighbouring independent African states and those fleeing wars of national liberation. It is generally agreed that the reception and settlement of these various groups of refugees was motivated substantially by the ideologies and policies of the Tanzanian President, Julius Nyerere.[2] It is therefore important to outline these principles before turning to Tanzania's response to the arrival of these diverse groups of refugees.

According to Zarjevski, 'from the start, the settlement of refugees in Tanzania was guided by the concepts of permanence and productivity, stemming, no doubt, from the principles on which the President, Julius Nyerere, hoped to develop his country' (Zarjevski, 1988, 137). These principles, collectively known as *ujamaa na kujitegema* (socialism and self-reliance) were adopted as Tanzania's national policy on 5 February 1967 through the Arusha Declaration (Coulson, 1982; and Ofcansky and Yaeger, 1997). Among other provisions, the Declaration called for the establishment of *ujamaa* farming collectives to encourage self-reliance and the reorganization of the education system 'in order to serve the mass of the population rather than to train a privileged elite' (Matthews, 2004, 1114). It also placed particular emphasis on the free provision of social services – health care, clean water, and especially standardized and nationalist education – throughout the country.

To put *ujamaa* into practice, Nyerere issued an agricultural policy on 13 September 1967 calling for a 'nation of *ujamaa* villages', to be designed around the principle of mutually dependent blocks of ten huts, cooperatively farming both subsistence food crops and cash crops. Voluntary implementation of the policy was slow, until Nyerere announced a 'villagization' policy whereby 'the whole rural population should live in villages' by the end of 1976 (Coulson, 1982, 249). This policy was implemented by force, and many cases of Tanzanians being forcibly relocated were reported in the mid-1970s. By the end of 1976, 13 million Tanzanians, 75 per cent of the mainland Tanzanian population, were living in *ujamaa* villages.

The external dimension of Nyerere's philosophy was pan-Africanism, centred on a belief in African solidarity and the objective of ending minority and white-rule throughout Africa. In 1963, Dar es Salaam became home to the OAU's Liberation Committee. In 1964, Tanzania initiated 'a strategy of encouraging and supporting armed struggles by the African populations of these colonized and otherwise oppressed countries' (Nnoli, 1978, 80). By the end of 1966, Tanzania hosted a wide range of liberation movements.[3]

Taken together, these internal and external policy priorities of *ujamaa* and pan-Africanism came to form the 'idea' of the Tanzanian state under Nyerere. They also clearly informed Tanzania's approach to both refugees from independent states, who were received and organized into settlements adhering to the *ujamaa* model, and to freedom fighters from wars of national liberation, who were hosted as an extension of Tanzania's foreign policy. It is against this background that Tanzania's response to key refugee populations can be more fully understood.

Refugees from independent African states

As highlighted by Rutinwa (2002a, 74), 'Tanzania began grappling with refugee crises almost at the same time that the country gained its independence.' As a result of pre-independence violence in Rwanda, Tutsi refugees began arriving in Ngara, in Tanzania's Northwestern Kagera Region, as early as 1959. By 1962, refugees were arriving in Ngara at the rate of 50 to 100 a day as part of a wider exodus of some 130,000 refugees from Rwanda.[4] Two main settlement sites were identified to accommodate these refugees: Kimuli and Bushubi. The establishment of the Kimuli settlement, in Karagwe, was largely successful, as refugees were assigned 10-acre plots and participated in the planning and construction of their settlement. In stark contrast, the establishment of Bushubi was problematic. According to Rutinwa (2002a, 77), 'the choice of the Bushubi area was dictated by a government desire to clear the bushes that harboured tsetse flies, lions, wild pigs and antelopes, and which had led to serious depopulation and consequent absence of economic activity in the area.' When the refugees resisted relocating to the new site, food rations were withdrawn from refugees who refused to relocate and refugee leaders who opposed the relocation were arrested and deported (Gasarasi, 1990, 91). Such coercion, while not as openly practised in other refugee settlements, was not dissimilar to the force used by Tanzanian officials to relocate nationals during the villagization programmes of the 1970s.

Some authors (Holborn, 1975; Tunga, 1987; and van Hoyweghen, 2002) have linked Tanzania's willingness to host refugees from Rwanda during this period to its view that refugees represented an opportunity to attract the resources necessary to encourage the settlement and economic development of under-populated regions of the country. This view, coupled with a desire to buttress regional security, was largely responsible for Tanzania's agreement in 1964 to resettle 10,000 Rwandan refugees from the Congo, and settle them in Mwesi, 'an area...already earmarked for development' (Cuénod, 1989, 223). To realize the development benefits of hosting refugees, however, mechanisms were required to keep refugees in designated settlements and secure external financial and technical support for the settlements until they achieved self-sufficiency. These requirements were met through the Refugees (Control) Act of 1965 and the Tripartite Partnership Model of refugee settlements.

Rutinwa (1996, 292) notes that the Refugees (Control) Act of 1965 is 'one of the most oppressive laws on the Tanzanian statutes book' and was 'introduced not to provide refugees with rights, but to control them'. The Act granted the government wide powers to deport refugees, and provided for the detention of refugees who are believed to have 'prejudiced peace, order or foreign relations, or who are believed to have committed offences outside Tanzania' (Article 10). Crucially, the Act also required all refugees to reside in either a designated reception area or in a refugee settlement, and provided sweeping powers to officials appointed by the Office of the President to control and manage refugee settlements. As a result of these provisions, the government was able to retain a high degree of control over the refugee population. Largely as a result of this control, there were fewer self-settled refugees in Tanzania in the 1970s than in any other host country in Africa (Holborn, 1975, 1150).

While the Refugee Act provided the mechanism to ensure that refugees remained in settlements, the Tripartite Partnership Model ensured that the costs associated with the settlements were not borne exclusively by Tanzania (Gasarasi, 1987; Gasarasi, 1984; and Rutinwa, 2002a). In 1964, Tanzania entered into a tripartite agreement with UNHCR and the Tanganyika Christian Refugee Service (TCRS) for the management of the Mwesi settlement, established to accommodate the Rwandan refugees resettled from the Congo. Under this agreement, Tanzania provided the land for the settlement, staff support, basic tools, access to community services and a waiver on import duty for goods related to the settlement. In turn, TCRS assumed responsibility for managing the settlement, while UNHCR provided the necessary funding and technical advice. In the following years, similar tripartite agreements were concluded for settlements to accommodate refugees from Rwanda, Burundi, Mozambique, and elsewhere. Between 1963 and 1979, 13 settlements were managed through such tripartite agreements, hosting an estimated 182,000 refugees.

As a financial burden sharing mechanism, the tripartite approach appeared to have been successful. Gasarasi (1987, 103) estimates that UNHCR contributed over US$11 million to the 13 settlements between 1963 and 1979. In contrast, Tanzania was responsible for a much smaller share of the financial costs. In a speech to the National Assembly during the 1972/73 budget session, the Minister for Home Affairs acknowledged that Tanzania incurred some expenses associated with the hosting of refugees, but that the majority of the costs were incurred by UNHCR, TCRS and WFP (Tanzania, 1972). The Minster reported that the combined value of commitments from UNHCR, TCRS and WFP for the period 1972/73 was TSh. 5,532,140. For its part, the Minister asked the National Assembly for TSh. 821,000, meaning that the government was expecting to contribute some 14 per cent of the total cost of the settlements in 1972.

The links between the tripartite model and Tanzania's *ujamaa* policies were strengthened in 1973 with the announcement of Nyerere's villagization policy, coupled with the arrival of thousands of refugees fleeing the 'selective genocide' in Burundi (Lemarchand and Martin, 1974). For some, the government's response to the arrival of these refugees confirmed that the settlement of refugees in remote areas was 'a strategy of the Tanzanian government to develop and exploit these new areas' (van Hoyweghen, 2002, 317). Daley (1989; and 1992) believes that the creation of these settlements contributed both to regional security, by containing the refugee population, and to the development and exploitation of a remote region of the country. In fact, refugee settlements were organized not only to produce subsistence crops but also export-earning crops, such as coffee and tobacco, which were sold through parastatals, gaining valuable foreign currency for Tanzania. Situating the establishment of settlements within a broader context, she argues that:

> the sudden influx of huge numbers of landless peasants in the form of refugees could be seen as a blessing by the state as it has sought to intensify the productivity of peripheral areas. Not only could peasant commodity production be under state control, but the capital for land settlement could be acquired via the less competitive and more accessible route of humanitarian aid ... The presence of refugees also offers the opportunity to attract long-term development aid to remote areas and to fill rural casual labor demands. (Daley, 1992, 138–9)

Refugees from wars of national liberation

While this approach to refugees from Burundi and Rwanda illustrates Nyerere's willingness to use refugees as a tool of domestic policy, his approach to refugees fleeing wars of national liberation illustrates his willingness to also use them as a tool of foreign policy. As outlined above, support for liberation movements in Southern Africa was a central element of Tanzania's foreign policy under Nyerere. Not only was the OAU Liberation Committee headquartered in Dar es Salaam, but Tanzania also hosted many refugees fleeing wars of national liberation. For example, Tanzania received approximately 6000 South Africans affiliated with either the ANC or the PAC (Pan-African Congress). While recognized as being hospitable to these refugees, however, Matthews (1970) emphasizes that only refugees who were members of one of the South African movements based in Tanzania were granted asylum by the government, and that refugees who ceased to be involved in the liberation movement once in exile were liable to be deported.

Similar restrictions were placed on Mozambican refugees who fled to Tanzania to escape the war of national liberation waged by FRELIMO against the Portuguese from 1964 to 1974 (Zolberg et al., 1989). As the war progressed, the number of Mozambican refugees in Tanzania steadily climbed from 10,000 in 1966 to 50,000 in 1972. These refugees were also settled through tripartite arrangements, but unlike the Rwandan and Burundian settlements, internal administrative control of the settlements was retained by the liberation movements. In turn, FRELIMO was based out of these settlements and, with the support of Tanzania, waged a guerrilla war in northern Mozambique for over a decade.

This review of Tanzania's refugee policy in the 1960s and 1970s is not intended to detract from the fact that Tanzania hosted tens of thousands of refugees during this period while simultaneously developing strategies to meet the significant needs of its own population. While refugees were primarily received and settled in a manner guided by Nyerere's domestic and international priorities, these refugees lived, for the most part, without fear of *refoulement* from Tanzania for two decades. In fact, the mass naturalization of 36,000 Rwandan refugees in December 1980 is an important reminder of the extent to which Tanzania practised an open asylum policy during this period (Gasarasi, 1990). As outlined in the next section, however, this hospitality proved difficult to sustain as the economic underpinnings of *ujamaa* began to erode.

Economic decline and changes in Tanzania's asylum policy in the 1980s

The 1980s was a tumultuous decade for Tanzania's economic and political landscape. As with many other African states during this period,

Tanzania's balance of payments began to suffer in the early 1980s as the global price of important cash crops – including coffee, sisal and tobacco – began to fall relative to the cost of imports. The resulting diminishment of Tanzania's terms of trade made basic consumer goods more expensive and *per capita* income decline. As a result, Tanzania's economic performance in 1985 was its worst since independence (Campbell and Stein, 1992).

In the early 1980s, Nyerere tried to sustain *ujamaa* while addressing the economic crisis. The National Economic Survival Programme (NESP) was launched in 1981 with the objective of boosting exports. The plan, however, proved unsustainable and was abandoned in 1982 in favour of a Structural Adjustment Programme. Publicly, Nyerere opposed the involvement of the IMF, knowing that its involvement would bring an end to *ujamaa*, but the government knew that continuing *ujamaa* while stimulating economic recovery constituted a near impossible balancing act. As outlined by Campbell and Stein, 'essentially, the Structural Adjustment Programme embraced the contradiction of trying to meet the requirements of the [International Monetary] Fund and the World Bank while holding defensively to the official ideology of socialism and self-reliance. This balancing act was taking place in a situation of deteriorating social services in education and sanitation and decreased delivery of healthcare and those material goods on which the hegemony of *ujamaa* was predicated' (Campbell and Stein, 1992, 9).

In the end, the balancing act could not be sustained, and Nyerere stepped down as President. Ali Hassan Mwinyi was elected President on 1 November 1985. Six months later, Mwinyi launched the Economic Recovery Programme (ERP), leading to further currency devaluations, removal of import restrictions, increases in producer prices for food and export crops and an intensive campaign against corruption and inefficiency (Ofcansky and Yeager, 1997, 72–3). In response, the IMF announced US$800 million in stand-by credits in July 1986, followed by additional loans in 1987. Increased IMF involvement in the Tanzanian economy through the late 1980s was associated with a range of austerity measures aimed at reducing public spending. The result was an erosion of the 'material underpinnings' of *ujamaa*, especially in the areas of education, health care and the provision of clean water (Messkoub, 1996).

These changes also affected the provision of services in the refugee settlements. The ultimate objective of the tripartite model was to make refugees living in settlements self-sufficient, at which point the international agencies would withdraw and return control of the settlements to the Tanzanian government. The government would then be required to provide public services to the settlement in exchange for taxes paid by the inhabitants, as with any other Tanzanian village. By the time of Tanzania's economic crisis, all 13 of the refugee settlements had been handed over to the government. If the Tanzanian government was unable to provide basic services to its own nationals, concern was raised as to its ability to fulfil its obligations to the refugees. To investigate this concern, UNHCR deployed a team of consultants to the settlements to assess the impact of the economic crisis on the refugee population. The consultants concluded that 'the severity and duration of the economic crisis [raised] a number of specific issues on the economic viability of the refugee communities' (Antoniou et al., 1987, 23–4).

At the same time, the government's public position on the hosting of refugees began to change. Government officials began to draw attention to 'the refugee problem as it may necessarily affect, in a multiple of ways, the socio-economic, political and cultural aspects' of the host country (Ayok Chol and Conrad, 1987, 8). Internationally, Ministers began to call for greater burden sharing with Tanzania, emphasizing that 'given the current economic decline facing many developing countries, Tanzania being no exception, assistance from the donor communities becomes more important' (Tanzania, 1990). By 1990, Amnesty International reported a 'hardening of attitudes towards refugees from Burundi' by the Tanzanian authorities (AI, 1990, 1). This change in attitude was most clearly articulated in February 1990 when President Mwinyi, in his bid for re-election, 'called for the immediate deportation of immigrants from Burundi and Rwanda who had entered the country without official permission since 1986' (AI, 1990, 1), notwithstanding their *prima facie* recognition as refugees by the Minister of Home Affairs.

This overview illustrates the scale of the economic crisis facing Tanzania in the 1980s, and the resulting structural changes in the national economy. There were also a number of domestic political changes, most notably the resignation of Nyerere and the erosion of services central to the maintenance of *ujamaa*. The government's position towards refugees also began to change during this period, as illustrated not only in government speeches but also in increasingly restrictive policies aimed at rounding-up and sometimes expelling refugees. It was against this backdrop that Tanzania received hundreds of thousands of refugees from Burundi and Rwanda in the 1990s.

The Great Lakes crisis and further changes in the 1990s

Nearly a million refugees fled to Tanzania as a result of the maelstrom of violence that gripped Rwanda, Burundi and Zaire in the mid-1990s. The first mass arrival was in the last week of October 1993 with the arrival of some 250,000 refugees from Burundi. Tanzania then received hundreds of thousands of refugees as a result of civil war and genocide in Rwanda. The scale of this movement was staggering: between 28 and 29 April 1994 alone, some 250,000 Rwandan refugees crossed the Rusumo bridge into Ngara, Northwestern Tanzania. It was 'the largest and fastest movement of refugees in modern history' (UNHCR, 1997b, 8). Eventually, there were approximately 700,000 Rwandans living in camps in the Kigoma and Karagwe regions of Tanzania. According to UNHCR, Tanzania's refugee population climbed from 292,100 at the end of 1992 to 883,300 at the end of 1994 (UNHCR, 2000a, 312). As with the situation in Eastern Zaire, outlined in Chapter 2, conditions in both the camps and in the surrounding regions were marked by increasing instability by mid-1994. The Deputy Director of UNHCR's Great Lakes Unit later reported that suspected perpetrators of the genocide and members of the FGoR 'mingled freely with genuine refugees' and that the local population watched 'with increasing frustration as large tracts of forest and agricultural land were destroyed' (Mahiga, 1997, 15). Shortly thereafter, Tanzania's long-standing 'open-door' refugee policy changed dramatically.

Tanzania's first change in policy came on 31 March 1995 when, almost a year after the initial influx, and in the lead-up to the country's first multiparty elections, the government closed its border with Burundi to prevent additional Rwandan refugees from fleeing renewed conflict in Burundi. Then, in December 1996, Tanzania announced that all Rwandan refugees would be required to leave the country by the end of the year (UNHCR, 2000a, 265). Many refugees requested a delay in the deadline to determine for themselves the viability of return to Rwanda, but as it became clear that the deadline would not be reconsidered 'Rwandans sought other methods to avoid repatriation' (Whitaker, 2002a, 328). For example, an estimated 35,000 refugees left the camps and started moving further into Tanzania during the night of 11 December. This movement continued the following day. On 13 December, the Tanzanian army intervened 'forcing as many as 200,000 fleeing refugees to turn around and retrace their steps' (Whitaker, 2002a, 329). At the same time, the camps were closed and their inhabitants were forced back across the border. This mass exodus in reverse caused 'widespread dismay in the humanitarian world' (Mahiga, 1997, 16) and numerous human rights organizations were quick to criticize the repatriation (AI, 1997a; and HRW, 1996).

Explaining the change in policy: 1995–96

Several authors have considered Tanzania's decision to both close its border with Burundi and expel the Rwandan refugees (Mahiga, 1997; Rutinwa, 1996; and Whitaker, 2002a). There is general agreement that a range of factors contributed to the shift in policy, including multipartyism and the changes in Tanzanian political culture in the 1990s, consequent changes in foreign policy, the magnitude of the Rwandan and Burundian refugee populations, the nature of the populations, external and internal security, and the lack of international support. This section briefly outlines these arguments.

First, it is important to emphasize that Tanzania's change in policy came in the context of domestic political changes within Tanzania, not only as a result of economic liberalization, as outlined above, but also in the run-up to the country's first multiparty elections. In February 1992, a special congress of Tanzania's ruling party, CCM (Party of the Revolution),[5] endorsed the principle of a multiparty system of government, partially as a result of pressure from donor institutions. The first multiparty elections were scheduled for October 1995. In February 1995, the former Minister of Home Affairs and Deputy Prime Minister under Myinyi, Augustine Mrema, resigned from CCM and joined the opposition National Convention for Construction and Reform (NCCR). Given his strong views on national security, he was a popular candidate for NCCR, and received the party's nomination as Presidential candidate in mid-March 1995, just days before the closure of the border with Burundi (Ofcansky and Yeager, 1997, 133).

In July 1995, the CCM selected Benjamin Mkapa as their presidential candidate. Anti-refugee rhetoric was a common feature of the ensuing campaign, with all parties portraying themselves as the only party with the solution to the refugee crisis (Rutinwa, 1996, 299). More generally, CCM portrayed itself as the only party that could prevent the spread of violence from Rwanda and Burundi, while claiming that a vote for the opposition would lead to ethnic divisions within Tanzania (Kelsall, 1996; and Sundet, 1996). The final results gave CCM 186 of 232 seats in the National Assembly. Mkapa won 62 per cent of the presidential vote, compared to Mrema's 28 per cent, and was sworn-in as Tanzania's third president on 23 November 1996.

With the advent of multipartyism came changes in Tanzania's foreign policy. As outlined above, Tanzania's foreign policy under Nyerere was guided by pan-Africanism and support for liberation movements. Consequently, Nyerere was willing to host a number of refugee populations actively opposed to oppressive regimes in their country of origin, often at the expense of friendly regional relations and sometimes at the expense of Tanzanian security. Unlike Nyerere, the new regime in Tanzania 'pursued an active policy of maintaining good relations with all neighbours', regardless of their ideology (Rutinwa, 1996, 299). By the time of the Rwandan emergency, Tanzania had adopted a regional policy of cooperation and conciliation, making regional relations a higher priority. This policy carried through to the Rwandan expulsion, as the government did not want to exacerbate tensions between Kigali and Dar es Salaam.

While these political changes in Tanzania were *necessary* for the change in hosting policy, they alone were not, however, *sufficient*. Attention must also be paid to specific features of the Rwandan refugee population (Mahiga, 1997; Musoke, 1997a; Musoke, 1997b; and Rutinwa, 1996). First, the scale of the Rwandan influx must be appreciated, with some 700,000 refugees arriving in Tanzania in less than a year. Second, Tanzanian officials were frustrated by the increasingly protracted nature of the Rwandan and Burundian refugee situations. Third, there was a widely held suspicion that the camps were harbouring FGoR elements who were not fleeing persecution, but justice. The activities of these elements also extended beyond the camp boundaries, leading to more general concerns of law and order in the surrounding areas.

A number of other concerns also arose as a result of the burdens associated with the influx, especially the 'dramatic' physical and environmental damage (UNHCR, ExCom, 1998b). During the initial influx, crops were destroyed, and doors and window frames from schools and medical centres were used as firewood. Over time, water sources and forests were depleted through overuse and the indiscriminate felling of trees (Green, 1994). Local markets were also affected as the flood of aid into the region drove down the prices of some locally produced goods, thereby decreasing income, while driving up the cost of staple consumables. While there was considerable donor support for the response to the initial influx of refugees, this support waned over time leaving the local authorities to supplement food aid, and leaving the local environment and population vulnerable. This led Rutinwa to conclude that the 'failures of the international community to give adequate assistance to Tanzania was the main reason for the closure of the border' with Burundi, marking the change in Tanzania's refugee policy (Rutinwa, 1996, 298).

Even before the 1996 expulsion of the Rwandan refugees, government ministers cited these concerns as adequate justification for a change in asylum policy. Speeches from the Ministries of Foreign Affairs and Home Affairs around the time of the border closure in 1995 suggest significant agreement between government departments on the nature of the problem. Citing the strain on the environment, local economy, infrastructure, and concerns relating to internal and external security, the Minister of Foreign Affairs claimed that 'the problem has reached saturation point and can no longer be sustained' (Tanzania, 1995b, 3). Reflecting on Tanzania's history of hosting large numbers of refugees, another government representative argued in Geneva that 'though traditionally the local population has always been sympathetic to refugees, all this is now changing under the strain of the current load' (Tanzania, 1995a, 5). The Ministers of Home and Foreign Affairs both claimed that 'experience has shown that measures such as the granting of permanent asylum and citizenship to the refugees are not a panacea for a permanent solution to the refugee crisis' and that 'the solution lies in the countries of origin rather than the countries of asylum' (Tanzania, 1995a, 6; and Tanzania, 1995b, 9). Significantly, the Ministers of Home and Foreign Affairs both accused the international community of 'double standards' when condemning Tanzania for its policies, especially in light of restrictive policies in the West:

> There is a tendency by the International Community when dealing with the refugee crisis to impress upon the weaker countries of asylum to live up to their humanitarian obligations at the expense of their national rights and interest. The primary duty of a state is to preserve itself and to protect its citizens and their rights. Countries of asylum, be they weak or strong, poor or rich, have a sovereign right to exercise this duty. The international community must respect this right without bias or double standards. (Tanzania, 1995b, 7; and Tanzania, 1995a, 10)

Given the range of challenges stemming from the Rwandan influx, and based on the government position articulated in the speeches cited above, it is clear how extensively Tanzania's position on the refugee question changed as a result of the influx of refugees in the early 1990s. The emphasis on self-sufficiency and local settlement was replaced by a focus on repatriation, while the integration of refugees into the

Tanzanian political community was replaced by a desire to exclude them. Most significantly, refugees are no longer characterized as an asset to Tanzania, but as a burden.

For one long-time observer of Tanzania's refugee policy, the events of 1995–96 can 'only be described as a sea-change in Tanzania's approach to refugees' (interview, Dar es Salaam, 2004). In the years following the expulsion, however, it is clear that the objective of the government was not to return to the *status quo ante*. Instead, the period following the events of 1996 witnessed the formulation and implementation of a series of increasingly restrictive refugee policies, largely targeting Burundian refugees in Northwestern Tanzania. The following section will outline these policies, before turning to a consideration of how Tanzania has justified the continued implementation of restrictive asylum policies.

The state of asylum in Tanzania: 1997 to 2006

By December 1997, one year after the expulsion of the Rwandan refugees, Tanzania continued to host approximately 295,000 refugees, 230,000 of whom were from Burundi. This number continued to climb as thousands of Burundian refugees continued to flee to Tanzania throughout 1997, with 20,000 to 30,000 arriving in the first three months of the year. While USCR indicated that 'humanitarian conditions at the camps were generally fair', it added that 'political factions among the refugee population created tensions and occasional violence' leading to the death of some ten camp residents in early 1997 (USCR, 1998).

In response to rising security concerns within the camps and in the refugee-populated areas, Tanzanian authorities began to round-up Burundians living outside the camps, claiming that this was a necessary move to protect Tanzanians living in the border areas. One human rights group argued that there was, however, at the core of the operation, a 'presumption that all refugees [posed] a security threat and [could] therefore be indiscriminately rounded up and confined in camps' (HRW, 1999b, 1). The new policy, of 'rounding-up *all* refugees on the grounds that *some* may pose a security threat' (HRW, 1999b, 3), reflected a new blanket approach to refugees, especially to Burundian refugees. This approach was largely in response to Burundian government allegations that rebel groups were active in Northwestern Tanzania, and that the ensuing threat was best addressed by confining all Burundians to camps. This lack of differentiation between Burundians engaged in armed activities and Burundian refugees was further reinforced by the *prima facie* refugee status given to all Burundians, as the lack of individual status made it easier to paint all Burundian refugees with the same brush.

This increasingly securitized view of refugees motivated the passing of more restrictive refugee legislation in 1998. In response to regional and domestic fears that the Tanzanian government was not in control of the refugee situation, Kamanga (2005, 104) argues that the 1998 Refugees Act had two objectives: to 'signal disengagement from the Open Door policy of the Nyerere administration', and to 'assure the populace' that the government was 'determined to address the problem of seemingly endless refugee influxes'. In fact, restrictions on refugees, especially Burundian refugees, intensified after the coming into force of the Act in February 1999. For example, the Tanzanian military issued an order in late 1999 that all Burundian refugees should move to refugee camps, even those who had arrived in the 1970s.

Refugee camps became overcrowded as a result of the ensuing round-ups. Coupled with funding shortfalls to the refugee programme, overcrowding soon led to short-term food shortages in 1999 and 2000, which led, in turn, to an increase in crime in and around the camps as some refugees turned to illegal activities to cope with the shortfall in assistance. Security concerns, food shortages and increased government restrictions continued to cause concern for UNHCR and refugee protection advocates in 2001 and 2002. At the same time, Tanzania frequently raised concerns about the levels of crime in refugee-populated areas while Burundi continued to accuse Tanzania of allowing rebels to be based in and around the refugee camps. In response, Tanzanian officials strictly prohibited refugees from travelling more than four kilometres outside the camps. Refugees were consequently no longer able to seek wage-earning employment in neighbouring villages and towns, and practically all economic activity between refugees and the local population ceased. At the same time, the refugee population climbed to over 500,000 by the end of 2001, confirming Tanzania once again as the country with the highest refugee population in Africa.

Tanzanian officials became increasingly concerned about the growing and prolonged nature of the Burundian refugee population, and began to press for them to be repatriated. Given the prevailing insecurity in many regions of Burundi, however, UNHCR representatives did not agree to promote repatriation, and agreed only to facilitate repatriation for refugees wishing to return. Some 85,000 refugees repatriated from Tanzania to Burundi in 2003, with only 37,000 returning with UNHCR's assistance. Given that these returns coincided with sustained crime and insecurity in and around refugee camps, additional reductions in food rations, and increased restrictions on refugees' freedom of movement and economic activity, a number of refugee advocates – including AI, HRW and TCRS – questioned the voluntary nature of the repatriations, suggesting that conditions in the camps had become so unbearable that many refugees felt compelled to repatriate to Burundi, notwithstanding the prevailing insecurity there (IRIN, 2002a). There was a general feeling that while Tanzania could not expel the Burundians as it had the Rwandans in 1996, for fear of damaging relations with the donor community, it could pursue the same objective by placing additional pressure on refugees to return.

Many of these concerns were reinforced with the publication of Tanzania's 2003 National Refugee Policy. The National Policy codified a number of the restrictive elements of Tanzanian approach to asylum, including restrictions on freedom of movement and limitations on economic activity for refugees, which placed significant constraints on the livelihood of refugees. The constraints continued through to the end of 2006, leading UNHCR to report that 'the most pressing issues highlighted by camp-based refugees are restrictions on their freedom of movement and their right to work. These, combined with limited access to land for cultivation and insufficient food and other assistance, expose refugees to the risk of exploitation' (UNHCR, 2007b, 121). These concerns most clearly illustrate how dramatically Tanzania's asylum policy has shifted over the past 45 years, from a policy focused on encouraging economic self-reliance to a policy that confines refugees in isolated and insecure refugee camps.

Understanding Tanzania's shift in policy

Official Tanzanian statements since the mid-1990s have consistently argued that the number of refugees in Tanzania, coupled with the length of their stay, the burdens they impose, especially in the form of insecurity, and the lack of sufficient international engagement to share these burdens, have justified Tanzania's decision to adopt a more restrictive asylum policy (Rutinwa and Kamanga, 2003). As summarized by Tanzania (2000, 6) during the Millennium Session of the UN General Assembly in 2000:

> Tanzania finds itself in a very difficult situation of hosting more than 800,000 refugees, most of whom are products of the crisis in the Great Lakes region. This is a huge burden for a poor country like

> Tanzania. Besides, refugees pose many problems relating to security and environmental degradation. There is an urgent need for the international community to increase support to the refugees as well as the refugee-hosting countries. In the same vein, we reiterate our call for international burden sharing and responsibility in refugee situations.

Given the frequency and consistency with which these justifications are raised, it is important to critically examine the extent to which concerns relating to numbers, burden sharing and insecurity fully explain the degree to which Tanzania's policy has shift in recent years.

Numbers

Tanzania has been among the top five African asylum countries for as long as asylum statistics have been available (UNHCR, 2000a). Although Tanzania's refugee population was relatively fluid between 1997 and 2005, with thousands of new refugees arriving while others were repatriating, the total number of refugees in the country remained above 500,000 in the same period, peaking at 689,373 in 2002 (UNHCR, 2007c, 536). By the end of 2005, it continued to host the largest refugee population in Africa (see Figure 6.1).

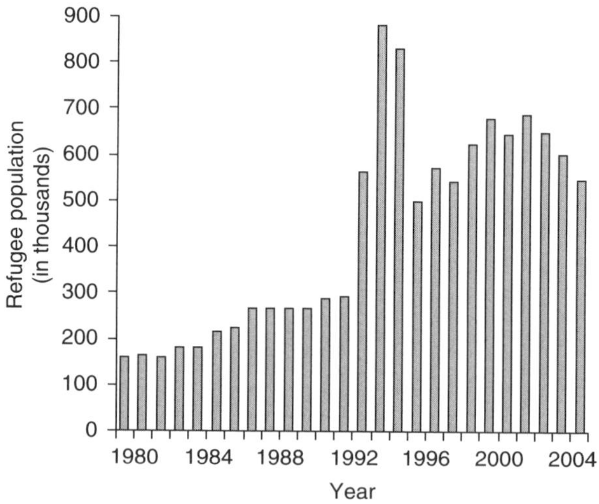

Figure 6.1 Refugee population in Tanzania (1980–2005) (UNHCR, 2000a; UNHCR, 2007c)

In addition, the government would add the approximately 218,000 Burundian refugees who have been in Tanzania since 1972. Since these refugees reside in the 'Old Settlements', not UNHCR-managed camps, they were not registered by UNHCR and consequently not included in UNHCR statistics. Accordingly, the government claims that Tanzania hosts over 800,000 refugees. In addition to the scale of the refugee population, Tanzania is also concerned about the lack of solutions for refugees, and the recurrence of refugee influxes over many decades. Tanzania perceives the refugee populations not only to be large and protracted, but part of a never-ending cycle of displacement.

Burden sharing

A number of concerns have been raised in recent years about diminishing donor engagement in the refugee assistance programme in Tanzania and levels of financial burden sharing. UNHCR has consistently reported since 2000 that its programme in Tanzania has been adversely affected by limited and unpredictable donor support. In 2001, UNHCR's Tanzania programme was forced to reduce its budget by some 20 per cent (UNHCR, 2002a, 137). In 2003, UNHCR reported that it 'struggled to maintain a minimum level of health care, shelter and food assistance to the refugees in the face of reduced budgets' (UNHCR, 2004b, 165). Likewise, in 2005, UNHCR reported that 'not all refugees' needs were met, a consequence of UNHCR's overall funding shortage' (UNHCR, 2005a, 141). Similar concerns were repeated in 2006, when 'UNHCR's Tanzania programme suffered from budget reductions' leading UNHCR to 'drastically reduce its activities in support of host communities' (UNHCR, 2007a, 198).

Similar shortages have also affected food distribution in the camps, with refugees receiving only 76 per cent of their required food ration in 2006 (UNHCR, 2007a, 197). Such shortages are, however, not new as dwindling support for WFP has led to a reduction in the amount of food distributed to refugees on numerous occasions in recent years. Lack of donor engagement resulted in interruptions to food distributions in July and again in September 2000. WFP was forced to significantly reduce food distribution to refugees in November 2002 and again in February 2003, resulting in a distribution of only 50 per cent of the normal ration (UNHCR, 2003d). In the midst of these cuts, the government reported that food shortages in the camps resulted in an increase in crime in the refugee-populated area. The

Minister of Home Affairs responded to the cuts by stating that the government was:

> afraid that we may have riots in the refugee camps because of hungry refugees. They might then leave their camps and run rampant in the villages. We have said that we would not be prepared to be put in such a situation, and the alarm has been sounded. Should things deteriorate to this extent, we may have to consider the possibility of repatriating the refugees forcefully. (cited in IRIN, 2003c)

Sensitive to these recurring shortfalls in donor support, the government has frequently stated that it will only continue hosting refugees if the international community provides the necessary support. As Mkapa reportedly told a meeting of foreign diplomats in Dar es Salaam, Tanzania's 'sympathy in assisting refugees should be supported by the international community because it was its responsibility' (IRIN, 2001a). For many, the 2003 shock to the food supply implied that the deal had been broken.

The burdens and benefits of hosting refugees

To highlight these concerns relating to burden sharing should not, however, lead to the conclusion that the protracted presence of refugees in Tanzania has had only negative implications for the refugee-populated areas. In fact, as Landau has argued, 'the longer-term economic and physical impact of the humanitarian influx has been two-sided, providing opportunities for some while further impoverishing others' (Landau, 2002, 275). The arrival of refugees attracted a range of humanitarian agencies, creating employment in an area otherwise offering few economic opportunities. For a town like Kibondo, one of the operational centres for the refugee programme in Northwestern Tanzania since the early 1990s, the arrival of the humanitarian agencies has resulted in an economic boom. One NGO worker remembered that when he arrived in Kibondo in 1997, only two buses a week passed through the town, there were very few consumer goods for sale in the local shops, and there was only one telephone line out of the town. By 2004, there were three or four bus services a day, each bringing a wide range of fresh consumer goods into town, and two companies providing coverage for mobile telephones (interview, Kibondo, 2004; IRIN, 2002b). As with Dadaab in Northern Kenya, the prolonged presence of a refugee assistance programme in Northwestern Tanzanian towns like Kibondo has contributed to tangible economic benefits.

Research undertaken on behalf of the Prime Minister's Office in 1997 tried to capture a broad picture of the impact of refugees on the Kigoma region (Tanzania, 1997). The study identified a number of positive consequences stemming from the presence of refugees, including increased attention paid to the region by the international community, job creation, an increase in income generating activities, improved access to services, and an inflation in the price of food products, which benefited local producers. It concluded, however, that the negative impact on physical infrastructure, the environment, social services, schools, health services, food security, utilities, security and the administrative system were of far greater concern. In an attempt to mitigate these negative impacts, and as a means of countering local resistance to hosting refugees, UNHCR launched a series of programmes in the late 1990s specifically designed to target the needs of the local population. These programmes, collectively known as Special Programmes for Refugee Affected Areas (SPRAAs), targeted the environment, roads, schools, health, water, security, and support to local administration. Similar to LAPs in Northern Kenya, SPRAAs resulted in the investment of over US$3.3 million in Kibondo District alone between 1997 and 2003.

Mindful of the scale of these contributions, and concerned by the apparently limited impact these interventions have had on the government's anti-refugee rhetoric in recent years, the Centre for the Study of Forced Migration at the University of Dar es Salaam undertook an impact assessment of the presence of refugees in Northwestern Tanzania (Rutinwa and Kamanga, 2003). The objective of the study was to assess the extent to which the conditions in Northwestern Tanzania matched the claims being made by the government to justify restrictive asylum policies. On the question of the environment, the report concludes that 'while a lot has been done to remedy the environmental impact of the presence of refugees, a lot more still needs to be done in the coming years' (Rutinwa and Kamanga, 2003, 23). In considering the impact on infrastructure such as roads and transportation, the report notes that as a result of SPRAAs, 'the road infrastructure has improved significantly', but that 'the infrastructure works done have not always reflected the priorities of the local people' (Rutinwa and Kamanga, 2003, 25–7). The benefits are more clearly defined in the area of health, as the report concludes that 'one can easily say that the benefits of the presence of refugees to the health sector far outweigh its negative impact' to the extent that 'some of the local beneficiaries do not want to dare think of the day when these services would be withdrawn' (Rutinwa and Kamanga, 2003, 31). Similarly, the refugee programme has positively affected educational services, access to clean water, and the capacity of local administration.

From this analysis, it may be argued that the prolonged presence of the refugee programme in refugee-populated areas like Kibondo has had a number of advantages for the local population. Northwestern Tanzania 'emerged from the colonial period as a backward, underdeveloped area relative to other parts of the country' (Daley, 1989, 142), a relationship that continued well into the 1980s. Regions like Kibondo, on the geographic and political periphery of the state, have not been a priority of the central government, and have consequently received little in the way of investment, especially since the economic crisis of the mid-1980s. Consequently, the arrival of the refugee programme has brought investment into the region that would likely have not otherwise been made. Such a positive evaluation of the refugee presence, however, does not take into account the government's concerns relating to security.

Security concerns

The link between the presence of refugees and internal and external security concerns for the Tanzanian state is not only the most frequently cited justification for restrictions against refugees, but also constitutes the most significant refugee-related burden for Tanzania. As outlined above, the influx of refugees from Rwanda in the mid-1990s constituted a number of direct and indirect security concerns for Tanzania, many of which continued after the forced return of the Rwandan refugees in 1996. As outlined in this section, significant security concerns have been documented in recent years. There have been a number of direct concerns, relating to allegations of the presence of armed elements in and around the refugee camps in Kibondo and the link between refugees and the flow of small arms into Tanzania. There have also been a number of indirect concerns, relating to the rise in crime, especially in the context of reductions in assistance to refugees, and tensions between refugees and the local population.

The direct security concerns faced by Tanzania relate to allegations that Burundian armed elements were based in and around the camps, and the belief that the presence of refugees facilitated the flow of small arms into Tanzania. Neither of these concerns are new to Tanzania, especially given its active support of liberation movements in the 1960s and 1970s. Given that these security concerns are no longer tied to support for liberation struggles, however, and given that they have been a source of regional and international frustration, not pride, for Tanzania, they are of increasing concern to the government.

The presence of Burundian refugees and armed elements led to attacks on Tanzanian territory by Burundian forces as early as the 1970s (Daley, 1989; and Malkki, 1995). According to the International Crisis Group (ICG), the 1972 Burundian refugee population 'spawned the first organized Hutu armed groups, Palipehutu and Frolina, which launched cross-border incursions against Burundi beginning in the 1980s' (ICG, 1999, 2). It is believed that both groups drew support not only from Hutu refugees living in towns like Kigoma, but also from those refugees transferred to settlements. It is also reported that these groups based training and cross-border incursions from remote border areas close to refugee settlements.

In the aftermath of the conflict in the Great Lakes region in the 1990s, and in particular the eruption of conflict in eastern Zaire in 1996, the presence of Burundian refugees, and allegations of support to Burundian rebel groups, became a sustained security concern for Tanzania. ADFL-led attacks on refugee camps in Zaire in late 1996 disrupted the bases of a number of Burundian rebel groups. Seeking somewhere to regroup, it is believed that a number of them travelled to Tanzania (ICG, November 1999, 4). Tanzania's decision to close its border with Burundi in March 1995 was partially in response to allegations that rebel groups had crossed into Kigoma Region along with Hutu refugees in 1993. Tanzanian troops were deployed to the border in May 1995 in response to reports that Burundian troops were crossing into Tanzania, and by July 1995, both countries had significant numbers of troops deployed in the border area. Such movements did not, however, prevent the Burundian government from claiming that Tanzania was providing shelter to rebel groups. Frustration with these allegations may partly explain why Tanzania launched the 1997 round-up operations.

These allegations were, however, supported by the ICG when, in 1999, it reported that 'Western Tanzania is the central, external base of the Hutu rebellion against the Buyoya regime' in Burundi (ICG, November 1999, 10). The ICG claimed that while 'most of the more militant activities [occurred] outside the domain of the camps', there was convincing evidence that 'Western Tanzania [was] a focal point for key activities of the rebellion, including: military mobilization, recruitment, training, fund-raising, political strategizing, communications, arms trafficking, resource distribution, medical treatment, naval operations and the launching of cross-border attacks' (ICG, November 1999 10–11). In response to these activities, the Burundian army established a five kilometre buffer zone along the border, effectively placing Tanzanian villages close to the border in a military zone. Several cases of Tanzanians being injured or killed by Burundian forces in this zone were documented. For example, in 2002, it was reported that three Tanzanian villages close to the border had been shelled by the Burundian army (BBC, 2002b).

In addition to these security concerns in the region, there was strong evidence that a number of other activities were carried out in the camps, including recruitment, fundraising and political activities. In addition to anecdotal evidence,[6] there has been documented evidence of groups of young male refugees leaving the camps to fight in Burundi and cases of recruitment (IRIN, 2001b; IRIN, 2000a). A number of refugees also reported that they were taxed by some of the rebel groups, that exiled political groups were active in the camps, and that a number of camp residents were the family of rebels still fighting in Burundi. In light of these activities, UNHCR identified ensuring 'the civilian character of camps' as one of its main objectives in Tanzania as recently as 2007 (UNHCR, 2007a, 195). Since 1998, UNHCR has invested approximately US$1.4 million a year to support a special programme designed to provide material and monetary support to some 287 policemen and women active in the refugee camps in Northwestern Tanzania. While the programme has been generally successful in improving law and order within the refugee camps, it was found to have had little discernible impact on security in the refugee-populated area as a whole (Crisp, 2001a, 2).

A second direct security concern affecting the refugee-populated area has been the proliferation of small arms. In 2003, President Mkapa stated that 'the proliferation of small arms [in Tanzania] is a result of refugees entering our country' (IRIN, 2003d). Small arms proliferation is certainly a growing concern in Tanzania, especially in refugee-populated areas (Mogire, 2006), with a marked tendency to link this problem to the presence of refugees. According to Rutinwa and Kamanga, however, evidence from Western Tanzania indicates that refugees and small arms flows are both the result of conflict and porous borders, not the other way around (Rutinwa and Kamanga, 2003, 16). Notwithstanding this evidence, there is a strong public perception that a link does exist, especially after the President's public declaration in 2003 which scapegoated the refugees.

Indirect Security Concerns: crime, grievances and local tensions

There are, however, a number of instances where refugees have caused indirect security concerns in Tanzania. The first is the link between refugees and illegal activities such as theft and prostitution, especially in the context of reductions in food rations in the camps. As noted above, government policies practically eliminated the possibility for refugees to engage in legal, wage-earning employment, making them almost fully dependent on international assistance. When this assistance is interrupted or reduced, as with food distribution on several occasions in recent years, refugees must turn to coping mechanisms to survive. For example, a 2004 study undertaken for WFP found that 98 per cent of refugee households employ one or more coping mechanisms to deal with food shortages (Collins, 2004). Surveys conducted in all twelve camps in Tanzania found that most refugee households (81 per cent) either limited portion sizes at meal times or reduced the number of meals eaten in a day to cope with reduced food rations. Fewer households (24 per cent) answered that they sent a family member out to beg. Significantly, eight per cent of households admitted engaging in prostitution or theft as a coping mechanism. Likewise, UNHCR reported in 2007 that 'chronic reductions in food rations [and] restrictions on refugees' movements outside the camps' have resulted in an increase in 'negative coping mechanisms, such as survival sex' (UNHCR, 2007a, 198).

There is, however, a danger of blaming all crime and insecurity in refugee-populated areas on refugees, especially in the context of decreased rations. In May 2001, *The Guardian (Tanzania)* reported that the police 'did not have enough officers to control the refugees who had abandoned their camps because they did not have enough food' (cited in IRIN, 2001c). Crime statistics from Kibondo did not, however support these claims. Between January and December 2000, 59 out of 232 cases of robbery (25 per cent) in Kibondo were attributed to refugees. Given that the refugees account for 25 per cent of the local population, however, 'the proportion of refugee cases is almost the same as the proportion of refugees in relation to the total population' (Rutinwa and Kamanga, 2003, 15–16).

The second way that refugees may indirectly cause insecurity relates to tensions with the local population, especially when the local population perceives that the refugees receive preferential treatment. Drawing on research from the late 1990s, Landau (2002, 276) cautioned that 'while there are claims that members of the local population were mobilizing politically on the basis that refugees were entitled to better services, free food and the like, it is not clear to what extent this indeed occurred.' The presence of SPRAAs, coupled with a policy of allowing local residents to access hospitals and feeding centres in refugee camps, seemed to have mitigated much of the local frustration towards refugees. Fieldwork in Kibondo in 2004, however, suggested that this kind of grievance was on the rise, notwithstanding cutbacks in the camps and the benefits Kibondo derived from the presence of the refugee programme. These tensions have become more significant in the context of competition over scarce resources, especially public services and food. A specific source of resentment is the need for Tanzanians to now pay for services like health care and education, which were free under the *ujamaa* system, while refugees receive these services for free. Several authors have recently highlighted the poor state of Tanzania's social services as a result of economic decline and the pressures of structural adjustment (Wangwe and Arkadie, 2000; and Temu and Due, 2000). As a result, Tanzanians are now receiving a lower level of services at a higher cost to the user. Coupled with the relatively high levels of services in the refugee camps, one NGO worker in Kibondo suggested that the local population was getting frustrated that 'refugees [were] getting services for free that they, as citizens, now need to pay for' (interview, Kibondo, 2004). Many of these concerns are further reinforced by the anti-refugee rhetoric of local Members of Parliament.

This overview of the security concerns perceived by the government in relation to the presence of refugees reveals two important features of the government's construction of refugees collectively as a threat to Tanzanian security. First, the perception that all refugees are a security threat has justified restrictive actions against all refugees. As indicated by the 1997 round-ups, little effort appears to be taken to screen those refugees detained to determine if containment in a camp is necessary. While it is generally believed that much of the violence in Northwestern Tanzania has been caused by non-refugee elements crossing from Burundi, there is a sense that the government does not differentiate between illegal immigrants and refugees because it is not in their political interest to do so. In fact, the government continues to find the use of *prima facie* refugee status to be politically useful, as it serves to blur the lines between 'Burundian in Tanzania' and 'Burundian refugee'. While these lines are blurred, it is easier for the government to scapegoat an outside factor that it is taking active steps to contain.

Second, while the rhetoric in Tanzania constructs all refugees as a real or potential security concern, the state's response to different nationalities of refugees has not been consistent. For example, many of the restrictive measures being imposed on the Burundian refugees, including restrictions on freedom of movement and economic activity, were not applied to the Congolese refugees in and around

Kigoma. Likewise, urban refugees in Dar es Salaam have not been subjected to any systematic sweeps or round-ups. While they exist on the edges of society (Sommers, 2001), and are not able to claim any of the material benefits provided to refugees in camps, urban refugees felt that they could generally work undetected so long as they spoke Swahili (interviews, Dar es Salaam, 2004). The fact that the restrictive measures are not applied to all refugees would seem to suggest that not all refugees are seen as threats by the Tanzanian government, but that the scapegoating of some refugees as threats is of particular political utility.

Conclusion

This chapter has examined the various phases of Tanzania's asylum policy from independence to 2006 to argue that while the nature of Tanzania's asylum policy shifted from an open policy under Nyerere to a restrictive policy under Mkapa, the factors underlying the policy have remained constant. Domestic, regional and international factors have played the dominant role in determining Tanzania's asylum policy for the 40 years following independence. Given the twin elements of the idea of the Tanzanian state under Nyerere – *ujamaa* and pan-Africanism – refugees fleeing both conflict in neighbouring countries and wars of national liberation were welcomed in Tanzania. Tanzania perceived the presence of these refugees as an economic asset, in the case of Rwandan and Burundian refugees, and as a political asset, in the case of Mozambican and South African refugees. The twin pressures of economic liberalization and democratization, however, resulted in a change in the idea of the Tanzanian state, and a consequent change in its asylum policy. These changes were coupled with the mass arrival of Burundian and Rwandan refugees in the mid-1990s. Following the expulsion of the Rwandan refugee population in 1996, Tanzania came to perceive the prolonged presence of Burundian refugees as an unending burden and as a security concern. Notwithstanding the benefits experienced in refugee-populated areas like Kibondo, Tanzania responded to various domestic, regional and international pressures by pursuing an increasingly restrictive asylum policy.

This response highlights the significant role that broader political factors played in the formulation of Tanzania's asylum policy. Just as these broader factors played a role in the development of a more restrictive asylum policy, they may also play a role in the encouragement of a more open approach. As UNHCR and donor countries consider their response to Tanzania's 2008 offer to naturalize some 218,000 Burundian refugees, they should be especially mindful of these broader factors, and consider how a more comprehensive engagement with the interests and priorities of Tanzania may help encourage a more open response.

7
Guinea

For most of the 1990s, Guinea was an island of relative stability, as conflict and warlordism engulfed its southern neighbours, Liberia and Sierra Leone. From the first arrival of refugees from the Liberian civil war in January 1990, through the outbreak of the Sierra Leonean conflict in 1991, the 1997 *coup d'état* in Freetown and the resumption of the Liberian war in 1999, Guinea provided refuge for well over 500,000 refugees. Many of these refugees lived in a patchwork of settlements in Southern Guinea, and most became self-sufficient. The refugee programme in Guékédou, Southern Guinea, was UNHCR's largest refugee programme in Africa in 1999. For many, it was also the most successful.

This situation changed dramatically in 2000. In response to a series of seemingly coordinated cross-border incursions from Liberia and Sierra Leone, the President of Guinea, Lansana Conté, called on all Guineans to round-up and expel the refugees, whom he blamed for the violence. In response, thousands of refugees were beaten and detained in the capital, Conakry. Refugees elsewhere in the country were also profoundly affected, both as a result of the popular frustrations fanned by the President's speech and as a result of the ongoing conflict. By April 2001, a tenuous calm returned to Guinea, but the implications of the events of the previous year were significant. The conflict had left an estimated 1500 Guineans dead and tens of thousands internally displaced. The country's refugee population was scattered, and the tradition of asylum had seemingly been irreversibly changed.

Given the scale of the violence in Guinea between September 2000 and April 2001, the fact that the President identified refugees as the cause of the violence, and limited donor engagement to deal with the aftermath of the incursions, it may have been reasonable to expect

Guinea to adopt a restrictive asylum policy. Guinea has not, however, pursued this course. In fact, Guinea has, since 2003, pursued an open asylum policy, despite numerous security concerns and limited financial burden sharing. In fact, since 2005, Guinea has pursued a policy of locally integrating remaining Liberian and Sierra Leonean refugees on its territory. This policy has continued, notwithstanding the cessation of refugee status for Sierra Leonean refugees and the alienation of Guinea by the international community following the bloodless coup that brought a group of army officers to power shortly after the death of President Conté in December 2008.

Given the trend towards more restrictive asylum policies elsewhere in Africa, why has Guinea continued to pursue a more open approach to asylum? By examining the factors that have affected Guinea's treatment of both Sierra Leonean and Liberian refugees from 1990 to 2006, this chapter argues that Guinea's approach can be more fully explained by placing the question of refugees within the context of broader historical and political dynamics. The chapter argues that Guinea has been willing to pursue an open asylum policy because it seeks leverage against a restrictive international donor community, because the hosting of refugees has played a central role in Guinea's foreign policy and strategic objectives in the sub-region, and because the nature of the Guinean state, inherited from Sékou Touré, gives the President a monopoly on power and the ability to pursue policy objectives in the absence of any meaningful political opposition. In this way, the case of Guinea furthers the argument of this book: African states do not formulate their asylum policies in isolation, but within the context of broader political considerations.

Guinea's asylum policy pre-September 2000

Little is known about Guinea's asylum policy between independence from France in 1958 and the end of the Sékou Touré regime in 1984 (Azarya and Chazan, 1987; Camara, 1976; O'Toole, 1978; and Rivière, 1977). The literature that does exist suggests that Touré's refugee policy, like that of Nyerere of Tanzania, was guided by the spirit of African solidarity and support for regional wars of national liberation. For example, Guinea granted not only asylum but also the honorary title of 'Co-President' to Kwame Nkrumah of Ghana after he was deposed in March 1966. An unknown number of Ghanaians followed Nkrumah into exile in Guinea, and were reported to have been encouraged by Touré to 'engage in activities to bring about a change in Ghana' (Hovet,

1970, 25). This policy was sustained, notwithstanding a number of retaliatory actions on the part of Ghana.[1] The Touré regime also provided support to Amilcar Cabral's *Partido Africano de Independencia de Guiné e Cabo Verde* in their war for the independence of Guinea-Bissau from Portugal in the late 1960s and early 1970s by allowing Cabral to establish his headquarters in Conakry. In retaliation, Portugal invaded Conakry in November 1970 in an attempt to assassinate Cabral (Le Vine, 2004, 222).

Guinea was also a refugee-producing country during the Touré regime. In contrast to the optimism that characterized the early years of independence (Adamolekum, 1976), the Touré regime undertook disastrous experiments with forms of socialism, including forced labour and the prohibition on commercial trade, coupled with authoritarianism, motivated by a perpetual fear of plots to overthrow the regime. According to O'Toole (1978, 60), 'the increasingly repressive measures adopted by the Government of Guinea in the 1970s continued to swell the ranks of those who had already left the country for political and economic reasons in the 1960s.' While estimates of the number of Guineans vary considerably, it is generally believed that between 2 million (Azarya and Chazan, 1987) and 600,000 (O'Toole, 1978) Guineans were living outside their country in the early 1970s, primarily in states bordering Guinea. Many of these émigrés, especially Mandingo traders, went to Liberia to escape Touré's restrictive economic policies in the 1960s and 1970s, only to return to Guinea in 1990 to escape from the Liberian civil war (van Damme, 1999, 39).

War in Liberia and the initial response: 1990

On 12 December 1989, the National Patriotic Front of Liberia (NPFL), led by Charles Taylor, crossed into Northern Liberia from Cote d'Ivoire, starting one of Africa's deadliest civil wars. The start of the Liberian civil war resulted in a mass influx of refugees into southern Guinea from January 1990 onwards, reaching 325,000 by year-end. The refugee population then peaked at roughly 670,000 refugees in 1996. By 1999, Guinea continued to host an estimated 450,000 refugees, making it the country with the largest refugee population in Africa that year (see Figure 7.1).

Given the response of Kenya and Tanzania to comparable mass influx situations, it is important to begin by emphasizing that Guinea did not respond to this large refugee population by establishing refugee camps. Instead, refugees were allowed to initially settle within the local population. Whereas other African states in the 1990s responded to the

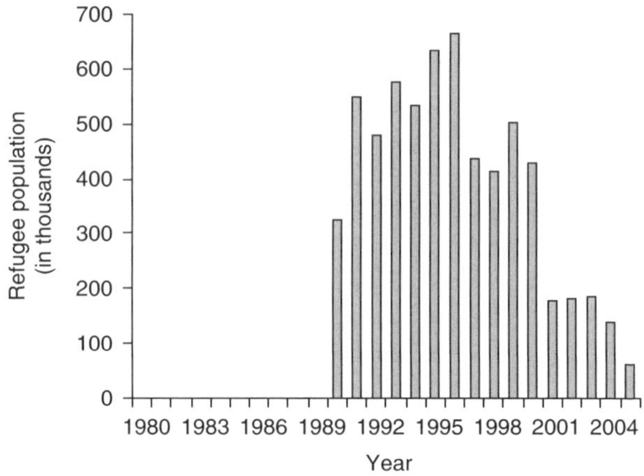

Figure 7.1 Refugee population in Guinea (1980–2005)
(UNHCR, 2000a; UNHCR, 2007c)

arrival of refugees by establishing camps, Guinea recognized the long-standing social, economic and linguistic links across the border and allowed refugees to settle in and around villages whose population typically belonged to the same ethnic group as the refugees. For example, when 10,000 ethnic Mano Liberians fled to Guinea in January 1990 to escape the fighting in Northern Liberia, they were settled in ethnic Mano Guinean villages. By March 1990, it was estimated that some 100,000 refugees had arrived in Guinea and that most had settled in approximately 60 villages (UNHCR, Technical Support Service, 1990a).

While van Damme (1999) has described the local dynamics of this settlement pattern, which built on pre-existing cultural, linguistic and economic ties, it is also important to consider the government's response to the influx. Unlike previous relations between Guinea and the UN system,[2] Guinea appealed to UNHCR for assistance and cooperated closely with UNHCR in the early stages of the crisis. Indeed, UNHCR later noted that from the beginning of the emergency 'the [Guinean] authorities ... welcomed the involvement of UNHCR in assisting as co-ordinator and facilitator of the emergency response' (UNHCR, Technical Support Service, 1990a, 2). This collaboration was formalized through a number of agreements in the early days of the crisis, including the accreditation of the first UNHCR Chargé de Mission for Guinea in March 1990 and the signing of a UNHCR's Branch Office agreement on 14 April 1990. These developments, in both practice and policy, highlight Guinea's willingness to engage with the refugee question. It is important to also note that while this response may be partially explained by the scale of the influx, it may also be the result of political changes in Guinea since the end of the Touré regime in 1984, and the desire of its new President, Lansana Conté, to pursue a policy of fostering closer relations between Guinea and Western countries.

Additional arrivals and a system close to breaking: 1991–2000

Van Damme (1999) outlines four major periods of refugee arrival in 1990–91, bringing some 350,000 refugees to Guinea, with 'rural refugees [fleeing] to rural areas, and urban dwellers settled mainly in the cities' (van Damme, 1999, 36). This pattern continued in the early 1990s, especially following the spillover of the Liberian conflict into neighbouring Sierra Leone. These arrivals settled predominantly in the *Languette* region of Guinea, a sliver of territory south of Guékédou that juts into Sierra Leone and partially borders Liberia. Guékédou became the focus of the international response to successive waves of arrivals from both Sierra Leone and Liberia through the 1990s and the UNHCR Sub-Office in Guékédou grew to become UNHCR's largest Sub-Office in Africa in 1999. The Guékédou Office was responsible for over 280,000 refugees in March 2000, 63 per cent of Guinea's total refugee population. These refugees, mostly Sierra Leonean, lived in 95 refugee settlements, ranging in size from 250 to 25,000 refugees, forming a patchwork of refugee settlement throughout southern Guinea, as illustrated in Map 7.1.

During the 1990s, UNHCR's programme in Southern Guinea, in general, and in Guéckédou, in particular, was seen by many to be a possible alternative to the refugee camps being established elsewhere in Africa. Instead of refugees being dependent on food distributions, UNHCR encouraged refugees to become self-sufficient by funding 'a number of agricultural programmes to promote cultivation of rice and other crops by refugees to meet the goal of self-sufficiency' (Black and Sessay, 1997, 595). As early as 1992, 87 per cent of refugees were engaged in some form of economic activity, while 50 per cent of refugees had achieved or were close to achieving self-sufficiency (Oularé and Keita, 1992, 13). On the basis of these findings, some, like van Damme (1995), asked if the settlement pattern in Guinea provided an alternative to refugee camps, pointing to the low cost of providing health-care to refugees, the contribution to the local economy and the degree of self-sufficiency enjoyed by refugees. These successes stood in particularly stark contrast to the vulnerability of Rwandan refugees in camps in Zaire and Tanzania during the same year.

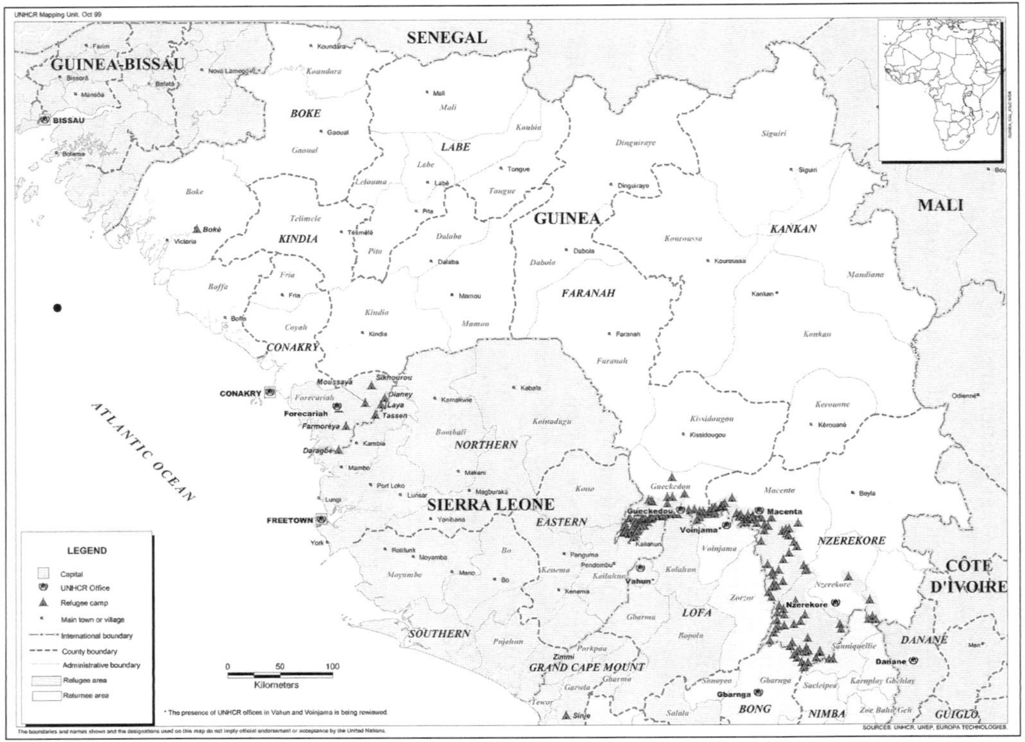

Map 7.1 UNHCR operations in Guinea (March 2000) (UNHCR, Mapping Unit, "Guinea: As of 7 March 2000", March 2000.)

By 1997, however, concerns were raised about the sustainability of this approach to refugee settlement. Black and Sessay (1997) highlighted how large-scale access to land for refugees had been motivated largely by short-term economic interests, and that the pattern of distribution could lead to longer-term concerns about environmental sustainability. They noted that while the immediate result of this large-scale access was an increase in food production, leading UNHCR 'to conclude that the refugees [were] capable of being self-sufficient' (Black and Sessay, 1997, 605), they cautioned that UNHCR and the Guinean government would eventually have to intervene to balance the short-term benefits of livelihoods for refugees and the local population with longer-term concerns about environmental sustainability.

The government and UNHCR soon came to share many of these concerns, and the UN Environment Programme (UNEP) was consequently requested to undertake a review of the programme. UNEP's preliminary report noted that 'high population densities in the rural areas and urban centres, mainly – but not solely – caused by the refugee influx, has resulted in a very high pressure on natural resources in southern Guinea' and that 'the apportion of the resources is unsustainable, leaving increasingly less natural resources available for an increasing population' (UNEP, 2000, 3). Crucially, the report noted that this situation was not the result of a lack of awareness of environmental issues, but highlighted instead the lack of burden sharing with Guinea to help mitigate the impact of the increasingly protracted nature of the refugee populations, noting that, 'after ten years, the situation seems to have become a permanent one, which according to many organizations present in Guinea and the Guinean Government cannot be sustained' (UNEP, 2000, 7).

These concerns about sustainability, combined with reduced donor support, came to place the refugee programme under greater strain by the end of 1999. UNHCR's programmes for both Liberian and Sierra Leonean refugees in the region were under-funded by 30 to 50 per cent in 1999, leading to cuts in the field.[3] According to a programme review conducted in 2000, this lack of donor engagement had a dramatic impact on the viability of the programme as a whole (Kaiser, 2001). The review noted that the programme worked under a number of constraints, including low levels of staffing and a dwindling capacity to support the 'relatively weak state structures with which UNHCR works' (Kaiser, 2001, 4). Indeed, it was found that these and other constraints, compounded by concerns relating to the environment first raised in 1997, had brought the whole premise of the programme into doubt.

The issue of insecurity also began to figure prominently in Guinea by the late 1990s, stemming largely from Guinea's involvement in the conflicts in Sierra Leone and Liberia. The May 1997 *coup d'état* in Freetown, Sierra Leone, which brought the Armed Forces Revolutionary Council (AFRC) to power, the ECOMOG (ECOWAS Monitoring Group) intervention in February 1998 and the attack on Freetown in 1999 by the Revolutionary United Front (RUF) all brought successive waves of refugees not only into southern Guinea, but also into Conakry. As under the Touré regime, Conté granted asylum to a deposed friend as the President of Sierra Leone, Ahmed Tejan Kabbah, fled to Conakry after the AFRC *coup*.

In the following months, two groups coalesced around Conté, on the one hand, and President Charles Taylor of Liberia, on the other (Kamara, 2001a, 3). The first grouping consisted of the Presidents of Guinea and Sierra Leone, with the support of *Kamajors* and members of the armed movement United Liberation Movement for Democracy (ULIMO).[4] The second consisted of Taylor, with the support of the RUF and, to a lesser extent, the AFRC.[5] Refugee protection and assistance became an important aspect of the struggle between these two groupings. The line between refugees and rebels became blurred, as *Kamajors* and ULIMO fighters helped the Guinean military patrol its borders and screen those seeking asylum in Guinea, while assistance to refugees was allegedly directed to support the campaigns of the two groups in Sierra Leone and Liberia (LCHR, 2002, 55–72). In response, the RUF launched cross-border incursions into Guinea in September 1998, targeting Tomandou refugee camp, 80 km from Guékédou, and killing ten people, including seven refugees (AI, 2001).

By the end of the 1990s, two issues were of increasing concern to Guinea: the impact of dwindling donor support on the sustainability of the refugee programme and an increase in security concerns relating to the militarization of the refugee question. In fact, these two themes were the focus of Guinea's statement to UNHCR's Executive Committee in October 1999. Guinea emphasized that it was 'the largest asylum country in the world proportional to its population [and] continues to suffer the negative impact of the presence of a large refugee population' (Guinea, 1999, 3, author's translation). It continued that Guinea's greatest concern was security, warning that 'if a solution is not found quickly that can guarantee our internal security, it is believed that the host population, already exhausted by the massive and prolonged presence of refugees, will not be able to suppress a feeling of rejection' (Guinea, 1999, 4, author's translation). Guinea also highlighted the perceived unequal treatment of African refugees, relative to refugees in the Balkans and East Timor, warning that 'the humanitarian fatigue of which we speak in other areas risks spreading in Africa, especially in Guinea ... if this indifference of the international community is allowed to continue' (Guinea, 1999, 7, author's translation).

In contrast with other African host countries, however, Guinea did not announce its intention to enforce encampment policies, enact tougher domestic legislation or push for the early repatriation of refugees. Instead, it stated it would enact a national refugee bill to codify its open approach to asylum. In fact, Guinea adopted *Loi L/2001/012 relative au statut des réfugiés* on 10 August 2000 (Guinea, 2000). The new law entitled recognized refugees to rights equivalent with those of Guineans, including freedom of movement and the right to work. In fact, notwithstanding concerns about security and declining donor engagement, Guinea continued to pursue an open asylum policy – until the events of September 2000.

The 2000–01 cross-border incursions

Between September 2000 and March 2001, Guinea suffered more than 30 cross-border attacks, resulting in an estimated 1500 civilian deaths, the internal displacement of between 100,000 and 350,000 Guineans, and the dispersal of tens of thousands of refugees. These events profoundly affected the protection of refugees in Guinea and the course of conflict in the sub-region, but have not figured prominently in the refugee literature. With the exception of some reporting by human rights organizations (AI, 2001; HRW, 2001a; HRW, 2002b; and LCHR, 2002) and limited consideration of these events in the francophone literature (Bangoura, 2001; Ellis, 2001; and McGovern, 2002), a detailed analysis of these events appears to be missing from the literature. One objective of this section is therefore to address this gap and present a detailed account of these events. Drawing from news wires, press releases and interviews in Guinea,[6] this section will chronicle the events of this important period and the responses from a range of actors before outlining the interventions of UNHCR and other actors to help Guinea address the security implications of the incursions.

Cross-border incursions: September 2000–March 2001

Between 1 and 2 September 2000, the Guinea border town of Massadou, to the east of Macenta, was attacked, allegedly by pro-Taylor Liberian elements supported by the RUF. An estimated 47 Guineans were killed in the attack, which marked the start of a rapid chain of events. On 3 and 4 September, Madina Woula, on the border with Sierra Leone and south-east of the regional centre of Kindia, was attacked, resulting in another 40 deaths. On 6 September, Pamalap, the border town near Forécariah and only 120 kilometres from Conakry, was attacked and held, allegedly by the RUF. The attack, which killed some 27 people and targeted an army garrison, was 'significant in that it marked the first attack in the border regions near Conakry' and threatened to strike at the very core of the Conté regime (AI, 2001, 3).

These seemingly coordinated attacks, spanning the length of Guinea's border with Sierra Leone and Liberia, caused panic in the capital. Local residents attacked Liberian and Sierra Leonean refugees and numerous anti-refugee demonstrations were held in Conakry in response to rumours that refugees were aiding the insurgents. Amidst this upheaval, UNHCR appealed to the international community to support what it identified as Guinea's security concerns. Likewise, in a meeting with foreign diplomats in Conakry on 7 September 2000, Moussa Solano, the Guinean Minister for Territorial Administration, blamed the attacks on Liberia and Burkina Faso, along with the RUF and Guinean dissidents, and called on the international community to condemn the attacks. He reportedly received a sceptical response.

On 9 September 2000, President Conté addressed the nation on radio, saying:

> I am giving orders that we bring together all foreigners... and that we search and arrest all suspects... They should go home. We know that there are rebels among the refugees. Civilians and soldiers, let's defend our country together. When you catch these people, these enemies, crush them. Wait for nothing. I order it![7]

According to Amnesty International (2001, 3), 'the President's speech is widely seen as a decisive turning point in national policy but also as implicit permission to the military, and the Guinean public, to go on the offensive against refugees in Guinea.' Refugees in Conakry were particularly affected. Some 5000 refugees were detained in community centres and police stations around the capital in the days following the speech. Many more were evicted from their homes and subjected to harassment and abuse by their neighbours, the police, and youth militias.

The President's speech was not only an effort to scapegoat refugees for the violence, thereby deflecting attention from Guinea's role in the regional conflict (McGovern, 2002), but reflected the feeling within the government that the Guinean army – lacking motivation, poorly trained and under-equipped – would not be able to repel the invasion without additional support. It found support in two groups. First, the alliance between Guinean forces and ULIMO fighters was reinforced, and ULIMO elements mobilized along with the Guinean army to defend Macenta and Guékédou. Many of these fighters had previously been refugees in Guinea, were drawn directly from the refugee population, or had family members within the refugee camps, especially Kouankan refugee camp, near Macenta. Second, thousands of young Guineans were recruited into local militias to reinforce the border defences. These youths, known as 'Young Volunteers', came primarily from Prefectures along the border; they were recruited by the local Prefects, armed, and sent to fight at the front-line with little or no training. No central registry was kept, so it is impossible to know how many Young Volunteers were recruited, but estimates range from 7000 to 30,000. With the support of the Young Volunteers and ULIMO, the Guinean military waged a six month campaign against the incursions. This began on 12 September 2000, when an offensive was launched to retake Pamalp, which included an attack on the Farmoréya Camp near Forécariah.

On 17 September 2000, the town of Macenta was attacked by elements from Liberia, resulting in many civilian casualties, including Mensah Kpognon, the Head of the UNHCR Macenta Office. A second UNHCR worker, Sapeu Laurence Djeya, was abducted and later released inside Liberia.[8] During the attack, the UNHCR Office in Macenta was looted. In response, UNHCR announced increased security restrictions, ordering all non-essential staff to remain in their homes and withdrawing all international staff to Conakry. This evacuation of international humanitarian workers was completed by 19 September, leaving national Guinean staff to deal with a near-impossible humanitarian situation.

Additional attacks on Macenta and Forécariah continued in September. In response, Guinean forces began shelling northern Liberia with heavy artillery on 22 September 2000. As Liberia claimed that Guinea's actions were 'tantamount to a full-scale war', a ranking Guinean officer was reported to have said that the army had been instructed to pursue any rebels attacking Guinea, 'even if it means entering Liberia and Sierra Leone' (IRIN, 2000b). In October and November, the fighting continued in southern Guinea, with attacks on Koyama, Balezia, and on the outskirts of Macenta and Guékédou.

A number of other related developments occurred in October. On 4 October, members of the ECOWAS (Economic Community of West

African States) Mediation and Security Council agreed, in principle, to send a military observer mission to patrol Guinea's borders with Liberia and Sierra Leone. As if to emphasize the need for such a deployment, Liberia claimed on 10 October that an armed group had attacked locations in Lofa County in Northern Liberia from bases located inside Guinea. At the same time, a delegation from the UN Security Council visited the sub-region in an effort to end the mounting violence. The mission met with Conté, who both 'denied that Guinea had ever supported Liberian dissidents' and 'requested that the international community take steps to dissuade President Taylor from this course of action' of backing the incursions into Guinea (UNSC, 2000c, 8). During the same meeting, Conté 'welcomed the decision in principle of ECOWAS to deploy troops on his borders, but noted that resource constraints would hamper the implementation' and therefore 'suggested that the United Nations assist in their deployment' (UNSC, 2000c, 8–9).

In early November, Guinean troops began to bomb villages in northern Sierra Leone in an attempt to undermine RUF activities. By the end of November, RUF fighters pushed deeper into Guinea, and almost captured the important regional town of Kissidougou after holding the town of Yendé, south of Kissidougou, for one week. Refugee settlements were also targeted in the fighting. According to Amnesty International (2001, 4), 'Katkama Camp, where the RUF reportedly attempted to recruit refugees to fight, was one of the camps particularly hard hit.'

The fighting reached Guékédou on 6 December. RUF fighters attacked from the south and west, as pro-Taylor Liberian and Guinean dissident elements reportedly joined from the east. The UNHCR Sub-Office in Guékédou, the base for one of the largest refugee operations in Africa, was attacked, looted and partially burned. The fight for Guékédou lasted several weeks and resulted in the virtual destruction of the town. The government later reported that 86 people, including 54 civilians, were killed, and that an estimated 100,000 Guineans fled the fighting and became internally displaced.

Fighting in the area continued through the first quarter of 2001. The last significant attack in the *Languette* was on 8 and 9 March, when RUF fighters attacked the Nongoa area, 30 kilometres west of Guékédou. The government's announcement on 19 March 2001 that it had repelled the attack brought to a close months of localized fighting in the Forest Region of Southern Guinea – stretching from Kissidougou to N'Zérékoré – and in and around Forécariah. Government officials estimated that the conflict resulted in the death of some 1500 Guineans and the internal displacement of well over 350,000 (interviews, Conakry, 2004).[9]

The conflict also had significant implications for the refugee population. First, tens of thousands were themselves displaced by the fighting. While UNHCR tried to gain access to approximately 92,000 displaced refugees in mid-December 2000, thousands more began to arrive spontaneously in Conakry seeking UNHCR assistance. In addition, the majority of the more than 90 refugee settlements in the *Languette* were destroyed, along with the refugees' livelihood. In the midst of the conflict, refugees were subjected to harassment, forced recruitment, physical and sexual abuse, arbitrary detention, and direct attacks by all sides of the conflict. Finally, the killing of the UNHCR Head of Office in Macenta resulted in the evacuation of UNHCR's international staff from Forécariah, Guékédou, N'Zérékoré, and Macenta, and a consequent suspension of all UNHCR activities outside of Conakry, leaving some 400,000 refugees without assistance for months. Addressing the protection and assistance needs of these refugees, and reinforcing the institution of asylum in Guinea, became a significant priority for a number of actors in the aftermath of the incursions, especially UNHCR.

UNHCR's response: Relocation, facilitated return, and resettlement

As the violence subsided in early 2001, UNHCR began to chart its response to the upheaval. It developed a three-pronged strategy to restore stability to the refugee population and to address the protection needs of the refugees. First, a massive relocation exercise was planned to find refugees scattered throughout Southern Guinea and to transport them to new refugee camps in the Albadaria and Lola Prefectures, both more than 50 kilometres from the borders with Sierra Leone and Liberia. Second, a series of options were considered to facilitate the safe return of Sierra Leonean refugees to Freetown. Third, additional resources were committed to the identification and processing of an estimated 30,000 refugees in need of resettlement to a third country. This section will briefly outline the evolution of these initiatives before turning to the responses of other actors.

In October 2000, UNHCR drafted an initial plan to relocate refugees from the border region and urban areas to newly established camps located at a safe distance from the border. The budget for the emergency transfer of some 125,000 refugees was estimated at US$11,398,000. Under-funding, insecurity and logistical problems caused delays, and a full-scale relocation exercise did not consequently begin until 27 April 2001. Between 27 April and the end of the relocation exercise on 27 May 2001, some 57,000 refugees were moved from the *Languette* to the newly established camps of Kountaya, Boréah and Telikoro near Kissidougou.

Sembakounya camp, near Dabola, was established to accommodate refugees relocated from Forécariah and Conakry. Starting in August 2001 and running into early 2002, Liberian refugees from Yomou and Diéké were relocated to the newly established Kola and Lainé camps, north of N'Zérékoré. Kouankan Camp, established in March 2000 before the attacks, remained open.

Specific activities were incorporated into the relocation exercise to help promote refugee and regional security. First, the Guinean military, under the supervision of the *Bureau National pour la Coordination des Refugiés* (BNCR), was involved in the exercise, responsible for screening refugees for weapons before the relocation. Second, military escorts for the relocation convoys ensured the security of refugees during the relocation.[10] Third, the new camps benefited from more proactive planning for refugee security. With the cooperation of the BNCR, a 'Mixed Brigade' (BMS) was formed from the police and gendarmerie to assume the responsibility of security in the camps.

The second prong of UNHCR's response was to facilitate the return of refugees to Sierra Leone, either by boat from Conakry to Freetown or overland through the establishment of a humanitarian corridor through RUF territory and into southern Sierra Leone. Returns by ferry from Conakry had started in late 2000 with a Sierra Leonean-chartered vessel. The International Organization for Migration (IOM) and UNHCR assumed responsibility for the operation on 9 January 2001, and facilitated the return of some 4800 refugees by the end of the month. The concern about this approach, in the absence of reliable access to the *Languette*, was that it forced refugees to make the perilous 1200 kilometre journey to Conakry, subjecting themselves to abuse and extortion along the way, to make a relatively short trip across the border to Sierra Leone.

To address this concern, the newly appointed High Commissioner for Refugees, Ruud Lubbers, made the establishment of a humanitarian corridor from Southern Guinea into Sierra Leone a priority during his visit to the region in February 2001. He received the support of Conté in Conakry and Kabbah in Freetown, while indications emerged that the RUF would also respect such a corridor. By the time Lubbers brought the proposal to the UN Security Council in March 2001, however, the support of key states had evaporated. The US stated that it 'did not support the creation of safe corridors or safe passages through rebel territory' as 'the risk to refugees' lives was too great and the RUF was not trustworthy' (UNSC, 2001a). Concerns were also expressed at Sierra Leone's ability to cope with large-scale return, and the amount of time required to prepare and deploy the necessary troops. Proposals for a humanitarian corridor were thereafter dropped, and small-scale returns by boat continued. By mid-2001, UNHCR estimated that some 55,661 persons of concern to UNHCR had returned to Sierra Leone, either by boat or spontaneously by foot.

The third prong of UNHCR's response was to refer as many as 30,000 vulnerable refugees for resettlement to a third country. Following the deployment of additional staff to Guinea in March 2001, an update on resettlement activities and populations in need of resettlement was presented at the Annual Tripartite Consultations on Resettlement in Geneva in June 2001. The update argued that 'increased stability within the refugee population, resulting from the relocation...will enable UNHCR-Guinea to more systematically identify refugees [for resettlement] in the coming months' (UNHCR, Guinea, 2001, 2). Following increased engagement by donor and resettlement countries, UNHCR's resettlement activities in Guinea grew significantly in following years. In fact, the number of refugees resettled from Guinea grew from 64 in 2000 to 1931 in 2005 (UNHCR, 2007c, 350). By 2006, however, that number had fallen back to 22 (UNHCR, 2007a, 275), meaning that UNHCR's Guinea programme fell well short of addressing the estimated 30,000 refugees in need of resettlement.

Broader engagement in Guinea: 2001–02

In addition to this response from UNHCR, offers of assistance and debt relief, both bilateral and multilateral, were extended to Guinea in late 2000 and throughout 2001 as a means of encouraging the government to keep hosting refugees and to keep its borders open to additional arrivals. The largest monetary contributions were made by the World Bank and IMF who, in the midst of the cross-border incursions, announced US$800 million in debt relief for Guinea. This assistance was estimated to equal about one-third of Guinea's debt service obligations between 2000 and 2019. While the package was reported to be part of a comprehensive debt reduction package for Guinea under the enhanced Heavily Indebted Poor Country Initiative, the World Bank linked the assistance to the incursions, recognizing Guinea's effort to address 'adverse external developments in the past eighteen months, including an increase in the frequency and the violence of rebel attacks from Sierra Leone and Liberia' (World Bank, 2000). A number of other bilateral financial contributions followed this announcement. In particular, the US made a number of humanitarian contributions to Guinea in early 2001, including over US$7 million of emergency assistance through the US Agency for International Development (USAID) and an additional US$5 million in emergency assistance from the US State Department.

In addition to these financial contributions, representatives of the Guinean government and donor government missions in Conakry highlighted the importance of solidarity with the regime during the incursions. A senior official of the Ministry of Security subsequently noted in 2004 that he believed that Guinea felt encouraged by the 'statements of solidarity' extended to it by the UN Secretary General, the President of the UN Security Council, the UN High Commissioner for Refugees, the OAU, and partner governments like the US, UK and France (interview, Conakry, 2004). Likewise, a diplomatic representative in Conakry believed that 'sympathetic rhetoric' from foreign governments was a source of comfort to the Guinean government (interview, Conakry, 2004). It is generally believed that this level of financial and diplomatic engagement with Guinea during the crisis, especially from the US government, provided the donor community with the leverage required to ensure that Guinea remained committed to the principle of *non-refoulement*, especially following the temporary closure of the Liberian border in May 2001 in response to an escalation of the conflict in Northern Liberia.

In addition to these examples of financial burden sharing, a range of actors supported efforts to respond to a number of Guinea's security concerns. These efforts targeted the security arrangements in refugee camps, training for the Guinean army, and the impact of armed elements remaining in Guinea after the incursions, including the Young Volunteers. For example, the Canadian government undertook an agreement with UNHCR to deploy two federal police officers (RCMP – Royal Canadian Mounted Police) to southern Guinea to train the BMS in basic policing and human rights principles (Herrmann, 2003). Likewise, to address the limited capacity of the Guinean armed forces and to ensure that Guinea would not be drawn into the conflicts that had plagued the sub-region for a decade, the US military began to train members of the Guinean armed forces in October 2000 (Berman, 2003). Finally, UNICEF (United Nations International Children's Emergency Fund) initiated a demobilization programme for the Young Volunteers in 2001. The objective of the programme was to address the reintegration needs of 5000 Young Volunteers, arguing that a failure to reintegrate the Young Volunteers would 'represent a serious threat to the country's stability' (UN-OCHA, 2001, 59). There was limited donor response to this appeal, and UNICEF was only able to demobilize 350 Young Volunteers in 2002. Subsequent appeals for 2003 and 2004 received practically no donor support. While UNICEF believed that a failure to resolve the problem of Young Volunteers contributed to 'a phenomenon of youth gangs who intimidate and threaten the population and show complete disregard for any authority' (UN-OCHA, 2003, 56), and that remaining youth could provide a fertile base for recruitment into new armed groups, it was unable to secure sufficient donor support. As a result, UNICEF's programmes for the Young Volunteers closed in June 2004.

Addressing the other armed elements in Guinea

Perhaps the most enduring consequence of the incursions, and Guinea's response, is the lingering presence of foreign armed elements in Southern Guinea. In 2001, Kamara noted that the conditions in Southern Guinea, characterized by 'large-scale displacement and non-existent economic opportunities, provided a reservoir of disaffected youths ready to be recruited into rebel armies and state-backed vigilante groups' (Kamara, 2001b, 12). According to 2004 reports, Liberian armed elements remained in southern Guinea, especially around N'Zérékoré and Macenta, and were engaged in criminal and political violence (IRIN, 2004a). There were also persistent rumours in 2003–04 that pro-Taylor, anti-Conté, groups were recruiting former Liberian combatants and Guinean youths for training in Southern Guinea, posing a potential challenge to the Conté regime (ICG, 2003). Combined with the potentially destabilizing presence of the Young Volunteers, the presence of foreign fighters remained one of the most potent legacies of conflict in the sub-region, and potentially a significant cause of instability in the region (ICG, 2005; and UN-OCHA, IRIN, 2005). In fact, the presence of armed elements, combined with political instability and a dramatic rise in the price of rice and oil, contributed to a significant increase in violence in the area in 2006 and 2007. Many of these concerns remain following Conté's death in 2008.

The largest armed group active in southern Guinea in 2000–04 was Liberians United for Reconciliation and Democracy (LURD), which emerged as a mysterious replacement to ULIMO during the cross-border incursions. While LURD's activities had a significant impact on security in the region and the course of the conflict in Liberia, they also had a direct impact on refugee protection in Guinea. Human Rights Watch (2002b) reported that a significant number of Liberian asylum seekers were stopped at border towns by Guinean officials and handed over to LURD commanders. These asylum seekers were then forced to carry arms, ammunition and supplies across the border to LURD bases in Northern Liberia. Many reported collecting the weapons from Guinean military trucks and being forced to make the return journey into Liberia up to 20 times before being allowed to seek asylum in Guinea.

It was also reported that LURD elements were present in the Kouankan refugee camp in 2002, and benefited from the material assistance distributed to refugees. According to Human Rights Watch (2002b, 10), 'numerous refugees gave detailed descriptions of the presence of armed LURD combatants in the refugee camp of Kouankan, where often uniformed and sometimes armed LURD rebels moved freely in and out of the camp.' LURD used the camp as a base for their families, as a destination for rest and relaxation, and as a source for supplies, especially food and medicine.

The rise and fall of the ECOWAS plan

Given Guinea's concerns about the porousness of its southern border, especially its border with Liberia, it is important to understand why the ECOWAS plan to deploy an ECOMOG force along the border was never implemented, notwithstanding Conté's initial support. In fact, when the ECOWAS observer mission was first announced on 4 October 2000, at the height of the incursions, it appeared to be the most effective way of stopping the attacks. In considering the rise and fall of the ECOWAS plan in light of the role that refugees played in the LURD supply chain, as outlined above, this section begins to highlight how the Conté regime's use of foreign armed elements to further its foreign policy and strategic objectives in the sub-region had an impact on Guinea's asylum policy.

At the end of December 2000, ECOWAS announced that an ECOMOG force of 1676 would be deployed to Guinea within a month. Meetings in mid-January to plan the deployment, however, coincided with renewed attacks on Guékédou. Given the delays in deploying the force, and concerns about its ability to fulfil its mandate if deployed, Conté grew impatient and pursued a dual strategy of artillery attacks on northern Sierra Leone and backing the LURD attacks on northern Liberia to create the buffer zone promised by ECOWAS. On 31 January 2001, it emerged that the Guinean army and air force had launched a series of attacks on RUF territory in Northern Sierra Leone, with the tacit agreement of the Kabbah regime in Freetown. Then, on 3 February 2001, the Liberian Defence Minister confirmed that Voinjama, the capital of Lofa County neighbouring Guinea, had been attacked by LURD forces based in Guinea.

As Guinea's military successes, proxy and otherwise, increased in Sierra Leone and Liberia, Conté support for the ECOWAS deployment faded. In fact, a deployment of ECOWAS troops after March 2001 would have hindered Guinea's objectives in Liberia. By the time the Guinean army, supported by irregular and foreign elements, regained control of Southern

Guinea in March 2001, Guinea ceased to support the ECOWAS plan, and pursued the defeat of the RUF and Charles Taylor through military means. This strategy seemed to work. The end of the incursions into Southern Guinea in March 2001 coincided with the LURD capture of Voinjama. In May 2001, reports emerged that the RUF had been forced into a ceasefire by the combined pressure of the Guinean attacks and the expansion of UNAMSIL (United Nations Assistance Mission in Sierra Leone) activities. Finally, on 11 August 2003, Charles Taylor stepped down as President of Liberia, and went into exile in Nigeria. The following week, a peace agreement was signed in Accra, ending Liberia's civil war.

The state of asylum in Guinea: 2004–08

The end of conflict in both Liberia and Sierra Leone, coupled with the expansion of peacebuilding activities in Sierra Leone and the election of Ellen Johnson-Sirleaf as President of Liberia in November 2005, had significant implications on the refugee populations in Guinea. Most specifically, it led to the repatriation of more than 130,000 refugees to Sierra Leone and Liberia between 2003 and 2006. As a result, only 33,200 refugees remained in Guinea at the start of 2007 (UNHCR, 2007a, 276). Conversely, while the end of the civil wars in its two southern neighbours certainly reduced the levels of insecurity in Southern Guinea, the region remained volatile. With a wide range of security concerns in the region, as outlined above, and the lack of donor support for reconstruction, it may be surprising that Guinea has remained committed to an open asylum policy since 2004, extending to the local integration of remaining refugees. This section examines the state of asylum in Guinea in recent years, especially within the context of ongoing concerns about domestic security and diminishing donor support for the refugee programme in Guinea.

One of the most striking elements of Guinea's approach to refugees in recent years has been the government's willingness to pursue the local integration of nearly 12,000 refugees. To facilitate this process, Guinea drafted new refugee legislation in November 2006. Then, in August 2007, the BNCR was replaced by a new government agency – *le Commission Nationale pour l'Intégration et le Suivi des Réfugiés* (CNISR) – responsible for monitoring the process of integration. This level of support for local integration is a clear demonstration of the openness of Guinea's asylum policy.

Guinea's primary concern, however, appears to be the willingness of donors to support integration programmes. During a visit by the UN

High Commissioner for Refugees in January 2005, for example, the Minister of Territorial Administration, Kiridi Bangoura, expressed his concern that the international community would ignore Guinea once it ceased to be a major refugee hosting country. While he acknowledged the importance of supporting reconstruction and peacebuilding programmes in Sierra Leone and Liberia, he called on UNHCR to mobilize donors to support rehabilitation, reconstruction and local development initiatives in areas of Southern Guinea that continued to host refugees (UNHCR, 2005c).

For its part, UNHCR has provided assistance to Guinea's integration and rehabilitation efforts in direct and indirect ways. While UNHCR's budget for Guinea has been reduced considerably in recent years, falling from US$25 million in 2003 to US$9.5 million in 2007, a portion of this budget has been specified for the costs associated with the legal and logistical process of integration. Indirectly, UNHCR has donated surplus resources and turned-over infrastructure as it closes refugee camps and offices, following the reduction of the refugee population. For example, UNHCR donated medical supplies, sewing machines, furniture and other items to the local population following the closure of its Kissidougou office in October 2006. More recently, UNHCR handed over the infrastructure of two refugee camps to the Guinean government in January 2008. This infrastructure included administrative buildings, health centres and water outlets.

That said, UNHCR appeared to share a number of the Minister's concerns about the sustainability of donor interest, stating that while Guinea had been trying to attract donor support for rehabilitation programmes in the refugee-populated areas for more than a decade, it 'failed to get a positive response from the international community, which has been linking its help to conditions like better governance and better management of public funds' (UNHCR, 2005c). In fact, donors appear to have become reluctant to support the refuge programme in Guinea, and contributed only 30 per cent of UNHCR's requested budget for Guinea in 2007. This prompted UNHCR to argue that while the government remains open to local integration as a solution for the remaining refugees, 'the success of local integration remains contingent upon the support of the international community' (UNHCR, 2007a, 278).

Local integration efforts have also been undermined by a deterioration in the political, economic and security situation in Guinea since 2006. Violent protests against the Conté regime in February and June 2006, fuelled by high inflation and the sacking of Guinea's Prime Minister, left an estimated 23 people dead. In response to renewed protests in early 2007, Conté declared a state of emergency in February 2007. It is estimated that some 140 people were killed and 1700 wounded in the ensuing violence. Some semblance of calm was restored following the appointment of Lansana Kouyaté to the post of Prime Minister, but the political and economic situation in Guinea remained highly precarious (UN-OCHA, IRIN, 2005; and ICG, 2005). Guinea was again thrown into turmoil in December 2008 following the sudden death of President Conté. Shortly after Conté's death, a small group of army officers led by Captain Moussa Dadis Camara seized power in a bloodless coup, leading to Guinea's suspension from the African Union and ECOWAS. Not only have these developments created a difficult work environment for humanitarian and development agencies, they have also further eroded the willingness of donor governments to invest in Guinea.

The apparent reluctance of the donor community to support local integration initiatives in Guinea points to a number of recurring burden sharing concerns, coupled with an apparent donor preference to contribute to reconstruction efforts in Sierra Leone and Liberia. More generally, it would appear that the refugee programme has been penalized as a result of the donor community's disengagement from Guinea, initially due to their frustration with the poor governance and human rights record of the Conté regime and, more recently, with a return to military rule since Conté's death. For example, the European Union decided in 2004 to suspend a €300 million aid package for Guinea, citing corruption and poor governance. As an extension of this frustration, donors appeared unwilling to fund programmes designed to support local populations in refugee-populated areas.

Explaining Guinea's position

In light of these concerns relating to burden sharing and security, perhaps compounded by Conté's death, it is striking that Guinea has remained willing to host refugees, receive additional refugees in the future, and locally integrate those who cannot return home. Guinea's open asylum policy would appear to contradict the hypothesis that African countries are restricting asylum when confronted with protracted refugee situations, failures of burden sharing and security concerns. Guinea has faced all these concerns, and has arguably paid a heavy price for sharing borders with Liberia and Sierra Leone. Given the findings from Kenya and Tanzania, it would seem likely that these countries would have increased the restrictiveness of their asylum policies, not the openness, if confronted with the insecurity faced by Guinea during the incursions. Guinea has not pursued a policy of abdicating responsibility for refugees, like Kenya, but has remained engaged through the work of the BNCR and CNISR. In response to security concerns, Guinea has not sought to confine refugees to camps, like Tanzania and Kenya, but has allowed freedom of movement for refugees. In response to the protracted presence of refugees, Guinea has not pushed for early repatriation, but has allowed them to locally integrate.

For these reasons, the case of Guinea illustrates the importance of situating the asylum policies of African states within a broader historical and political perspective. States, like Guinea, do not formulate their refugee policies in a vacuum, but rather devise and carry them out within a particular historical and political context, and in relation to broader internal and external factors and objectives. This section will outline how such broader historical, domestic and international factors have had played a predominant role in the formulation of Guinea's asylum policies.

The enduring legacy of Sékou Touré

The legacy of the Touré regime has influenced Guinea's approach to refugees in a number of ways. The first inheritance, and the one most often mentioned by Guineans, is the tradition of the Guinean exile under Touré. As outlined above, hundreds of thousands of Guineans fled the Touré regime, and many of these exiles were received into extended families and communities in neighbouring countries. Many of these exiles began to return to Guinea following the end of the Touré regime in 1985 and the outbreak of the Liberian civil war in 1989. When Guinea then started to receive refugees from the very regions that had hosted Guinean exiles, many felt obliged to return the hospitality. It should also be emphasized that the number of refugees in Guinea during the 1990s never exceeded even the most cautious estimation of the number of Guinean exiles under Touré of 600,000.

Second, Guinea remains a political community where the President holds significant, if not absolute, power, and where the mechanisms of the state are designed to ensure that this power can effectively be broadcast to the periphery of the state. This feature is, for some, the inheritance of the structures Touré developed to facilitate mass mobilization (Le Vine, 2004; and Kaba, 1977). Through these structures, Touré's party, the *Parti Democratique de Guinée*, was present in all parts of Guinea through a 'pyramid system of committees serving as points of articulation between the leadership and the masses' (Kaba, 1977, 29). This system, right down to the level of the *chef de quartier*, not only remains in Guinea, but retains the tradition of membership in the President's party and loyalty to the President. While many donors, especially the EU, see these structures as inhibiting good governance, they do, at least, ensure an open asylum policy when that openness is extended from the level of the President. As demonstrated by the events of 9–12 September 2000, however, these structures can equally harm refugees when the President sees it in his interest to pursue a restrictive asylum policy.

A third inheritance from Touré is the securitization of politics and the fear of the perennial plot. According to Le Vine (2004, 222), 'if anything epitomized the coercive atmosphere maintained by the Sékou Touré regime during most of its existence, it was the institutionalized paranoia of the "permanent plot", developed as an argument by Touré himself to explain the crises of Guinean society and to justify permanent revolutionary vigilance and repression.' From the first alleged assassination plot in April 1960 to the last in March 1984, Touré publicly claimed to have put down over 20 plots and conspiracies, many involving exiled Guineans seeking to undermine his regime. In a similar way, and certainly since a failed *coup* in 1996, Conté also adopted a prism of security, and justified a number of actions on the basis of countering the subversive activities of unknown, and somewhat mythical, 'Guinean elements' in the sub-region. In this sense, Conté appeared willing to subjugate all other interests to the priority of the survival of his regime. These concerns were heightened following an alleged assassination attempt in January 2005 and a series of general strikes and protests by sections of the military in 2006 and 2007.

Historically, Guinea's asylum policy has also been part of this struggle to retain power. According to LCHR (2002, 60), 'the control and management of refugees in Guinea is viewed as inherently a matter of national security. Only the President can make final decisions on refugee matters; nothing is decided or acted upon without his personal approval.' If, as argued below, he has identified hosting refugees as one means of ensuring regime survival, then other considerations of the positive and negative impacts of the presence of refugees would not matter. As argued by Bangoura (2001, 17–18), confronted with challenges to his regime throughout the late 1990s and magnified by the incursions, Conté clutched for every straw he could to remain in power. In doing so, he found great political utility in the presence of refugees.

Domestic pressures and opportunities

Another distinction between Kenya and Tanzania, on the one hand, and Guinea, on the other, relates to the openness of domestic politics and the state of democratization. As argued in the case of Tanzania, the process of democratization has had a negative impact on the government's openness to host refugees. In the case of Kenya, domestic and international pressure on the Moi regime contributed to the formulation of the 'abdication and containment' strategy. In the case of Guinea, steps towards effective opposition and democratization have been tentative at best. The leading opposition figure, Alpha Condé, was jailed shortly before the 1998 general elections and the 2001 referendum seeking a constitutional amendment to allow Conté to stand for a third term as President 'produced an implausible 98 per cent majority in favour of the change' (Melly, 2003, 1). Likewise, a flawed election in 2003 and the numerous changes in Prime Ministers in 2004–08 further eroded the credibility of the Conté regime in the eyes of donors. Simply put, Conté did not find himself in a position where he faced meaningful domestic electoral opposition before his death, and he consequently did not need to restrict asylum in an attempt to gain electoral favour, as is the case elsewhere in Africa.

The sub-regional context: An enemy of my enemy is my friend

In response to the 2000–01 incursions, Conté appears to have entered into an alliance with ULIMO and subsequently LURD. This alliance, while reportedly reinforced through the personal ties between Conté and LURD's leadership, may best be described as a marriage of convenience. Conté needed the support of LURD to stop the incursions. In turn, LURD needed Conté to support their war against Taylor. What held the two together was their common enemy in Charles Taylor. The presence of refugees in southern Guinea played an important role in the LURD campaign from late 2001. The refugee camps provided a secure home for LURD families, and a safe location for rest and relaxation. The assistance provided to the camps was known to have been redirected to LURD on a number of occasions. More importantly, as highlighted by Human Rights Watch, it appears as though the openness of the border and arrival of refugees also contributed to LURD's supply chain.

The granting of asylum was also an important political statement for Conté, not only with the hosting of Liberian refugees fleeing Taylor, thereby highlighting the failures of his regime, but also the hosting of Sierra Leonean refugees, and especially President Kabbah who was welcomed in Conakry following the 1997 AFRC *coup* in Freetown. This political dimension of hosting refugees – to provide shelter to friendly leaders and to refugees fleeing opposing regimes – has been repeated throughout Guinea's post-independence history. In this sense, it is interesting to consider how the politics of asylum in Guinea in the late 1990s was similar to that in the late 1960s, when Conakry was the home of Cabral's liberation movement. In both cases, Guinea supported an armed group dedicated to the overthrow of a neighbouring regime Conakry considered to be unfriendly: for LURD it was Taylor, the warlord; for Cabral it was Portugal, the colonizer. The hosting of both groups resulted in attacks on Guinea, the hosting of Cabral likely being the primary cause of the invasion of Conakry on 22 November 1970.

The international context: Playing the refugee card with donors

Finally, and most significantly, the presence of refugees in Guinea, and the government's willingness to host them, was a point of leverage between donor countries and the Conté regime for several years. As the overview of the donor response to the incursions suggests, multilateral and bilateral assistance to Guinea in the first half of 2001 was used to ensure that the government maintained the institution of asylum in the midst of the incursions. During this time, the donor countries used aid as leverage against Guinea. From the fall of Taylor in 2003 to Conté's death in 2008, it appeared as though Guinea tried to use the presence of refugees as leverage against the donor community. In much of the same way as Kenya allowed Somali refugees to enter its territory in 1991 to seek support from the donor community following the imposition of multiparty democracy, Guinea highlights its open asylum policy as a way of rebutting criticisms of its failures to combat corruption and promote good governance. Throughout the 1990s, the Conté regime gave the donor community few reasons to remain engaged apart from the presence of one of Africa's largest refugee populations. As noted above, flawed elections in 1993, 1998 and 2003 demonstrated little progress towards democratization. Given the regime's intransigence, coupled with Conté's failing health, it appeared as though many donor governments had adopted a 'wait and see' attitude to Guinea by suspending aid and waiting for the end of the Conté reign while preparing robust packages to facilitate the transition (ICG, 2003; and Melly, 2003). Given the return to military rule that followed Conté's death, it does not appear likely that donors are anxious to re-engage with Guinea.

In response to donor restrictiveness, Guinea appears to be 'playing the refugee card' by using its open asylum policy as way of thawing the frosty donors. Many believe that Guinea used the presence of refugees as diplomatic currency, especially with the US government. This engagement was linked to the change of regime in Monrovia, as Guinea was the most direct way for the US to engage in the Liberian conflict without directly engaging in Liberia. As political uncertainty continues following Conté's death, and as donors continue to express not only their reluctance to invest in Guinea but their preference to contribute to Sierra Leone and Liberia, Guinea must go to great lengths to ensure even modest donor engagement. As one of the few African countries to allow the local integration of refugees, Guinea may see broader political utility for continuing its open asylum policy.

Conclusion

This chapter has examined Guinea's approach to refugees from Sierra Leone and Liberia against the backdrop of regional instability. The chapter has argued that Guinea's asylum policy during the 1990s was guided predominantly by its engagement in the conflicts in the sub-region, leading to the politicization of asylum and the militarization of refugee camps. The chapter then chronicled the events surrounding the cross-border incursions of 2000–01, which prompted Conté to blame refugees for the spillover of conflict into Guinea. Given the scale of Guinea's security concerns during this period, coupled with its renewed concerns about declining donor engagement, it is striking that Guinea has not pursued a restrictive asylum policy. Instead, Guinea has pursued an open asylum policy because it is seeking leverage against a restrictive international donor community, because asylum has played a central role in Guinea's strategic objectives in the sub-region, and because the nature of the Guinean state, inherited from Sékou Touré, gives the President a monopoly on power and the ability to pursue policy objectives in the absence of any meaningful political opposition. In this way, this chapter has argued that historical, regional and international factors have played a significant role in the formulation of Guinea's asylum policy. As Guinea faces the challenges of a post-Conté era, and as donors continue to concentrate efforts on peacebuilding in Sierra Leone and Liberia, it will be important to understand how these dynamics continue to affect Guinea's asylum policy.

8
The Politics of Asylum in Africa

As illustrated by the cases of Kenya, Tanzania and Guinea, host states in Africa do not formulate their asylum policies in a political vacuum. Instead, asylum policies are affected by a range of political, economic and historical factors, often unrelated to the presence of refugees. While the importance of these factors is clearly recognized by representatives of African host states, they have not been given the prominence they deserve in research on refugees in Africa. In fact, a critical understanding of these factors, their origins and how they interact has not figured prominently in the literature on asylum in Africa. Given the changing nature of asylum policies, however, and the range of factors unrelated to the presence of refugees that can affect the quantity and quality of asylum afforded by a host state, a more critical understanding of these broader factors is crucial for a more effective engagement with the question of asylum in Africa.

In response to this importance, the goal of this chapter is to outline a framework for understanding the politics of asylum in Africa. This framework will highlight the range of factors that influence the asylum policies of host states in Africa, and the extent to which some factors may be more significant than others in the formulation of asylum policies. Drawing from the historical, conceptual and empirical chapters of this book, this chapter argues that political factors unrelated to the presence of refugees tend to play a greater role in the formulation of asylum policies than refugee-specific factors. Given the vulnerability of states in African to internal and external pressures, states like Kenya, Tanzania and Guinea have a tendency to incorporate decisions on asylum into a broader political calculus. For example, while the presence of refugees may, in a number of circumstances, constitute a burden, host states may see advantages in downplaying the benefits of hosting refugees as part of broader efforts to address external pressures from donor states. Likewise, as part of broader efforts to address internal pressures, host regimes may see benefits in portraying *all* refugees as security concerns, thereby justifying restrictive measures. Instead of simply condemning states for acting in this way, it is essential to understand the factors and dynamics that lead them to adopt more restrictive policies. Such an understanding does not excuse states for failing to meet their obligations under international refugee and human rights law, but rather reveals the full complexity of asylum policy formulation and the broad range of factors that need to be addressed if more open asylum policies are to be encouraged.

To support this argument, this chapter begins by re-emphasizing the importance of placing the host state more directly at the centre of the study of asylum, and focusing on the characteristics of the particular state as the point of departure for understanding asylum policies. The chapter then reviews the responses of Kenya, Tanzania and Guinea to the presence of refugees, highlighting their approach to both the quality and quantity of asylum, before presenting the elements of a framework for understanding the politics of asylum in Africa. This framework is based on a consideration of the broader range of factors that need to be incorporated into future research on African asylum policies. While it would be problematic to argue that the cases of Kenya, Tanzania and Guinea are representative of the continent of Africa as a whole, the findings from these cases do provide insight into which factors need to be included in the examination of other refugee situations in Africa.

Asylum and the state in Africa

This book has focused on the response of states in Africa to the arrival and prolonged presence of significant refugee populations. As argued in Chapter 1, this focus on the perspective of the host state, especially from a comparative perspective, has been lacking in scholarly work on the refugee problem in Africa. As a result, the interests and motivations of the host state have been relegated to a position of secondary importance in scholarly efforts to understand the problem of refugees in Africa. This should not be taken to mean that the host state should be excluded from any examination of asylum. On the contrary, as the cases of Kenya, Tanzania and Guinea illustrate, host states have played a significant role in determining asylum policies on their territory. Given the importance of the state, coupled with the political history of the state in Africa, it is important to begin by understanding the characteristics of the host state and governing regime, and those factors that influence state behaviour. Ayoob (1995, 2) argues that in the context of Third World states, 'state behaviour... is largely determined by the insecurity that is aggravated by the overwhelming feeling of vulnerability, if not impotence, among its state elites.' Given this condition, the primary objective of Third World regimes is to 'reduce the deep sense of insecurity from which [they] suffer domestically and internationally' (Ayoob, 1995, 3). These dynamics have clearly been present in Kenya, Tanzania and Guinea.

In the case of Kenya, the history of conflict between the state and its Somali population, coupled with the suspension of international aid in 1991, put pressure on the weakened Moi regime at the time of the mass arrival of the Somali refugees. The regime responded by implementing an open approach to the quantity of asylum, thereby satisfying the donor community, and a restrictive approach to the quality of asylum, by seeking to contain refugees on the periphery of the state. In the case of Tanzania, the end of the *ujamaa* model in 1985, coupled with the introduction of multiparty elections in 1995, resulted in changes in the idea of the Tanzanian state and challenges to the CCM regime. In response, Tanzania placed restrictions on the quantity and quality of asylum it provided to refugees from Rwanda and Burundi, both in an attempt to pressure the donor community to engage in more burden sharing and as a means of responding to increased domestic political competition. In Guinea, the Conté regime clung to power by engaging in regional conflicts and limiting domestic opposition. With the fall of the Taylor regime in Liberia and continued political instability following Conté's death, however, donors appear to have decreased interest in Guinea and have suspended aid in light of the country's poor governance record. In response, Guinea has sought concessions from donors by highlighting its open approach to the quantity and quality of asylum, but with seemingly little effect. In all three cases, feelings of vulnerability have contributed significantly to the formulation and implementation of particular asylum policies.

The most significant implications of state and regime vulnerability for asylum policies arise when they affect the state's perception of the costs associated with granting asylum. Loescher (1989, 8) argues that 'the formulation of refugee policy involves a complex interplay of domestic and international factors at the policy-making level and illustrates the conflict between international humanitarian norms and the sometimes narrow self-interest calculations of sovereign nation states.' The vulnerability of African states plays a significant role in shaping these 'self-interest calculations', and largely defines the political space within which asylum policies may be formulated. While Loescher (1992, 42) argues that states are more likely to grant asylum when it is likely to increase their power relative to other actors who might otherwise challenge the regime, the vulnerability of African states makes it more likely that they will only be willing to implement open asylum policies when it is not to the detriment of the host state or governing regime. Conversely, African host states could be expected to adopt restrictive asylum policies in cases where the arrival and presence of refugees negatively affects state boundaries, state institutions, governing elites, or weakens 'the capacity of states and regimes to act effectively in the realm of both domestic and international politics' (Ayoob, 1995, 9). Such calculations have clearly affected the nature of the asylum policies of Kenya, Tanzania and Guinea.

State response to refugee movements

While states may be said to adopt an open or restrictive asylum policy, the case studies illustrate that policies rarely fall exclusively into one of these categories, but rather fall along a spectrum between open and restrictive. To add clarity to the description of asylum policies, it is useful to also describe their effect on the *quantity* and *quality* of asylum. The quantity of asylum relates to the approach of the host state to physical access to its territory by refugees and asylum seekers. In contrast, the quality of asylum relates to the rights afforded to those permitted to enter and remain in a host state. Disaggregating asylum policies into open and restrictive approaches to the quality and quantity of asylum may provide a clearer understanding of the specific ways in which a state responds to the arrival and prolonged presence of refugees.

States may adopt a restrictive approach to the quantity of asylum in a number of ways. At the extreme, it may expel entire refugee populations, as in the case of Tanzania's expulsion of Rwandan refugees in 1996, or close its borders to prevent the arrival of additional refugees, as Tanzania did with its border with Burundi in March 1995. It can also push for the repatriation of refugees on its territory in advance of the promotion of repatriation by UNHCR, as Tanzania has recently done with Burundian refugees. In contrast, Kenya demonstrated an open approach to the quantity of asylum from 1992 onwards. While pushbacks were carried out in 1989 and 1990, and while smaller groups of Somali arrivals were returned to Somalia in 1990 and 1991, Kenya has generally allowed Somali refugees to enter its territory subsequent to the suspension of international aid in November 1991. Similarly, Guinea has demonstrated an open approach to the quantity of asylum for much of its experience with Sierra Leonean and Liberian refugees. It was only in the aftermath of the President's September 2000 speech and the closure of the Liberian border in late 2000 and early 2001 that Guinea placed limits on the quantity of asylum. As argued in Chapter 7, donor pressure on the Conté regime in the midst of the incursions appears to have played a significant role in ensuring that Guinea pursued this open approach to the quantity of asylum.

Host states may also adopt open or restrictive approaches to the quality of asylum they offer to refugees. As highlighted by Jacobsen (2005, 31–3) and the US Committee for Refugees (2005), a number of social and economic rights afforded to refugees by the 1951 Convention have been denied to refugees by a number of states, especially in the context of protracted refugee situations. These rights include the right to earn a livelihood and freedom of movement.[1] As detailed by Crisp (2003a, 11–13), it is by curtailing these rights that African states have been most restrictive in their asylum policies.

In concert with restrictions it has placed on the quantity of asylum, Tanzania has placed a number of restrictions on the quality of asylum it offers to refugees by prohibiting refugees from travelling more than four kilometres from refugee camps, by denying refugees access to local markets and by rounding up refugees who had previously been settled outside the refugee camps. The containment of refugees in the Dadaab camps, thereby denying them freedom of movement, has been a hallmark of Kenya's approach to Somali refugees. This policy has been reinforced by regular police sweeps in Nairobi and other urban areas. In contrast, Guinea has generally pursued an open approach to the quality of asylum. With the exception of the state-sanctioned backlash against refugees in September 2000 and the incorporation of Liberian refugees into the LURD supply chain, Guinea's official position has been to extend a high quality of asylum to refugees. Both during the pre-September 2000 settlement phase and subsequent to the relocation exercises, Guinea has generally allowed refugees freedom of movement and the right to work outside refugee camps. Unlike Kenya or Tanzania, Guinea also permits refugees to reside in Conakry, at the political core of the country. Finally, the local integration of Sierra Leonean and Liberian refugees is a significant example of the degree to which Guinea has pursued an open approach to the quality of asylum, although it remains to be seen if and how this policy will be sustained following Conté's death.

The politics of asylum in Africa

Given these distinctions between open and restrictive approaches to the quantity and quality of asylum, how do states decide what form their asylum policy should take? To answer this question, it is important to develop a more rigorous conceptualization of the politics of asylum in Africa. At the core of such an approach is a more critical understanding of the full range of factors that a host state considers when formulating its asylum policy. Given the primary objective of reducing vulnerability to internal and external pressures, host states both interpret the impact of refugees through the lens of these pressures and incorporate the question of refugees into a broader political calculus. As such, states formulate their response to refugees mindful of the furtherance of broader political objectives, with the paramount objective being the survival of the governing regime. It is, therefore, likely that asylum policies are primarily the product of an instrumental calculation of how to ensure regime survival and mitigate internal and external pressures. As a result, factors unrelated to the presence of refugees are not only likely to play a more influential role in the formulation of asylum policies, but are also likely to play a significant role in the characterization of refugees as either a burden or a security concern. To more fully explain this dynamic, it is important to consider how a number of refugee specific factors – including historical factors, quantitative factors, burden sharing factors and security factors – interact with broader domestic, regional and international factors. Drawing from the case studies, this section argues that the combination and interaction of these factors will determine the asylum policies adopted by states. While each of these factors may affect different states in different ways, a consideration of these factors, and the interplay between them, will illustrate how each played a role in determining the asylum policies of Kenya, Tanzania and Guinea.

Historical factors

A state's past experience with refugee movements may contribute significantly to its approach to the arrival of additional refugees, especially to those from the same country of origin. As argued by Jacobsen (1996, 660–1 and 669), if past refugee movements resulted in political or economic benefits for the host state and local community, coupled with a sustained engagement by the international community, there is a greater probability that future refugee movements will benefit from an open asylum policy. Likewise, if a state previously had a negative experience with the arrival of refugees, there is a higher probability that it will adopt a restrictive approach.

Tanzania's response to Burundian refugees in the 1970s may largely be understood in these terms. The arrival of Rwandan refugees in the 1960s boosted Tanzania's status regionally and internationally, while the Tripartite settlement model helped ensure that the refugee presence would attract development resources to underdeveloped regions of the country and ensure that the cost to the state would remain low. In another way, the experience of hundreds of thousands of Guineans having sought and received asylum in the region during the Touré regime likely informed the open approach of the Conté regime to the arrival of Liberian refugees in the early 1990s. At the same time, a positive historical experience does not always lead to an open asylum policy in the future. The history of Ugandan refugees in Kenya in the 1980s, and the general agreement that they made an important contribution to the Kenyan economy, did not appear to play a role in the formulation of the Moi regime's response to the arrival of Somali refugees.

However, it is more likely that a negative historical experience will lead to a restrictive asylum policy than a positive historical experience will lead to an open approach. This is particularly true if past experience results in the host state feeling that its hospitality has been 'slighted' or forgotten by refugees or the international community. After the RPF gained control of Kigali and formed a Tutsi-dominated government in 1994, a number of stories circulated of Rwandans who had been granted citizenship in Tanzania in the 1980s burning their Tanzanian passports and returning to Rwanda. While these stories have not been verified, they have nonetheless affected Tanzanian asylum policy. Some feel that this 'slighted hospitality' contributed significantly to Tanzania's post-1995 position that local integration and naturalization were no longer feasible for any refugee it hosts. At the same time, the belief that the engagement of the international donor community has waned over time resulted in feelings of 'forgotten hospitality'. In particular, feelings that the international donor community previously left the host country to shoulder a refugee burden alone will likely lead to a lack of willingness to trust the sustainability and dependability of burden sharing in future cases, as discussed below.

Quantitative factors

The changing nature and scale of refugee movements in Africa, however, may result in historical experiences not being seen as a useful precedent. For example, it is unlikely that the presence of 10,000 Ugandan refugees in Kenya in the 1980s could be viewed as useful for understanding the response of the Moi regime to the arrival of over 400,000 Somali refugees. In fact, concerns relating to the numbers of refugees and their length of stay were cited by officials in Kenya, Tanzania and Guinea as a key factor contributing to the state's approach to asylum. In this way, it is important to understand how the quantitative features of a refugee movement may affect the response of the host state.

As outlined in Chapter 4, a significant characteristic of the changing nature of conflict in Africa since the end of the Cold War has been the advent of so-called failed, fragile or collapsed states, where the nature of conflict has resulted in a breakdown of essential state structures (Rotberg, 2004; and Zartman, 1995). The dynamics of state failure and the changing nature of conflict in Africa in the 1990s not only resulted in the outflow of significant refugee populations to countries like Kenya, Tanzania and Guinea, but also frustrated efforts to find solutions for the refugee situations they produced. As conflict became more protracted, as state failure became more common, and as efforts to ensure stability in post-conflict societies proved more difficult (Ali and Matthews, 2004), the prospects of resolving refugee situations became more distant. For example, the collapse of state institutions in Somalia in the early 1990s continues to frustrate efforts to find a solution to the Somali refugee situation and, coupled with the lack of external engagement and the policy responses of host states, has led to one of Africa's most protracted refugee situations. In fact, a list of Africa's major protracted refugee situations doubles as a list of the most significant examples of protracted conflict and state fragility in Africa, as illustrated by Table 8.1 (below).

Not only are these conflicts proving difficult to resolve, but the refugee populations they produce are spending longer in exile. According to UNHCR (ExCom, 2004b, 2), the average duration of a major refugee situation has increased from nine years in 1993 to 17 years in 2003. As these situations become increasingly protracted, and as solutions remain elusive, host states come to perceive them as an unending burden. Such a perception may, in turn, affect the state's approach to asylum. For example, in both Kenya and Tanzania, the protracted nature of the refugee situation was identified as one of the principal concerns of the host state, and a justification for adopting a restrictive asylum policy. This fact highlights the need to formulate and implement comprehensive solutions to protracted refugee situations.[2]

The increase in numbers alone, however, cannot independently account for the nature of asylum policies adopted by states. For example,

Table 8.1 Major protracted refugee situations in Africa (1 January 2005) (UNHCR, 2006, 107)

Country of asylum	Country of origin	Total
Burundi	Dem. Rep. of Congo	48,000
Cameroon	Chad	39,000
Congo	Dem. Rep. of Congo	59,000
Côte d'Ivoire	Liberia	70,000
Dem. Rep. of Congo	Angola	98,000
Dem. Rep. of Congo	Sudan	45,000
Ethiopia	Sudan	90,000
Guinea	Liberia	127,000
Kenya	Somalia	154,000
Kenya	Sudan	68,000
Rwanda	Dem. Rep. of Congo	45,000
Sudan	Eritrea	111,000
Uganda	Sudan	215,000
United Rep. of Tanzania	Burundi	444,000
United Rep. of Tanzania	Dem. Rep. of Congo	153,000
Zambia	Angola	89,000
Zambia	Dem. Rep. of Congo	66,000

Guinea's refugee population climbed from 325,000 in 1990 to 670,000 in 1996 without prompting a change in policy from the regime in Conakry. Lessons may also be drawn from the politics of asylum in the West. In the context of Europe's trend towards restrictionism in the 1990s, Gibney (2001, 3) argues that 'rising numbers on their own fall well short of providing an adequate explanation for increased restriction.' The fact that Western governments continue to introduce restrictive asylum policies notwithstanding the fact that the number of asylum seekers arriving in all industrialized countries has fallen by half in the past five years raises further questions about the explanatory value of numbers alone. As Gibney (2001, 3) concludes, 'rising asylum claims tell us what governments have been reacting to, but they do not tell us why governments have grasped with such alacrity measures designed to restrict and prevent rather than include and manage those striving for asylum.' This conclusion applies with equal force to Africa, and points to the fact that other factors likely play a more significant role.

At the same time, it is important to recognize that the politics of refugee numbers are as potent in Africa as they are in the West. For example, Bariagaber (1999, 603) notes that host countries in the Horn of Africa were thought to inflate their refugee statistics in the 1980s and 1990s as a means of both attracting additional material resources from humanitarian organizations and embarrassing a neighbouring regime. Similar concerns were raised in Guinea in 1999, as humanitarian workers believed that Guinea had inflated the refugee population in the Guékédou settlements as a means of inflating the assistance budget. Crisp (1999b, 8) argues that these concerns were expressed across Africa in the 1990s, as aid agencies were frequently suspicious that host countries made 'exaggerated claims about the number of refugees present on their territory' to embarrass neighbouring regimes, attract additional material and financial assistance, justify large refugee assistance programmes and bureaucracies, and 'to cast the most favourable light possible on the country's commitment to humanitarian norms, thereby bolstering its international reputation and external support'. Such concerns indicate that broader political factors may motivate host states to present inflated refugee statistics, and that refugee statistics are consequently just as susceptible to politicization as the characterization of refugees as a security concern or a burden.

Burden sharing factors

In all three cases, government officials claimed that the mass arrival and prolonged presence of refugees had a negative impact on the refugee-populated area, while also expressing concern about declining donor engagement and failures in burden sharing. This section applies the framework presented in Chapter 3 to examine how perceptions of burden sharing contributed to the asylum policies adopted by Kenya, Tanzania and Guinea.

Evidence from the cases suggests a wide scope of burden sharing in the three cases, both in terms of financial and physical burden sharing. In Kenya, donor engagement has supported programmes as diverse as the Firewood Project, the security package, assistance to the local population through LAPs, and the largest resettlement programme in Africa. While there is less engagement in resettlement from Tanzania, there is a wide scope of financial burden sharing, with support for the security package and assistance to the local population through the SPRAAs. The scope of burden sharing was more limited in Guinea.

In contrast, the scale, sustainability and dependability of burden sharing in all three cases have caused concern for host states. In Kenya, limited and unpredictable donor support has meant that UNHCR was struggling to 'maintain minimum standards of emergency assistance' more than a decade after the 'end' of the Somali refugee emergency (UNHCR, 2004b, 191). Similar concerns were evident in Tanzania, with significant shortfalls in donor support since the late 1990s. In contrast, the scale of burden sharing in Guinea in 2001–03 was significant, with donors sometimes contributing more funds than requested by UNHCR and other implementing partners. The scale and dependability of this engagement, however, changed with the fall of the Taylor regime in Liberia in August 2003. With the change of circumstances in Liberia, donor interest has shifted away from Guinea and towards reconstruction in Liberia, highlighting a lack of dependability.

These experiences support Crisp's more general conclusion that 'donor states can be said to have exacerbated the decline in protection standards in Africa by making it increasingly clear that they are no longer prepared to support long term refugee assistance efforts' (Crisp, 2000, 7). Such concerns are reinforced when considering what aspects of asylum donors were seeking to ensure in these host states. In all three cases, it would appear that donors were targeting their assistance to ensure a high quantity of asylum as opposed to a high quality of asylum. In both Kenya and Guinea, donor engagement was most pronounced amid fears that the borders of the host state would be closed to refugees. This type of engagement was particularly evident in Guinea between September 2000 and March 2001.

At the same time, the three case studies illustrate that host states have tended to emphasize the burdens of hosting refugees, notwithstanding the evidence that their presence may, in certain circumstances, constitute a benefit. All three cases provide significant evidence that, in some respect, the prolonged presence of refugees and the refugee assistance programme has resulted in tangible benefits for the refugee-populated area. These benefits have taken the form of investment in local services and infrastructure, especially through the LAPs in Kenya and the SPRAAs in Tanzania, and the creation of employment opportunities. In Guinea, where refugees enjoy the right to work, they have contributed directly to the local economy, especially in market towns like N'Zérékoré. These benefits associated with the presence of refugees have not been articulated by representatives of the host state in international fora such as UNHCR's Executive Committee, where host states tend to emphasize that the hosting of refugees has resulted only in burdens.

Given that this tactic is believed to have been employed as a means of trying to leverage additional support, it may be argued that host states characterize refugees exclusively as a burden as a means of trying to influence the level of assistance they receive from the international donor community. As noted in Chapter 3, African host states have consistently advocated for monetary compensation from the international community for hosting refugees since the 1970s. Since the ICARA process, however, donor states have refused to provide financial burden sharing either as compensation or at the levels requested by host states. The inability of African states to shift the terms of the burden sharing debate over the past 25 years suggests that the dynamics of the debate are largely dictated by donors and determined by the nature of relationship between African states and the donor community as opposed to any objective characterization of the African refugee burden, as argued below. Given donor interest in a high quantity of asylum, African states should consider how they can best engage with the interests of donor states to ensure more dependable burden sharing. As recent evidence from Uganda and Zambia might suggest, open asylum policies leading to local integration may be used by host states to create such an opportunity.

Security factors

Security concerns have also played an important role in the formulation of asylum policies, with both Kenya and Tanzania justifying restrictive asylum policies on the basis of perceived refugee-related insecurity. It is, however, important to understand the nature of these security concerns, consider the extent to which refugees are the cause of these concerns, and identify other factors that may contribute to the securitization of the refugee question. This section applies the framework presented in Chapter 4 to examine how perceptions of refugees as direct and indirect security concerns contributed to the asylum policies of Kenya, Tanzania and Guinea.

In all three cases, it was not refugees that caused direct security concerns, but the presence of armed elements either within or close to the refugee population. In fact, there is little evidence suggesting that direct security concerns are caused by the presence of refugees. In the case of Kenya, a long history of conflict between the ethnic-Somali Kenyan population and the Kenyan state has reinforced a public distrust of Somali refugees and a popular belief that their presence could facilitate the spillover of violence from Somalia to Kenya. On the basis of this association, and the fact that terrorism in the region and small arms proliferation have roots in Somalia, Somali refugees are perceived as direct security threats. Likewise, security concerns relating to the presence of refugees are not new to Tanzania, especially given its active support of African liberation movements in the 1960s and 1970s, or for Guinea, given its history of hosting foreign armed elements. As Tanzania's security concerns are no longer tied to support for liberation struggles, and refugees have been a source of regional and international frustration, not pride, for Tanzania since the 1990s, they are of increasing concern to the CCM regime, which has, in turn, securitized the presence of Burundian refugees. In Guinea, the President's 'speech act' in September 2000 masked the fact that the Conté regime had entered into an alliance with foreign armed elements, especially LURD.

In all three cases, the identification of refugees as a cause of direct security concerns stems more from the perceptions and policy choices of the host state and governing regime. The political decision to securitize the refugee population has often been used as a means to divert attention from regime action in other areas, as in the case of Guinea, or to divert attention from government inaction, or its inability to control related security concerns, as with the proliferation of small arms in Kenya and Tanzania. While the proliferation of small arms and the presence of armed elements in volatile border areas do constitute legitimate security concerns, they are not directly caused by refugee movements. As such, evidence from the cases would suggest that the identification of refugees as a direct security concern in Kenya, Tanzania and Guinea is more the result of a 'scapegoat strategy', as described by Job (1992, 29), than a legitimate security concern. This dynamic will be discussed in greater detail below.

In contrast, the three case studies demonstrate how the presence of refugees, coupled with other factors, has resulted in indirect security concerns for host states. Shortcomings in burden sharing, combined with restrictive asylum policies, have led refugees in Kenya and Tanzania to pursue their own coping strategies. Notwithstanding the fact that these strategies are often more harmful for refugees than for the local population (Crisp, 2003a, 19–22), some of these coping strategies have created legitimate security concerns for host states. This is especially true in the case of Tanzania, where interruptions in food distribution to encamped refugees have resulted in instances of refugees turning to theft and banditry as a coping strategy.

In a similar way, two other indirect security concerns are more the consequence of factors unrelated to the presence of refugees than a result of the actions of refugees themselves. First, grievances arising from the perception that refugees receive preferential treatment, most evident historically in the case of Tanzania, largely result from economic liberalization and structural adjustment programmes. A common characteristic of structural adjustment programmes is the limiting of access to social services, especially as governments introduce user fees for access to services such as health and education. Such fees can act as a barrier to access, especially for poorer members of society. In such cases, the fact that the local population must now pay for services which the refugees continue to receive for free has resulted in tensions between the two groups, notwithstanding the significant contribution to the local community made through SPRAAs. Similarly, shocks in Guinea's economy, which provoked the dramatic increase in the cost of rice, are believed to have increased tensions between the local population and refugees, although it may be too soon to tell how lasting these tensions will be.

Second, perceptions that the presence of refugees has prompted shifts in the balance of power either between the governing regime and domestic challenger groups, or between the core and periphery of the state, are best understood within the context of democratization and political liberalization. As argued by Mkandawire (1999, 124), 'periods of transition tend to render more transparent challenges to the legitimacy of the state, as hitherto unarticulated or muted claims are openly voiced.' Governing regimes consequently face additional pressures to meet the political and economic demands of a range of challenger groups and regions of the country. The fact that large refugee movements in the 1990s coincided with the early stages of democratization has not meant that refugees have affected political opportunity structures. Instead, changes in the political opportunity structure have affected refugees, as challenger groups have sought to create political opportunity by linking the presence of refugees to a range of social, economic and security concerns. At the same time, governing regimes, in a bid to retain power when confronted with democratization, have employed additional 'scapegoat strategies' and politicized the refugee question for their political benefit, as discussed below.

This analysis of the burden sharing and security concerns of host states indicates that factors unrelated to the presence of refugees have played a significant, if not the predominant role, in determining the asylum policies of states. In particular, the changing nature of conflict in Africa, the inability of African states to exert pressure on the international donor community, and the consequences of limited state capacity, economic liberalization, and democratization all appear to have crucially influenced the nature of asylum policies adopted by Kenya, Tanzania and Guinea. For this reason, any understanding of asylum policies in Africa must consider these broader domestic, regional and international factors.

Domestic factors

As illustrated by the cases of Kenya, Tanzania and Guinea, various dynamics resulting from democratization and the consequent increase of domestic pressure on the governing regime have limited the space within which asylum policies have been formed. At the same time, some governments have sought to politicize the presence of refugees as a way of countering sources of domestic pressure and demonstrating their control over domestic affairs. This section seeks to highlight these dynamics by drawing on similar tensions in Western states and by emphasizing the growing significance of nationality laws in Africa.

Rutinwa (1999) cites three factors to explain increasing xenophobia in a number of African states during the 1990s. First, he points to declining feelings of solidarity between local populations and refugees, due primarily to the fact that refugees were no longer fleeing wars of national liberation. Second, he emphasizes the dual impact of the African economic crisis and economic liberalization on the well-being of citizens in refugee-populated areas, noting that the curtailment of services to citizens has 'made it difficult for the people to accept the same services being provided for free to refugees' (Rutinwa, 1999, 2). Third, he notes that xenophobia has 'emerged at a time when most of Africa is democratizing and governments are compelled to take into account public opinion in formulating various policies' (Rutinwa, 1999, 2). Crisp (2000, 8) makes a similar point by noting that 'prior to the 1990s, authoritarian governments and one party states in Africa were relatively free to offer asylum to large refugee populations when they considered such a policy to be consistent with their own interests.' In fact, it is no coincidence that the era of open asylum policies in Africa in the 1960s and 1970s overlapped with the era of the 'monopoly state' in Africa (Clapham, 1996, 56–62), with virtually no sources of domestic opposition. In this way, it is significant that it is the least democratic of the three cases – Guinea – that has maintained the most open asylum policy.

To better understand this dynamic, lessons may be drawn from the experience of Western asylum countries. In considering the rise of more restrictive policies in Western states in the 1990s, Gibney (2001, 7) argues that a number of factors eroded the autonomy of state leaders to set asylum policies and led to 'a *democratization of asylum policy* in Western states, with domestic political actors (the public, the media and opposition parties) increasingly calling the tune.' As Gibney argues (2001, 7):

> The results were not pretty. As asylum became part of the cut and thrust of domestic politics, government leaders found themselves facing more pressures to restrict entry. With little incentive to resist ... governments implemented an increasingly retrograde set of control measures to prevent and deter the arrival of asylum seekers.

As a consequence of this process, the politics of asylum in the West has increasingly come to focus on the government's ability to demonstrate control, with public perception that the admission of refugees is neither orderly nor controlled having the potential to undermine the government's legitimacy in the eyes of the electorate (Gibney, 2004; Spencer, 2003; and Weiner, 1995). In democratic states, this loss of legitimacy may have electoral consequences as 'political elites believe that if they fail to control asylum, it will contribute to or cause their electoral defeat' (Gibney, 2001, 7).

While similar dynamics are at play in African states, the reduced ability of the state in Africa to broadcast its authority to the periphery of the state, as argued by Herbst (2000), results in different outcomes. In Western states, governments have sought to demonstrate their control over the asylum question through the introduction of increasingly stringent screening procedures and more differentiated categorizations of individuals permitted to enter and on what terms. Unlike European states, however, African states do not have the same capacity to broadcast authority and must consequently seek alternate means of demonstrating control (Herbst, 2000, 13–28). In such cases, it is to the benefit of African regimes that refugees have only *prima facie* refugee status, as the lack of individualized status not only facilitates the securitization of refugees, as outlined above, but their politicization as well. Whereas European states seek greater precision in refugee definitions, African states tend to seek greater ambiguity as a means of facilitating securitization, thereby justifying blanket control.

This is yet another way that Job's 'scapegoating strategy' (Job, 1992) informs an understanding of asylum policies. Given the vulnerability of African regimes to internal pressures, the portrayal of *all* refugees as security concerns, thereby justifying encampment, for example, allows the government to demonstrate control. This is the instrumental value of portraying refugees, collectively, as a security concern: the governing regime can demonstrate its ability to 'control' a security 'threat' by imposing encampment, thereby using the presence of refugees to address a domestic source of pressure in the context of democratization. This dynamic is especially evident in Kenya's portrayal of Somalis, Tanzania's portrayal of Burundians, and Conté's portrayal of Sierra Leonean and Liberian refugees in his speech of 9 Septmeber 2000.

It is also important to compare the role that a number of other actors have played in domestic asylum debates in both the West and Africa. In particular, both the media and NGOs have played key roles in the Western asylum debate (Tazreiter, 2004). While the media is often seen to fan the flames of restrictionism, Western NGOs have frequently been the only means through which the needs and interests of refugees can be voiced (Gibney, 2001, 8). This is true at the national, regional and international level, with groups like the British Refugee Council, ECRE and Amnesty International representing the needs and rights of refugees to different levels of governing authority. While the media has been found to play an equally potent role in shaping popular anti-refugee sentiments in Africa, as illustrated by Nyamnjoh's work on the role of the media in the articulation of a more exclusionary idea of citizenship (Nyamnjoh, 2005, 17–24), a striking difference between the asylum debate in Africa and the West is the role of domestic and regional NGOs. In particular, domestic refugee NGOs have been found to have a very limited presence, if any at all, in many host countries in Africa. As argued by ECRE and USCR (2003, 20), 'an important constraint in the ability to offer a secure asylum environment for refugees [in regions of refugee origin] is the extremely limited roles of NGOs and civil society.' Findings from the cases support this conclusion. No domestic NGOs focusing specifically on refugee and asylum issues were active in either Tanzania or Guinea between 1995 and 2004. While RCK was an active commentator on asylum issues in Kenya, funding limitations curtailed its ability to play a more influential role. This lack of an active NGO presence to voice the concerns of refugees and asylum seekers, coupled with the political benefits of securitizing refugees for governing regimes facing the internal pressure of democratization, will likely have continued implications for the state of asylum in Africa.

More fundamentally, however, asylum policies have been affected by what Gyimah-Boadi (2004, 21) has termed 'a new and more nationally oriented citizenship', which has accompanied the rise of democratization and economic liberalization in Africa. Herbst (1999) argues that the combined effect of these forces was the primary cause of the increased significance of citizenship laws in Africa during the 1990s, designed to enhance the division between citizen and foreigner. For Herbst (1999, 267), 'the wave of democratization sweeping across Africa…has made citizenship laws even more publicly controversial than in the past, because it suddenly matters a great deal who can and cannot vote.' While 'all the [African] state can do through citizenship laws is provide a basic, lower-common-denominator identity', Herbst (1999, 277) argues that 'this basic identity may still be important to non-citizens, even if the advantages of being a citizen are far fewer than in more developed countries.' As witnessed in the increasing differentiation between ethnic Somalis from Kenya and Somalia and between ethnic

Ha in Tanzania and Burundi, this increased emphasis on national citizenship as a result of political transformations in Africa during the 1990s has affected asylum by increasing the differentiation between refugee and non-refugee.

As argued in Chapter 4, ethnic affinity between refugees and the local population has been understood to be central to peaceful cohabitation between the two groups. Whereas the accepted logic has been that populations separated by artificial colonial borders shared a sense of distributive justice that bound them together, and when refugees arrived in a region of an ethnically similar local population they would be welcomed as ethnic kin, this would appear to no longer necessarily be the case in the context of countries undergoing political and economic liberalization. In fact, findings from Kenya and Tanzania indicate the extent to which nationality and citizenship have come to be more defining identities than ethnicity, thereby eroding affinity between the local population and refugees. In contrast, in countries like Guinea that are not subject to such pressures, similar divisions between ethnically related nationals and refugees do not appear to be as entrenched.

In this way, the relationship between democratization, changing notions of political membership and the adoption of restrictive asylum policies highlights the need to develop a more critical understanding of the implications of democratization on human rights for non-citizens in Africa. While Young (1999) has outlined how democratization can lead to an erosion of human rights, most scholarly literature on democratization in Africa views the process as one that is necessarily good. Findings, especially from Tanzania, however, would suggest that, like South Africa (HRW, 1998), the process of democratization can have a negative impact on the human rights of non-citizens in Africa. Just as Zakaria (1997) argues that democratization does not always lead to liberal democracies, and Snyder (2000) argues that democratization does not always lead to peace, the relationship between democratization and asylum policies in Africa is not always good for human rights.

Regional factors

In addition to these domestic factors, the three cases highlight the significant role of regional factors in the asylum policies of Kenya, Tanzania and Guinea. In some cases, like Guinea, the granting of asylum was used both as a means of highlighting the failure of neighbouring regimes and as a cover for providing support to elements opposed to the neighbouring regime. In other cases, like Tanzania, changing relations between the host state and the country of origin resulted in the prioritization of regional relations over the needs of refugees. Finally, for states like Kenya, the inability to resolve prolonged refugee situations is compounded by neighbouring a state with no functioning central government. Most significantly, the changing nature of conflict in Africa has been closely associated with the spillover of insecurity into neighbouring states, and the regionalization of previously intra-state conflict. As argued by Stedman and Lyons (2004, 143), events of the 1990s indicate that 'wars in Africa are increasingly becoming regionalized and the distinction between civil war and international war less meaningful.' As such, it is important to more critically understand the role that relations between neighbouring African states have played in formulating particular asylum policies.

Here, it is important to emphasize the significance of the end of wars of national liberation for asylum policies in Africa. Just as issues relating to refugees and asylum were largely addressed as issues of foreign policy by Western states during the Cold War (Loescher and Scanlan, 1986), the response of Guinea and Tanzania to refugees fleeing colonial regimes in the 1960s and 1970s was dictated substantially by their anti-colonial foreign policies. Just as 'by portraying refugee admission as an issue of *raison d'état*, Western elites were able to carve out a significant degree of autonomy from the domestic politics of their states' during the Cold War (Gibney, 2001, 6), African leaders such as Nyerere and Touré were able to appeal to the idea of the anti-colonial African state as a justification for their approach to many refugees and liberation movements.

Such considerations were, for some, indicative of a wider trend. Wright (1999) argues that prior to the 1990s, African foreign policies were largely influenced by factors such as the impact of colonialism, solidarity and non-alignment, and opposition to apartheid South Africa. In contrast, since the end of the Cold War and the political transition in South Africa, other issues have come to dominate African foreign policy agendas. In contrast, contemporary foreign policy is increasingly guided by concerns relating to changing state capacities, economic crisis, the proliferation of security concerns, the impact of democratization, and the regionalization of conflict. In this way, it may be argued that the arrival and prolonged presence of refugees may reluctantly draw a host state more fully into a 'regional security complex' (Buzan, 1992), whereby states are unable to insulate themselves from insecurity in neighbouring states. Given the regionalization of conflict, otherwise relatively peaceful states like Kenya and Tanzania would likely not want to be drawn into the regional security complexes of the Horn of Africa and the Great Lakes region. This may be one reason that these states have been actively involved in trying to resolve conflicts in countries of origin, specifically Somalia and Burundi, by hosting peace negotiations. Given the limited literature that exists on African foreign policies, however, additional research is needed to fully explore this dynamic.

International factors

Finally, the cases of Kenya, Tanzania and Guinea clearly illustrate the role of international factors in the formulation of their asylum policies. In particular, all three states have developed their asylum policies in light of a number of external factors and constraints. Paramount among these constraints, as outlined above, is the power imbalance between the host state and the donor state, with the interests and priorities of the donor state playing the dominant role in determining the nature of burden sharing with the host state. This section considers how these international factors have affected asylum policies by considering in greater detail the predominant role that the power imbalance between host and donor states plays in the formulation of asylum policies.

The distribution of power in the donor-host relationships illustrated in the three case studies reflects the broader pattern of power distribution in the North-South relationship, as characterized by Ravenhill (1990), Krasner (1985) and others. Krasner (1985, 30) characterizes the relationship between South and North as being between 'weak and vulnerable states on the one hand and strong and resilient ones on the other'. As a consequence, he believes that 'a deep asymmetry of power' between South and North 'leaves almost all developing countries exposed to shocks from the international environment' (Krasner, 1985, 294). Largely as a result of this power imbalance, African states were unable to insulate themselves from pressures to pursue economic and political liberalization by the end of the 1980s, as outlined in Chapter 1. As Clapham (1996, 193) argues, this 'metamorphosis' resulted from a number of pressures 'which made it extremely difficult for them to cling to their previous insistence on unfettered sovereignty in the international arena combined with monopoly statehood in the internal one'. Tordorff (2002, 237) claims that by the beginning of the 1990s, 'Western governments sought to deny African states the freedom to choose the political and economic systems which their leaders believed would best suit their countries' individual circumstances and needs.' Responding to the scale of these external pressures is a significant challenge for African states.

In some cases, African regimes have used the presence of refugees to seek leverage against an otherwise restrictive international donor community, both to extract material benefits and to ensure their survival. Perhaps the best example was the Conté regime's practice of highlighting the openness of its asylum policy as a way of seeking concessions from the European Union. Similarly, Moi's decision to allow a high quantity of asylum to Somali refugees in 1991 was linked to its desire to seek support from the donor community following the suspension of international aid. In each of these cases, host states attempted to 'link' the presence of refugees to other areas of negotiation with donor states in order to seek concessions, a process known as 'issue-linkage' (Betts, 2005b; and Hasenclever et al., 1997).

Efforts by Kenya, Tanzania and Guinea to employ issue-linkage to extract greater burden sharing from donor states have, however, met with very limited success. This is likely due to the fact that they have placed an emphasis on restricting the quality of asylum, as opposed to the quantity of asylum, which appears to be of greater interest to donors. Given more than 25 years of concerns about burden sharing on the part of host states in Africa, it is striking that African states, independently and collectively, have not resorted to action similar to that of South-East Asian states and Macedonia and threatened to disregard the principle of *non-refoulement* as a means of extracting burden sharing commitments from donor states. In fact, there is no evidence to suggest that Tanzania's expulsion of the Rwandan refugees was a tactic to gain leverage against the donor community. In reviewing the cases, it would appear that Kenya accepted the constraints placed upon it by the international donor community and Guinea relied on its strategic importance as a guarantee of sustained donor engagement. In the long run, neither strategy appears to have been successful.

Indeed, host states are typically caught between two contradictory pressures when formulating their asylum policies. Domestically, and especially in the context of democratization, there is pressure for the host state to demonstrate control over refugee populations by restricting asylum. Internationally, however, host states face pressure from UNHCR and the international donor community to provide asylum for refugees fleeing neighbouring conflicts. The question of how states negotiate between these two, often contradictory, sets of factors is a question that requires significant additional research. There is, however, a dominant view among state officials in Kenya, Tanzania and Guinea that it is not possible for aid-dependent states to approach the question of refugees without considering the foreign policy implications. In such cases, states do not feel free to pursue unilateral action for fear of jeopardizing relations with the donor community, upon whom they are dependent.

Towards a more effective response to asylum in Africa

This overview illustrates how a broad range of factors have combined to affect the asylum policies of states like Kenya, Tanzania and Guinea. While these factors will affect different states in different ways, factors unrelated to the presence of refugees tend to play a predominant role in the formulation of asylum policies as host states incorporate decisions on asylum into their broader political calculus. These factors, in turn, are influenced significantly by the state's ability to respond to a range of internal and external pressures that have the potential to exacerbate the vulnerability of African states and governing regimes. It is for this reason that the state must be more closely integrated into the study of refugees in Africa and that the political dynamics of asylum policies need to be more fully addressed. As the case studies have illustrated, the politics of the state in Africa has played a significant role in determining the quality and quantity of asylum afforded to refugees; future research on refugees in Africa therefore ignores the state at its peril.

In fact, while their particular approaches have differed, Kenya's approach to Somali refugees, Tanzania's approach to Rwandan and Burundian refugee and Guinea's approach to Liberian and Sierra Leonean refugees have obeyed a similar logic. While representatives of all three states have pointed to factors such as the scale and duration of the refugee problem, burden sharing and security as justifications for the quality and quantity of asylum they have provided, the case studies found that responses of these states to refugees have primarily been the result of broader political factors. In this way, the case studies support the conclusion that the asylum policies of states like Kenya, Tanzania and Guinea are influenced more by factors unrelated to the presence of refugees than by refugee-specific factors.

This is not to suggest that factors relating to the presence of refugees – such as the scale and protracted nature of refugee populations and concerns about burden sharing and security – are irrelevant to the study of asylum in Africa. Instead, as outlined in Chapter 2, these factors have been central aspects of the asylum question in Africa since the 1960s. What is necessary, however, it to understand these factors in a more critical way, mindful of the political context within which asylum policies are formulated. Issues relating to burden sharing and security are typically conditioned by factors unrelated to the presence of refugees. These broader factors are the result of changes in the African political landscape since the 1980s, which have exacerbated a number of internal and external pressures on the African state, as outlined in Chapter 1. These pressures have increased the vulnerability of many governing regimes in Africa, and have, in turn, indirectly had an impact on the formulation of asylum policies. In particular, these pressures have often led the governing regime to portray refugees collectively as a burden, as a means of seeking leverage against the international donor community, and as a security concern, as a means of demonstrating control in light of domestic pressures.

To understand these dynamics, it is important to recognize the politics of asylum in Africa. Such an approach affords the state a more central role in the study of asylum in Africa, while recognizing the broader spectrum of factors that affect the asylum policies of states, especially political factors unrelated to the presence of refugees. As a result of the prevailing sense of vulnerability experienced by many regimes in contemporary sub-Saharan Africa, regimes tend to see the arrival of refugees as a potential threat to their survival. Facing such threats, but under pressure from the international donor community to provide asylum, African states must balance a range of factors and interests when formulating their asylum policies. Adopting the politics of asylum as a conceptual framework leads to important conclusions not only for the study of asylum in Africa, but also for the future of the refugee protection regime in Africa. While part of the solution to the crisis of asylum in Africa surely lies in addressing the scale and protracted nature of the refugee problem, burden sharing and security, part of the solution also lies in engaging in broader political and economic forces that influence a state's asylum policies.

Implications for the study of asylum in Africa

For the study of asylum in Africa to more effectively engage with the changing nature of asylum policies in Africa, it needs to more fully engage with the politics of host states. As outlined in Chapter 1, such an approach has generally been lacking, especially from a comparative perspective. While commentators have acknowledged that political factors affect the asylum policies of African states, the literature in this area remains remarkably limited, especially when compared to the literature elsewhere. The cases of Kenya, Tanzania and Guinea, however, demonstrate the predominant role played by the politics of the host state in determining the quality and quantity of asylum afforded to refugees. To better understand constraints on asylum, refugee studies should, therefore, develop more rigorous and critical understandings of the ways in which the interests, constraints and concerns of states affect their asylum policies, notwithstanding the obligations placed on them by international refugee and human rights regimes. Given the diversity of states and asylum policies in Africa, such understandings are likely best developed in a comparative perspective.

At the same time, it is important to recognize that such political dynamics are not exclusive to the study of asylum in Africa. In fact, as argued in the work of Gibney (2004), Weiner (1995) and others, the politics of asylum is an approach that is equally relevant in Western states. As outlined above, these understandings of the politics of asylum in Western states may help explain the dynamics of the politics of asylum in Africa. Further consideration should therefore be given to the benefits of a cross-regional comparative approach, and the benefit of more generally overcoming divisions between the study of asylum in the global North and the global South. In this sense, it is also important to understand the possible motivations for a continued conceptual division between the analysis of Western and African asylum policies. Chimni (1998a, 351) argues that the end of the Cold War witnessed a paradigm shift in refugee policy, law and research, centred on the 'creation of a myth of difference: the nature and character of refugee flows in the Third World were represented as being radically different from refugee flows in Europe since the end of the First World War.' To overcome this 'myth of difference', asylum in Africa should be 'de-exoticised' and further research undertaken on the benefits of understanding both the similarities and the differences between asylum in Africa and the West.

That said, research on asylum in Africa should draw on the rich literature on African comparative and international politics. As outlined in this chapter, the vulnerabilities of the African state, democratization, economic liberalization, and the changing pattern of relations between African states and the international donor community have all had a significant impact on the quantity and quality of asylum afforded to refugees. Each of these factors has, in turn, been considered in the broader literature of African politics. While the dynamics of asylum policy formulation may challenge the dominant views of some aspects of this literature, as with the findings on democratization and the human rights of non-citizens, research on asylum in Africa should draw on the broader literature, especially to understand those changes in the political and economic context of African states since independence which have, in turn, influenced the state's response to refugees.

Implications for the refugee protection regime in Africa

An approach that recognizes the politics of asylum also carries important implications for the future direction of the refugee protection regime in Africa. First, identifying both the burdens and benefits associated with the presence of refugees would help move beyond the rhetoric of refugees as exclusively a burden, as argued by the work of Rutinwa and Kamanga on refugees in Northwestern Tanzania (2003). As indicated by the Kenya case study, replicating their approach of identifying both the benefits and burdens associated with the presence of refugees would appear to be a more effective way of addressing the burden sharing concerns of host states. Through such an approach, donor engagement could be more effectively targeted to mitigate the burdens associated with the presence of refugees, like the negative impact on the environment, while additional programmes are developed to maximize the benefits associated with the presence of refugees, especially capitalizing on the benefits to the local economy.

A more politicized understanding of burden sharing, and the interests of African states more generally, also speaks to the question of recent proposals to 'externalize' European asylum policy, as outlined in Chapter 3. A range of European-driven bilateral and multilateral policy initiatives in recent years have focused on the two-fold assumption that programmes in Africa, and other regions of origin, can be developed as a means of reducing the number of spontaneous arrival asylum seekers reaching the EU and that countries of first asylum would be willing to participate in such schemes. Such assumptions fail to consider the willingness and ability of states in regions of refugee origin to participate in such schemes (Betts and Milner, 2006). In fact, domestic constraints faced by states like Kenya and Tanzania would likely mean that the domestic political cost of participating in such schemes would be too high, and that such states would not be able to provide the quality of asylum required. At the same time, the power imbalance between African and donor states will make it difficult for African states to resist such programmes, especially if European states link participation in such schemes with issues like aid and debt. While more research is required on how African states will balance these contradictory domestic and international pressures, an approach that recognizes the politics of asylum in Africa clearly forwards our understanding of one aspect of the 'new asylum paradigm'.

It is equally important for the refugee protection regime to engage more consistently with the range of security concerns associated with refugee movements. While a range of refugee-related security concerns are, in fact, motivated by attempts to counter sources of domestic pressure on the governing regime, this is not to say that host states and refugee-populated areas do not have legitimate security concerns relating to refugee movements. Kenya, Tanzania and, to a certain extent, Guinea were all found to have legitimate indirect security concerns in refugee-populated areas. These concerns typically resulted from tensions between local communities and refugee populations, stemming from either competition over scarce resources or the perception that refugees were receiving preferential treatment. Lessons should be learned from the apparent success of interventions in Kenya and Tanzania to mitigate these indirect security concerns, and similar targeted development assistance and local assistance projects incorporated into other refugee programmes, especially in cases of protracted refugee situations.

At the same time, it is important to recognize that while refugees are not, by definition, responsible for direct security concerns, refugee movements typically occur in a context of wider insecurity, stemming from the presence of armed elements in the refugee population, the spillover of conflict and the proliferation of small arms. These phenomena have a negative affect not only on the security of refugees, but also on the security of host states. As such, responses to these direct security concerns, involving a wider range of peace and security actors, need to be developed and implemented, not only to ensure the protection of refugees, but also to ensure the continued willingness of states to provide asylum.

Such responses, however, can only mitigate the concerns of states and the protection needs of refugees. Fundamentally, the most effective way of ensuring a convergence between the concerns of states and the protection needs of refugees is through the formulation and implementation of a comprehensive solution to the refugee situation itself. Building from the lessons of past comprehensive solutions (Betts, 2008; Betts, 2006; Betts, 2004; Loescher and Milner, 2008b; and Loescher and Milner, 2005), this approach would potentially employ the full spectrum of possible solutions for refugees – including repatriation, local integration and resettlement – and involve the sustained engagement of a wide range of actors, including peace and security, development and humanitarian actors. Such solutions would ultimately be the best way of addressing the concerns of host states and meeting the protection needs of refugees.

The formulation and implementation of comprehensive solutions to protracted refugee situations may be more effectively realized if they were incorporated into ongoing discussions on peacebuilding at the international and regional level. In response to the growing challenge of failed and fragile states, as outlined above, considerable attention has been paid in recent years to the importance of peacebuilding. As illustrated by cases as diverse as Angola, Burundi, Liberia and Mozambique, armed conflict has the potential to re-emerge and become more protracted if active steps are not taken to build a sustainable peace. While debates on definitions persist, recent discussions have generally revolved around developing ways to ensure stability in countries previously affected by conflict so as to prevent a slide back into war (Ali and Matthews, 2004).

Much of this debate has, however, focused exclusively on peacebuilding activities within the country in question, with little or no attention paid to the regional nature of conflict and the regional dynamics that should consequently be addressed as part of a successful peacebuilding programme. This is especially striking given the growing literature on the regional nature of conflict and insecurity in the global South. As argued by Ayoob (1995), Buzan (1992) and others, intra-state conflict in the global South has the demonstrated potential to 'spillover' into neighbouring, and equally vulnerable, states, thereby regionalizing conflict. For example, civil conflict in Sierra Leone and Burundi not only affected these two countries but other countries in the Mano River Union in West Africa and the Great Lakes region of Central Africa, as illustrated by the cases of Guinea and Tanzania. It is important to address these regional dynamics, and to more fully understand the relationship between protracted refugee situations, regional insecurity and the regional dynamics of peacebuilding. In fact, the presence of refugee warriors within refugee populated areas and the potential for early and forced repatriation by the country of asylum have both proven to have the potential to undermine peacebuilding efforts, while the experience of exile may enable refugees to contribute to various stages of the peacebuilding process. Not only could the incorporation of refugees into peacebuilding discussions lead to more effective peacebuilding programmes, but such an approach could also be an effective way of engaging with the broad range of actors required to formulate and implement comprehensive solutions for protracted refugee situations (Loescher and Milner, 2008b; and Loescher et al., 2007).

This approach would, however, need to be especially mindful of the interests, concerns and constraints on host states. Indeed, host states must balance and respond to a range of pressures and interests when formulating their asylum policies, many of which are not related to the presence of refugees. Accordingly, comprehensive engagement in refugee situations must also address the broader political and economic constraints faced by host states. To this end, a more comprehensive response to the crisis of asylum in Africa would need to situate the question of refugees within the wider context of North – South negotiations, including trade, aid, debt, governance, human rights, defence, and development. Incorporating asylum into this broader constellation of issues would not only recognize the full range of factors that affect a state's asylum policies, but also create opportunities for the formulation of 'win-win' outcomes through the potential linking of asylum to wider benefits for the host state.

More fundamentally, however, there is a profound imperative for additional research on asylum in Africa to contribute to efforts to find lasting solutions. Turton (1996) argues that research on questions relating to human suffering can only be justified if its objective is to alleviate that suffering. Given the proven ability of the international community to resolve cases of prolonged exile elsewhere in the world, the crisis of asylum in Africa is neither inevitable nor unchangeable. Research must therefore challenge the *status quo* by enhancing and refining our understanding of the complex interplay of factors that shape the asylum policies of states. It is on the basis of a more comprehensive understanding of the problem that better responses can be found, while a more rigorous understanding of the factors affecting asylum in Africa will contribute to the identification of possible solutions to the crisis. At the end of 2008, there were more than 2 million refugees trapped in protracted refugee situations in Africa. Given the scale of human suffering represented by this figure, a solution to their plight cannot come soon enough.

Notes

1 Understanding the State and Asylum in Africa

1. Engagement with the international donor and humanitarian community is taken to mean both bilateral relations with donor governments and broader multilateral engagement with the host state through UNHCR and operational NGOs active in refugee-populated areas.
2. This book uses the terms 'Third World' and 'global South' interchangeably. For a discussion of the continued relevance of the term 'Third World', see: MacFarlane, 1999.
3. In Kenya, this involved research in both Nairobi and Dadaab, the region of North Eastern Province that hosted the majority of the Somali refugee population. In Tanzania, this involved research in both Dar es Salaam and in Kibondo, the region of Northwestern Tanzania that hosted the majority of the Burundian refugee population. In Guinea, this involved research in both Conakry and N'Zérékoré, the region of Southern Guinea that hosted the majority of Liberian refugees.

2 A History of Asylum in Africa

1. For an overview of refugee movements in the Great Lakes region and in the Horn of Africa in the 1960s and early 1970s, see: Zolberg et al., 1989, 37–71. For an overview of UNHCR's response to these movements, see: Loescher, 2001, 114–26.
2. For discussion of the problems associated with refugee statistics in Africa, and some of the political interests behind these problems, see: Crisp, 1999b; and Kibreab, 1991, 8–15. The politics of refugee numbers will be discussed in Chapter 8.
3. For an overview of the zonal development approach, see: Adelman and Sorenson, 1994; and Gorman, 1993.
4. 'Member States of the OAU shall use their best endeavours consistent with their respective legislations to receive refugees and to secure the settlement of those refugees who, for well-founded reasons, are unable or unwilling to return to their country of origin or nationality.' Article II(1), 1969 OAU Convention.
5. 'Where a Member State finds difficulty in continuing to grant asylum to refugees, such Member State may appeal directly to other Member States and through the OAU, and such other Member States shall in the spirit of African solidarity and international co-operation take appropriate measures to lighten the burden of the Member State granting asylum.' Article II(4), 1969 OAU Convention.
6. For an early critique of the notion of 'traditional hospitality', see: Kibreab, 1985, 67–84.

7. This total was roughly half the amount requested by African states. The largest contributions were received from: USA (US$285 million), European Economic Community (US$68 million), West Germany (US$34 million), Japan (US$33 million), Saudi Arabia (US$30 million), Canada (US$18.8 million), Italy (US$17 million), the United Kingdom (US$13.8 million), and France (US$2.4 million) (Anand, 1993, 77).
8. For a detailed description of the refugee crisis in the Great Lakes region in the 1990s, see: Ogata, 2005, 172–275.
9. Herbst (2000, 255) notes that Musevini's capture of power in Uganda in January 1986 was 'the first time that power was seized in Africa by a leader who had gone back to the bush to form his own army', which, in this case, drew heavily from Rwandans in exile since the 1960s.

3 The Principle and Practice of Burden Sharing with Africa

1. 'Persons of concern' to UNHCR include refugees, asylum-seekers, returnees, some internally displaced persons (IDPs), stateless persons and some other individuals deemed to be in need of international protection (UNHCR, 2007a, 12).
2. For example, in 2004, UNHCR's Annual Programme and Supplementary Programme budgets combined totalled US$1.2 billion. Of that, US$27.7 million (2.3%) was met by resources made available through the United Nations Regular Budget. See: UNHCR, 2005a, 17.
3. 'Earmarking is a device by which a bilateral donor agency specifies the geographic or sectoral areas in which a multilateral agency or NGO may spend its contribution' (Smillie and Minear, 2003, 20).
4. Nine other countries had smaller resettlement programmes with no geographic quotas in 2003–04. Following is a list of resettlement countries (and their quotas) in 2003–04: Australia (4000), Brazil (100), Benin (n/a), Burkina Faso (n/a), Canada (7700), Chile (60), Denmark (500), Finland (750), Iceland (30), Ireland (10 families), the Netherlands (500), Norway (1145), New Zealand (750), Sweden (1000), United Kingdom (500), United States (70,000). Belgium, France, Spain and Switzerland resettled individual refugees referred by UNHCR in 2003. As such, the global resettlement quota for 2003 was approximately 90,000 refugees. See: UNHCR, Resettlement Section, 2003a.

4 Host State Security and Refugee Movements in Africa

1. While earlier works (Gordenker, 1987; and Loescher and Monahan, 1989) examined the links between refugee movements and international politics Loescher (1992) and Weiner (1993) were the first to specifically examine the link between refugee movements and security.
2. Morris and Stedman (2008) note that recent exceptions to the gap between refugee studies and security studies include Lischer (2005), Loescher and Milner (2005) and Stedman and Tanner (2003). It is important to also note the contribution of Jacobsen (2000) and Maluwa (1995).

3. For an examination of UNHCR's motivation for adopting a human security perspective, see: Adelman, 2001; Hammerstad, 2000; and Loescher et al., 2008, 55–9.

5 Kenya

1. This chapter uses the term 'Somali' to refer to the Somali ethnic group, and 'Somalian' to refer to the nationality. This distinction is important as a significant portion of Kenya's population is ethnically Somali. See: Pérouse de Montclos and Kagwanja, 2000, 220.
2. The primary countries of origin of refugees in Kenya (and their total in 2005) are: Somalia (173,700), Sudan (73,000), Ethiopia (16,400), Uganda (2800), DRC (2400), Rwanda (2300), and Burundi (1200). UNHCR, 2007a, 240. For a consideration of Kenya's response to Sudanese refugees, see: Kaiser, 2008.
3. As outlined below, the state of emergency had been imposed on the Northern Frontier District of Kenya (which includes the current North Eastern Province) thirteen days after Kenyan independence in 1964 in response to a secessionist movement by Kenyan-Somalis.
4. While there are very few official exceptions to this regulation, a significant number of refugees reside outside the camps without official permission. In her detailed research of Somali refugees in Kenya, Horst (2006) found that many Somali refugees reside in Eastleigh, a predominantly Somali suburb of Nairobi, for a variety of reasons. Some leave the camps to seek employment to support family members in the camps or possibilities for onward migration from Kenya, legal or illegal. Others leave the camps because they find the harsh and insecure environment of the camps too difficult, and would rather take the chance of a clandestine existence in Nairobi.
5. This section is based on interviews with long-serving UNHCR and CARE staff in Dadaab, conducted in Dadaab in 2004.
6. Information for this section is drawn from CARE Kenya and UNHCR programme documents and interviews with programme staff in Dadaab in 2004.
7. Meeting with long-serving CARE workers in Dadaab in 2004.
8. According to Africa Watch: '*Shifta* carries two meanings: it is the official term of reference for political opposition in the NFD; and it is a derogatory term, literally translated as bandit' (Africa Watch, 1991, 284).
9. Howard (1991, 83) argues that 'the post-coup detentions followed a pattern that suggested that the government was strongly worried by the emergence of an articulate, professional elite that had not been and could not be co-opted by the spoils of office.'

6 Tanzania

1. As of July 2009, the Tanzanian Immigration Department had received citizenship applications from approximately 165,000 Burundian refugees in the 'Old Settlements' of Katumba, Mishamo and Ulyankulu. The first of these applications were approved in early August 2009, when the Tanzanian

Minister of Home Affairs granted citizenship to 3,568 Burundian refugees, while pledging to finalise the remaining applications by the end of 2009. It is, however, important to note that this offer of naturalization has not been extended to the remaining 36,000 Burundian refugees who fled to Tanzania in 1993 (interviews, Dar es Salaam and Kasulu, 2009).
2. According to Chaulia, 'the imprint of Julius Nyerere's personality and ideals on the postcolonial state's refugee policy is overwhelming' (Chaulia, 2003, 154). According to Holborn, 'Tanzanian policy has been dominated by the spirit and philosophy of one man: Julius K. Nyerere' (Holborn, 1975, 1148).
3. These movements included: Front for the National Liberation of Mozambique (FRELIMO), the African National Congress of South Africa (ANC), the South West People's Organization of Namibia (SWAPO), the Zimbabwean African National Union (ZANU), and the People's Movement for the Liberation of Angola (MPLA) (Nnoli, 1978, 81).
4. Mendel explains that 'precise figures are difficult to obtain, in part because many of the migrants were absorbed by ethnically similar communities in the rural areas, but tens of thousands of refugees entered Tanzania between 1959 and 1964' (Mendel, 1997, 38).
5. *Chama Cha Mapinduzi*, Party of the Revolution, was formed in 1977 as a result of the merger of the ruling party of the mainland, TANU, and the ruling party of Zanzibar, ASP. CCM remained the only legal political party in Tanzania until May 1992.
6. During interviews in Kanembwa Camp, Kibondo, in 2004, refugees indicated that the rebel representatives were well-informed about economic activity in the camps, often arriving within hours of a financial transaction to demand a tax of ten per cent. One story was told of a refugee who sold a pig for TSh. 150,000. By the time he returned to his hut, a representative of CNDD-FDD was waiting for them to demand TSh. 15,000. Many refugees point to these events as evidence that the rebel group had a strong network within the camps.

7 Guinea

1. The most infamous retaliatory act by Ghana was the detention of Louis Lansana Beavogui, Guinea's Minister of Foreign Affairs, in October 1966 while Beavogui was transiting through Accra, en route to the OAU Conference in Addis Ababa (O'Toole, 1978, 10).
2. In 1978, it was noted that while 'Guinea [belonged] to most of the UN's specialized agencies, it received missions of the World Health Organization, UNESCO and other agencies with so many restrictions that they seldom [were] able to offer much assistance to the country' (O'Toole, 1978, 74–5).
3. UNHCR's regional budget for the Sierra Leone Operation had a budget of US$7,072,068 in 1999, but received only US$3,358,677 – a shortfall of 53 per cent. Likewise, UNHCR's Liberian Repatriation and Reintegration Operation had a budget of US$ 24,487,299 in 1999, but received only US$17,022,926 – a shortfall of 31 per cent (UNHCR, 2000b, 111–24).
4. The *Kamajors* were a pro-Kabbah militia operating in Northern Sierra Leone and Freetown, in opposition to the AFRC and the RUF (O'Neill, 2000). ULIMO

was founded in Freetown in 1991 by Liberians who had fled the advance of Charles Taylor (Ellis, 1998).

5. For the origins of the RUF and their links with Charles Taylor, see: Abdullah and Muana, 1998.
6. This section is based on fieldwork in Guinea in 2001 and 2004, a comprehensive review of UNHCR press releases, situation reports from the United Nations Office for the Coordinator of Humanitarian Affairs (UN-OCHA), reports by human rights groups (including AI and HRW) and related news-wire reports (*l'Agence France-Presse* (AFP), the UN Integrated Regional Information Network (IRIN), the Panafrican News Agency (PANA), and Reuters, covering events from 1 September 2000 to 1 April 2001.
7. The President's speech was unscripted, and no transcript of the speech appears to exist. This extract, by an unknown translator, has been cited by both LCHR and USCR (LCHR, 2002, 74; and USCR, 2000e).
8. For a detailed account of the events of 17 September 2000, including the killing of Kpognon and the abduction of Djeya, see: UNHCR, Inspector General's Office, 2000.
9. In contrast, USCR reported in 2002 that 'aid workers widely considered' the Government's estimate 'to be greatly inflated', and placed the number of displaced at the end of 2001 to be closer to 100,000 (USCR, 2002). The politics of numbers was a feature of the Guinea refugee programme prior to September 2000, as discussed in Chapter 8.
10. This security was notwithstanding a number of events during the relocation. On 23 May 2001, Guinean authorities arrested seven refugees at a roadblock during a relocation exercise on suspicion of belonging to a rebel group. UNHCR expressed concern about the event which occurred 'despite the agreement by Guinean military and local authorities that screening of baggage and refugees would take place before the departure of convoys from camps' (UNHCR, 2001c).

8 The Politics of Asylum in Africa

1. For example, Article 17(1) of the 1951 Convention provides that 'the Contracting State shall accord to refugees lawfully staying in their territory the most favourable treatment accorded to nationals of a foreign country in the same circumstances, as regards the right to engage in wage-earning employment.' Likewise, Article 26 of the 1951 Convention provides that 'each Contracting State shall accord to refugees lawfully in its territory the right to choose their place of residence and to move freely within its territory, subject to any regulations applicable to aliens generally in the same circumstances.'
2. For an overview of historical and contemporary efforts to formulate comprehensive solutions for protracted refugee situations, see: Betts, 2008; Loescher and Milner, 2008b; and Loescher and Milner, 2005, 67–84.

Bibliography

Abdullah, Ibrahim and Patrick Muana (1998) 'The Revolutionary United Front of Sierra Leone', in Christopher Clapham (ed.), *African Guerrillas*, Oxford: James Currey Ltd., 172–194.

Acharya, Amitav and David B. Dewitt (1997) 'Fiscal Burden Sharing', in James C. Hathaway (ed.), *Reconceiving International Refugee Law*, Nijhoff Law Specials No. 30, London: Martins Nijhoff Publishers, 111–154.

Adamolekum, 'Ladipo (1976) *Sékou Touré's Guinea: An Experiment in Nation Building*, London: Methuen and Company.

Adelman, Howard (2001) 'From Refugees to Forced Migration: The UNHCR and Human Security', *International Migration Review*, Vol. 35, no. 1, Spring, 7–32.

Adelman, Howard and John Sorenson (eds) (1994) *African Refugees: Development Aid and Repatriation*, North York: York Lanes Press.

Adelman, Howard and Awa Abdi (2003) 'How long is too long? Durable Solutions for the Dadaab Refugees', report prepared for CARE Canada, Toronto: Centre for Refugee Studies, York University, 30 June.

Adepoju, Aderanti (1982) 'The Dimension of the Refugee Problem in Africa', *African Affairs*, Vol. 81, no. 322, 21–35.

Africa Watch (1991) *Kenya: Taking Liberties*, New York: Africa Watch, July.

Ali, Taisier M. and Robert O. Matthews (2004) 'Conclusion: The Long and Difficult Road to Peace', in Taisier M. Ali and Robert O. Matthews (eds), *Durable Peace: Challenges for Peacebuilding in Africa*, Toronto: University of Toronto Press, 393–425.

Amate, C.O.C. (1986) *Inside the OAU: Pan-Africanism in Practice*, Basingstoke: Macmillan, 1986.

Ambrose, Brendalyn P. (1995) *Democratization and the Protection of Human Rights in Africa*, London: Praeger Publishers.

Amnesty International (2001) 'Guinea and Sierra Leone: No Place of Refuge', AI Index: AFR 05/006/2001, London, 24 October.

Amnesty International (1997a) 'Great Lakes Region: Still in Need of Protection: Repatriation, Refoulement, and the Safety of Refugees and the Internally Displaced', AI Index: AFR 02/07/97, London, 24 January.

Amnesty International (1997b) 'In search of safety: The forcibly displaced and human rights in Africa', London: Amnesty International, June.

Amnesty International (1990) 'Tanzania: Burundi Nationals Detained in Tanzania', AI Index: AFR 56/07/90, London, September.

Anand, Renu (1993) *African Refugees: An overview*, New Delhi: Khama Publishers.

Anker, Deborah, Joan Fitzpatrick and Andrew Shacknove (1998) 'Crisis and Cure: A Reply to Hathaway/Neve and Shuck', *Harvard Human Rights Journal*, Vol. 11, 295–310.

Antoniou, Jim, Brian Shorter and Trevor Sweetman (1987) *Tanzania: Burundi Refugee Settlements: A Planning Mission Report*, Basingstoke: Scott Wilson Kirkpatrick and Partners, July.

Aradau, Claudia (2001) 'Migration: The spiral of (in)security', *Rubikon*, March, http://venus.ci.uw.edu.pl/~rubikon/forum/claudia1.htm

Asres, Wondem (2007) *The State, the Crisis of State Institutions, and Refugee Migration in the Horn of Africa: The Case of Sudan, Ethiopia and Somalia*, Asmara: Red Sea Press.

Austin, Kathi (2002) 'Armed Refugee Camps as a Microcosm of the Link between Arms Availability and Insecurity', Draft Case Study for Discussion, SSRC Workshop on International Law and Small Arms Proliferation, Washington DC, 6 February.

Ayok Chol, Antony and Shayo Conrad (eds) (1987) 'Final Report on the International Conference on the Management of Planned and Spontaneous Refugee Settlements in Africa', Dar es Salaam: Faculty of Commerce and Management, University of Dar es Salaam.

Ayoob, Mohammed (1997) 'Defining Security: A Subaltern Realist Perspective', in Keith Krause and Michael C. Williams (eds), *Critical Security Studies: Concepts and Cases*, London: UCL Press, 121–146.

Ayoob, Mohammed (1995) *The Third World Security Predicament: State Making, Regional Conflict and the International System*, Boulder, CO: Lynne Rienner Publishers.

Azarya, Victor and Naomi Chazan (1987) 'Disengagement from the State in Africa: Reflections on the Experience of Ghana and Guinea', *Comparative Studies in Society and History*, Vol. 29, no. 1, 106–131.

BBC (2002a) 'News on-line: Kenya inquiry targets Somali militants', 30 November, http://news.bbc.co.uk/2/hi/africa/2529655.stm

BBC (2002b), 'News on-line: Tanzania protests Burundi shelling', 4 January, http://news.bbc.co.uk/2/hi/africa/1742151.stm

Bakewell, Oliver (2001) 'Refugee aid and protection in rural Africa: working in parallel or cross-purposes?', *New Issues in Refugee Research*, Working Paper No. 35, Geneva: UNHCR, March.

Bangoura, Dominique (2001) 'La Guinée face aux rebellions au sud de son territoire', *Afrique contemporaine*, No. 200, 4e trimester, 17–33.

Barber, Ben (1997) 'Feeding Refugees or War?: The Dilemma of Humanitarian Aid', *Foreign Affairs*, Vo. 76, no. 4, July, 8–14.

Bari, Shamsul (1992) 'Refugee Status Determination under the Comprehensive Plan of Action (CPA): A Personal Assessment.' *International Journal of Refugee Law*, Vol. 4, no. 4, 487–511.

Bariagaber, Assefaw (1999) 'States, International Organisations and the Refugee: Reflections on the Complexity of Managing the Refugee Crisis in the Horn of Africa', *The Journal of Modern African Studies*, Vol. 37, no. 4, December, 597–619.

Barkan, Joel D., and Jennifer G. Cooke (2001) 'US Policy toward Kenya in the Wake of September 11: Can New Antiterrorist Imperatives Be Reconciled with Enduring US Foreign Policy Goals?', *Africa Notes*, Number 4, Centre for Strategic and International Studies, Washington, December.

Barutciski, Michael and Astri Suhrke (2001) 'Lessons from the Kosovo Refugee Crisis: Innovations in Protection and Burden-sharing', *Journal of Refugee Studies*, Vol. 14, no. 2, 95–115.

Berman, Eric (2003) 'Peacekeeping policies towards Africa', *Security Dialogue*, Vol. 34, no. 2, June, 199–214.

Betts, Alexander (2008) 'Historical Lessons for Overcoming Protracted Refugee Situations', in Gil Loescher, James Milner, Edward Newman and Gary Troeller (eds), *Protracted Refugee Situations: Political, Human Rights and Security Implications*, Tokyo: United Nations University Press, 162–185.

Betts, Alexander (2006) 'Comprehensive plans of action: Insights from CIREFCA and the Indochinese CPA', *New Issues in Refugee Research*, Working Paper No. 120, Geneva: UNHCR, January.

Betts, Alexander (2005a) 'What does "Efficiency" Mean in the Context of the Global Refugee Regime?', Working Paper No. 9, Centre on Migration, Policy and Society, University of Oxford.

Betts, Alexander (2005b) 'International Cooperation Between North and South to Enhance Refugee Protection in Regions of Origin', RSC Working Paper No. 25, Oxford: Refugee Studies Centre, Queen Elizabeth House, University of Oxford, July.

Betts, Alexander (2004) 'International cooperation and the targeting of development assistance for refugee solutions: Lessons from the 1980s', *New Issues in Refugee Research*, Working Paper No. 107, Geneva: UNHCR, September.

Betts, Alexander and James Milner (2006) 'The Externalization of EU Asylum Policy: The Perspective of African States', Working Paper 36, Centre on Migration, Policy and Society, University of Oxford.

Black, Richard and Mohamed Sessay (1997) 'Forced Migration, Land-Use Change and Political Economy in the Forest Region of Guinea', *African Affairs*, Vol. 96, no. 385, October, 587–605.

Bratton, Michael and Nicolas van de Walle (1997) *Democratic Experiments in Africa: Regime Transitions in Comparative Perspective*, Cambridge: Cambridge University Press.

Brooks, Hugh C. and Yassin El-Ayouty (eds) (1970) *Refugees South of the Sahara: An African Dilemma*, Westport, CT: Negro University Press.

Buzan, Barry (1992) 'Third World Regional Security in Structural and Historical Perspective', in Brian Job (ed.), *The Insecurity Dilemma: National Security of Third World States*, Boulder, CO: Lynne Reinner Publishers, 167–189.

Buzan, Barry (1991) *People, States and Fear: An Agenda for International Security Studies in the Post-Cold War Era*, Second Edition, London: Longman.

Buzan, Barry, Ole Waever and Japp de Wilde (1998) *Security: A New Framework for Analysis*, Boulder, CO: Lynne Reinner Publishers.

Callamard, Agnès (1994) 'Malawian Refugee Policy, International Politics and the One-Party Regime', *Journal of International Affairs*, Vol. 47, no. 2, Winter, 525–556.

Camara, Sylvain Soriba (1976) *La Guinée sans la France*, Travaux et recherches de science politique No. 44, Paris: Presse de la Fondation Nationale des Science Politiques.

Campbell, Horace and Howard Stein (eds) (1992) *Tanzania and the IMF: The Dynamics of Liberalization*, Boulder, CO: Westview Press.

Carmody, Pádraig (2005) 'Transforming Globalization and Security: Africa and America Post-9/11', *Africa Today*, Vol. 52, no. 1, Fall, 97–120.

Carver, Richard (1994) 'Kenya: Aftermath of the Elections', *Refugee Survey Quarterly*, Vol. 13, no. 1, 30–55.

Centre for Refugee Studies (CRS) (1996) 'Common but Differentiated Responsibility: A Model for Enhanced International Refugee Protection within

Interest Convergence Groups', Discussion Paper, Refugee Law Research Unit, Centre for Refugee Studies, York University, Toronto, 25 March.

Chabal, Patrick (1994) *Power in Africa: An Essay in Political Interpretation*, Basingstoke: Macmillan.

Chambers, Robert (1986) 'Hidden Losers? The Impact of Rural Refugees and Refugee Programs on Poorer Hosts', *International Migration Review*, Vol. 20, no. 2, Summer, 245–263.

Chaulia, Sreeram Sundar (2003) 'The Politics of Refugee Hosting in Tanzania: From Open Door to Unsustainability, Insecurity and Receding Receptivity', *Journal of Refugee Studies*, Vol. 16, no. 2, 147–166.

Chazan, Naomi, Peter Lewis, Robert Mortimer, Donald Rothchild and Stephen John Stedman (1999) *Politics and Society in Contemporary Africa*, Third Edition, Boulder, CO: Lynne Reinner Publishers.

Chimni, B. S. (1999) 'From resettlement to involuntary repatriation: Towards a critical history of durable solutions to refugee problems', *New Issues in Refugee Research*, Working Paper No. 2, Geneva: UNHCR, May.

Chimni, B. S. (1998a) 'The Geopolitics of Refugee Studies: A View from the South', *Journal of Refugee Studies*, Vol. 11, no. 4, 350–374.

Chimni, B. S. (1998b) 'The Global Refugee Problem in the 21st Century and the Emerging Security Paradigm: A Disturbing Trend', in A. Anghie and G. Sturgess (eds), *Legal Visions of the 21st Century: Essays in Honour of Judge Christopher Weeramantry*, the Hague: Kluwer Law International, 283–299.

CIMADE, INODEP and MINK (1984) *Afrique, terre des refugiés: Que faire?*, Paris: Harmattan.

Clapham, Christoher (2005) 'Introduction', *International Affairs*, Vol. 81, no. 2, 2005, 275–279.

Clapham, Christopher (1996) *Africa and the International System: The Politics of State Survival*, Cambridge: Cambridge University Press.

Collins, Greg (2004) 'The Coping Strategies Index (CSI) Baseline Survey: World Food Programme (WFP) Assisted Refugees in Western Tanzania', prepared for WFP Tanzania, June–July.

Conteh-Morgan, Earl (1997) *Democratization in Africa: The Theory and Dynamics of Political Transitions*, London: Praeger Publishers.

Coulson, Andrew (1982) *Tanzania: A Political Economy*, Oxford: Clarendon Press.

Crisp, Jeff (2004) 'The local integration and local settlement of refugees: a conceptual and historical analysis', *New Issues in Refugee Research*, Working Paper No. 102, Geneva, UNHCR, April.

Crisp, Jeff (2003a) 'No solutions in sight: the problem of protracted refugee situations in Africa', *New Issues in Refugee Research*, Working Paper No. 75, Geneva: UNHCR, January.

Crisp, Jeff (2003b) 'Why Do We Know So Little about Refugees? How Can We Learn More?', *Forced Migration Review*, No. 18, September, 55.

Crisp, Jeff (2001a) 'Lessons Learned from the implementation of the Tanzania security package', Geneva: UNHCR, Evaluation and Policy Analysis Unit, EPAU/2001/05, May.

Crisp, Jeff (2001b) 'Mind the Gap! UNHCR, humanitarian assistance and the developmental process', *New Issues in Refugee Research*, Working Paper No. 43, Geneva: UNHCR, May.

Crisp, Jeff (2001c) 'The WHALE: Wisdom we Have Acquired from the Liberia Experience: Report of a regional lessons-learned workshop, Monrovia, Liberia, 26–27 April 2001,' Geneva: UNHCR, Evaluation and Policy Analysis Unit, EPAU/2001/06, May.

Crisp, Jeff (2000) 'Africa's refugees: patterns, problems and policy challenges', *New Issues in Refugee Research*, Working Paper No. 28, Geneva: UNHCR, August 2000.

Crisp, Jeff (1999a) 'A state of insecurity: the political economy of violence in refugee-populated areas of Kenya', *New Issues in Refugee Research*, Working Paper No. 16, Geneva: UNHCR, December.

Crisp, Jeff (1999b) 'Who has counted the refugees? UNHCR and the politics of numbers', *New Issues in Refugee Research*, Working Paper No. 12, Geneva: UNHCR, June.

Cuénod, Jacques (1989) 'Refugees: Relief or Development?', in Gil Loescher and Laila Monahan (eds), *Refugees and International Relations*, Oxford: Clarendon Press, 219–253.

Cuénod, Jacques (1967) 'The Problem of Rwandese and Sudanese Refugees', in Sven Hamrell (ed.), *Refugee Problems in Africa*, Uppsala: The Scandinavian Institute of African Studies, 45–53.

Czaika, Mathias (2005) 'A Refugee Burden Index: methodology and its application', paper presented at the conference 'Seeking Refuge, Seeking Rights, Seeking a Future', Oxford Brookes University, 13–14 May.

Daley, Patricia (1992) 'The Politics of the Refugee Crisis in Tanzania', in Horace Campbell and Howard Stein (eds), *Tanzania and the IMF: The Dynamics of Liberalization*, Boulder, CO: Westview Press, 125–146.

Daley, Patricia (1989) 'Refugees and Underdevelopment in Africa: The case of Barundi refugees in Tanzania', DPhil Thesis, Faculty of Anthropology and Geography, University of Oxford.

Davidson, Basil (1992) *The Black Man's Burden: Africa and the Curse of the Nation-State*, New York: Times Books.

Dowty, Alan, and Gil Loescher (1996) 'Refugee Flows as Grounds for International Action', *International Security*, Vol. 21, no. 1, Summer, 43–71.

Drysdale, John (1964) *The Somali Dispute*, London: Pall Mall Press.

Economic Community of West African States (ECOWAS) (1979) 'Protocol A/P.1/5/79 Relating to Free Movement of Persons, Residence and Establishment', Dakar, 29 May.

El-Ayouty, Y. (ed.) (1994) *The Organization of African Unity after Thirty Years*, London: Praeger Publishers.

Elizondo, Debbie (2001) 'Opening remarks by Ms. Debbie Elizondo, Chief, Resettlement Section', Regional Resettlement Meeting, Addis Ababa, 27 February.

Ellis, Stephen (2005) 'How to Rebuild Africa', *Foreign Affairs*, September/October, 135–148.

Ellis, Stephen (2001) 'Les guerres en Afrique de l'Ouest: le poids de l'histoire', *Afrique contemporaine*, No. 198, 2e trimester, 51–56.

Ellis, Stephen (1998) 'Liberia's Warlord Insurgency', in Christopher Clapham (ed.), *African Guerrillas*, Oxford: James Currey Ltd, 155–171.

Ellis, Stephen (1995) 'Liberia 1989–1994: A Study of Ethnic and Spiritual Violence', *African Affairs*, Vol. 94, no. 375, April, 165–197.

Englebert, Pierre (2004) 'Guinea: Recent History', *Africa South of the Sahara 2004*, 33rd edition, London: Europa Publications, 503–510.

Eriksson, L.G., G. Melander and P. Nobel (eds) (1981) *An Analysing Account of the Conference on the African Refugee Problem, May 1979, Arusha*, Uppsala: Scandinavian Institute of African Studies.

European Council on Refugees and Exiles (ECRE) and the US Committee for Refugees (USCR) (2003) *Responding to the Asylum and Access Challenge: An Agenda for Comprehensive Engagement in Protracted Refugee Situations*, Washington: USCR and ECRE, August.

Fonteyne, J.P. L. (1983) 'Burden-Sharing: An Analysis of the Nature and Function of International Solidarity in Cases of Mass Influx of Refugees', *The Australian Year Book of International Law*, Vol. 8, 162–188.

Furley, Oliver (ed.) (1997) *Conflict in Africa*. London: Tauris Academic Studies.

Gasarasi, Charles (1990) 'The Mass Naturalization and Further Integration of Rwandese Refugees in Tanzania: Process, Problems and Prospects', *Journal of Refugee Studies*, Vol. 3, no. 2, 88–109.

Gasarasi, Charles (1987) 'The Tripartite Approach to the Resettlement and Integration of Refugees in Tanzania', in John R. Rogge (ed.), *Refugees: A Third World Dilemma*, Totowa, NJ: Rowman and Littlefield, 99–114.

Gasarasi, Charles (1984) *The Tripartite Approach to the Resettlement and Integration of Rural Refugees in Tanzania*, Research report no. 71, Uppsala: The Scandinavian Institute of African Studies.

Gibney, Matthew J. (2004) *The Ethics and Politics of Asylum: Liberal Democracy and the Responses to Refugees*, Cambridge: Cambridge University Press.

Gibney, Matthew J. (2002) 'Security and the Ethics of Asylum after 11 September', *Forced Migration Review*, No. 13, June, 40–42.

Gibney, Matthew J. (2001) 'The state of asylum: Democratization, judicialization and evolution of refugee policy', *New Issues in Refugee Research*, Working Paper No.50, Geneva: UNHCR, October.

Goodwin-Gill, Guy (1996) *The Refugee in International Law*, Second Edition, Oxford: Clarendon Press.

Gordenker, Leon (1987) *Refugees in International Politics*, London: Croom Helm, 1987.

Gorman, Robert F. (1987) *Coping with Africa's Refugee Burden: A Time for Solutions*, Dordrecht: Martinus Nijhoff Publishers and UNITAR.

Gorman, Robert F. (1986) 'Beyond ICARA II: Implementing Refugee-Related Development Assistance', *International Migration Review*, Vol. 20, no. 2, 283–298.

Gorman, Robert F. (ed.) (1993) *Refugee Aid and Development: Theory and Practice*, Westport, CN: Greenwood Press.

Gould, W. T. S. (1974a) 'International Migration in Tropical Africa: A Bibliographical review', *International Migration Review*, Vol. 8, no. 3, 347–365.

Gould, W. T. S. (1974b) 'Refugees in Tropical Africa', *International Migration Review*, Vol. 8, no. 3, 413–430.

Grahl-Madsen, Atle (1983) 'Ways and prospects of international co-operation in refugee matters', *AWR Bulletin*, Vol. 23, no. 2/3.

Grahl-Madsen, Atle (1980) *Territorial Asylum*, Stockholm: Almqvist and Wiksell International.

Green, R.H. (1994) 'That They May be Whole Again: Off-setting Refugee Influx Burdens on Ngara and Karagwe Districts', Dar es Salaam: UNICEF, September.

Guinea (2000) Government of, National Assembly *Loi L/2001/012 relative au statut des réfugiés en Guinée*, 10 August.

Guinea (1999) Government of, 'Déclaration de S.E. M Mousa Solano, Ministre de l'Administration du Territoire et de la Décentralisation de la République de Guinée, devant la Cinquantième Session du Comité Executif du Haut Commisariat aux Réfugiés', Geneva, October.

Gyimah-Boadi, E. (2004) 'Africa: The Quality of Political Reform', in E. Gyimah-Boadi (ed.), *Democratic Reform in Africa: The Quality of Progress*, Boulder, CO: Lynne Rienner Publishers, 2004, 3–27.

Hammerstad, Anne (2000) 'Whose Security? UNHCR, Refugee Protection and State Security After the Cold War', *Security Dialogue*, Vo. 31, no. 4, December, 391–403.

Hamrell, Sven (1967) 'Introduction: The Problem of African Refugees', in Sven Hamrell (ed.), *Refugee Problems in Africa*, Uppsala: The Scandinavian Institute of African Studies, 9–25.

Hans, Asha and Astri Suhrke (1997) 'Responsibility Sharing', in James C. Hathaway (ed.), *Reconceiving International Refugee Law*, Nijhoff Law Specials No. 30, London: Martins Nijhoff Publishers, 83–109.

Harbeson, John W. and Donald Rothchild (2000) 'The African State and State System in Flux', in John W. Harbeson and Donald Rothchild (eds), *Africa in World Politics: The African State System in Flux*, Third Edition, Boulder, CO: Westview Press, 3–20.

Harman, Danna (2002) 'In a dire Kenyan camp, links to Al Qaeda', *Christian Science Monitor*, 18 December.

Harrell-Bond, Barbara (1986) *Imposing Aid: Emergency Assistance to Refugees*, Oxford: Oxford University Press.

Hasenclever, Andreas, Peter Mayer and Volker Ritterger (1997) *Theories of International Regimes*, Cambridge: Cambridge University Press.

Hatch, John (1970) 'Historical Background of the African Refugee Problem', in Hugh C. Brooks and Yassin El-Yahouty (eds), *Refugees South of the Sahara: An African Dilemma*, Westport, CT: Negro University Press, 1–20.

Hathaway, James C. (1997) 'Preface: Can International Law be made Relevant Again?', in James C. Hathaway (ed.), *Reconceiving International Refugee Law*, Nijhoff Law Specials No. 30, London: Martins Nijhoff Publishers, xvii–xxix.

Hathaway, James C. (1991) *The Law of Refugee Status*, Toronto: Butterworths, 1991.

Hathaway, James C. (ed.) (1997) *Reconceiving International Refugee Law*, Nijhoff Law Specials No. 30, London: Martins Nijhoff Publishers.

Hathaway, James C. and Alexander Neve (1997) 'Making International Refugee Law Relevant Again: A proposal for collectivized and solution-oriented protection', *Harvard Human Rights Journal*, Vol. 10, 115–211.

Helton, Arthur (2002) *The Price of Indifference: Refugees and Humanitarian Action in the New Century*, Oxford: Oxford University Press.

Herbst, Jeffrey (2000) *States and Power in Africa: Comparative Lessons in Authority and Control*, Princeton, NJ: Princeton University Press.

Herbst, Jeffrey (1999) 'The Role of Citizenship Laws in Multiethnic Societies: Evidence from Africa', in Richard Joseph (ed.), *State, Conflict, and Democracy in Africa*, Boulder, CO: Lynne Rienner Publishers, 267–296.

Herrmann, Roy (2003) 'Mid-term review of a Canadian security deployment to the UNHCR programme in Guinea', Geneva: UNHCR, Evaluation and Policy Analysis Unit, EPAU/2003/04, October.

Holborn, Louise W. (1975) *Refugees: A Problem of Our Time: The Work of the United Nations High Commissioner for Refugees 1951 – 1972*, Metuchen, NJ: The Scarecrow Press, Inc.

Horst, Cindy (2006) *Transnational Nomads: How Somalis Cope with Refugee Life in the Dadaab Camps of Kenya*, Oxford: Berghahn Books.

Horst, Cindy (2002) 'Vital Links in Social Security: Somali Refugees in the Dadaab Camps, Kenya' *Refugee Survey Quarterly*, Vol. 21, no. 1 and 2, 242–259.

Hovet, Thomas (1970) 'Boundary Disputes and Tensions as a Cause of Refugees', in Hugh C. Brooks and Yassin el-Ayouty (eds.), *Refugees South of the Sahara: An African Dilemma*, Westport: Negro University Press, 21–30.

Howard, Rhoda E. (1991) 'Repression and State Terror in Kenya: 1982 – 1988', in Timothy Bushnell (ed.), *State Organized Terror: The Case of Violent Internal Repression*, Boulder, CO: Westview Press.

Human Rights Watch (2003) 'Weapons Sanctions, Military Supplies, and Human Suffering: Illegal Arms Flows to Liberia and the June–July 2003 Shelling of Monrovia', New York: HRW Briefing Paper, 3 November.

Human Rights Watch (2002a) 'Kenya: Crackdown on Nairobi's Refugees After Mombasa Attacks', New York, 6 December.

Human Rights Watch (2002b) 'Liberian Refugees in Guinea: Refoulement, Militarization of Camps and Other Protection Concerns', New York: HRW, Vol. 14, no. 8 (A), November.

Human Rights Watch (2001a) 'Guinea: Refugees Still at Risk: Continuing Refugee Protection Concerns in Guinea', New York: HRW, Africa Division, Vol. 13, no. 5 (A), July.

Human Rights Watch (2001b) 'Press Release: Guinea Forces Kill, Wound Civilians in Sierra Leone', New York, 28 February.

Human Rights Watch (1999a) 'Forgotten Children of War: Sierra Leonean refugee Children in Guinea', New York: HRW, Vol. 11, no. 5 (A), July.

Human Rights Watch (1999b) 'In the Name of Security: Forced Round-Ups of Refugees in Tanzania', New York: HRW, Vol. 11, no. 4, July.

Human Rights Watch (1998) *'Prohibited Persons': Abuse of Undocumented Migrants, Asylum Seekers and Refugees in South Africa*, New York: HRW, March.

Human Rights Watch (1996) 'Press release: Human Rights Watch/Africa Calls on the Tanzanian Government and UNHCR to Respect International Law', New York, 17 December.

Human Rights Watch (1995) 'Somali Refugees in Kenya', in *The Human Rights Watch Global Report on Women's Human Rights*, New York: HRW.

Hurwitz, Agnès (2002) 'Responsibility-sharing Arrangements for the Protection of Refugees, with Particular Reference to Europe and the Determination of Claims for Refugee Status', DPhil Thesis, Faculty of Law, University of Oxford.

Huysmans, Jef (2000) 'Migration and the Politics of Security', in Sophie Body-Gendrot and Marco Martiniello (eds), *Minorities in European Cities: The Dynamics of Social Integration and Social Exclusion at the Neighbourhood Level*, Basingstoke: Macmillan, 179–189.

Hyndman, Jennifer (2000) *Managing Displacement: Refugees and the Politics of Humanitarianism*, Minneapolis: University of Minnesota Press.

Hyndman, Jennifer and Bo Viktor Nylund (1998) 'UNHCR and the Status of Prima Facie Refugees in Kenya', *International Journal of Refugee Law*, Vol. 10, no. 1 and 2, 21–48.

Hyslop, Jonathan (ed.) (1999) *African Democracy in the era of Globalisation*, Johannesburg: Witwatersrand University Press, 1999.

Ihonvbere, Julius O. (1994) 'The "Irrelevant" State, Ethnicity, and the Quest for Nationhood in Africa', *Ethnic and Racial Studies*, Vol. 17, no. 1, January, 42–60.

International Crisis Group (ICG) (2005), 'Stopping Guinea's Slide', Dakar: ICG Africa Report no. 94, 14 June.

International Crisis Group (ICG) (2003) 'Guinée: Incertitudes autour d'une fin de règne', Freetown: ICG Rapport Afrique no. 74, 19 December.

International Crisis Group (ICG) (1999) 'Burundian Refugees in Tanzania: The Key Factor to the Burundian Peace Process', ICG Central Africa Report No. 12, Nairobi: ICG, 30 November.

IRIN (2004a) 'Guinea: Economic crisis and Liberian gunmen threaten stability', 15 July, http://www.irinnews.org/Report.aspx?ReportId=50684

IRIN (2003a) 'Kenya: Feature-making communities safe from small arms', 29 October, http://www.irinnews.org/report.aspx?reportid=46951

IRIN (2003b) 'Burundi-Tanzania: Repatriations to include settled Burundians', 27 February, http://www.irinnews.org/Report.aspx?ReportId=41826

IRIN (2003c) 'Tanzania: Food situation in refugee camps 'dire'', 19 February, http://www.irinnews.org/Report.aspx?ReportId=41686

IRIN (2003d) 'Tanzania: President ties rise in small arms to refugee inflows', 1 September, http://www.irinnews.org/Report.aspx?ReportId=45867

IRIN (2003e) 'Liberia: LURD leader Sekou Conneh returns from Guinea', 24 September, http://www.irinnews.org/Report.aspx?ReportId=46315

IRIN (2002a) 'Burundi-Tanzania: IRIN special report on returning Burundian refugees', 8 May, http://www.irinnews.org/report.aspx?reportid=49519

IRIN (2002b) 'Burundi-DRC-Tanzania: Focus on positive aspects of refugee crisis', 28 June, http://www.irinnews.org/Report.aspx?ReportId=32724

IRIN (2001a) 'Tanzania: Mkapa calls for assistance for refugees', 10 January, http://www.irinnews.org/Report.aspx?ReportId=16606

IRIN (2001b) 'Tanzania: Burundi rebels attack refugee transit centre', 13 February, http://www.irinnews.org/Report.aspx?ReportId=17957

IRIN (2001c) 'Tanzania: Hungry Kibondo refugee reports 'exaggerated'', 18 May, http://www.irinnews.org/Report.aspx?ReportId=21304

IRIN (2000a) 'Tanzania: 165 Burundian refugees sentenced', 23 June, http://www.irinnews.org/Report.aspx?ReportId=16047

IRIN (2000b) 'IRIN Update 811 of events in West Africa', 25 September.

Isbister, John (2003) *Promises Not Kept: Poverty and the Betrayal of Third World Development*, Sixth Edition, Basingstoke: Palgrave Macmillan.

Jackson, Robert H. (1992) 'The Security Dilemma in Africa', in Brian Job (ed.), *The Insecurity Dilemma: National Security of Third World States*, Boulder, CO: Lynne Reinner Publishers, 81–94.

Jackson, Robert H. (1990) *Quasi-states: Sovereignty, International Relations, and the Third World*, Cambridge: Cambridge University Press.

Jackson, Robert H. and Carl G. Rosberg (1982) 'Why Africa's Weak States Persist: The Empirical and Juridical in Statehood', *World Politics*, Vol. 35, no. 1, October, 1–24.

Jacobsen, Karen (2005) *The Economic Life of Refugees*, Bloomfield, CT: Kumarian.

Jacobsen, Karen (2002) 'Can Refugees Benefit the State? Refugee Resources and African Statebuilding', *Journal of Modern African Studies*, Vol. 40, no. 4, 577–596.

Jacobsen, Karen (2001) 'The forgotten solution: local integration for refugees in developing countries', *New Issues in Refugee Research*, Working Paper No. 45, Geneva, UNHCR, July.

Jacobsen, Karen (2000) 'A Framework for Exploring the Political and Security Context of Refugee Populated Areas', *Refugee Survey Quarterly*, Vol. 19, no. 1, 3–22.

Jacobsen, Karen (1996) 'Factors Influencing the Policy Responses of Host Governments to Mass Refugee Influxes', *International Migration Review*, Vol. 30, no. 3, Autumn, 655–678.

Jacobsen, Karen and Loren Landau (2003) 'Researching refugees: some methodological and ethical considerations in social science and forced migration', *New Issues in Refugee Research*, Working Paper No.90, Geneva: UNHCR, June.

Jacobsen, Karen, with Steven Wilkinson (1993) 'Refugee Movements as Security Threats in Sub-Saharan Africa', in Myron Weiner (ed.), *International Migration and Security*, Boulder, CO: Westview Press, 201–227.

Jamal, Arafat (2003) 'Camps and Freedoms: Long-Term Refugee Situations in Africa', *Forced Migration Review*, No. 16, January, 4–6.

Jervis, Robert (1976) *Perception and Misperception in International Politics*, Princeton, NJ: Princeton University Press.

Job, Brian (1992) 'The Insecurity Dilemma: National, Regime, and State Securities in the Third World', in Brian Job (ed.), *The Insecurity Dilemma: National Security of Third World States*, Boulder, CO: Lynne Reinner Publishers, 1992, 11–35.

Joppke, Christian (ed.) (1998) *Challenges to the Nation-State: Immigration in Western Europe and the United States*, Oxford: Oxford University Press.

Juma, Monica Kathina (2002) 'Migration, Security and Refugee Protection: A Reflection', Paper Prepared for the Conference 'Refugee Protection in Africa: How to ensure security and development for refugees and hosts', Entebbe, 10–14 November.

Juma, Monica Kathina and Astri Suhrke (eds) (2002) *Eroding Local Capacity: International Humanitarian Action in Africa*, Uppsala, Sweden: Nordiska Afrikainstitutet.

Kaba, Lansine (1977) 'Guinean Politics: A Critical Historical Overview', *The Journal of Modern African Studies*, Vol. 15, no. 1, March, 25–45.

Kagwanja, Peter and Monica Juma (2008) 'Somali Refugees: Protracted Exile and Shifting Security Frontiers', in Gil Loescher, James Milner, Edward Newman and Gary Troeller (eds), *Protracted Refugee Situations: Political, Human Rights and Security Implications*, Tokyo: United Nations University Press, 214–247.

Kagwanja, Peter Mwangi (2002) 'Strengthening Local Relief Capacity in Kenya: Challenges and Prospects', in Monica Kathina Juma and Astri Suhrke (eds), *Eroding Local Capacity: International Humanitarian Action in Africa*, Uppsala, Sweden: Nordiska Africa Institute, 94–115.

Kaiser, Tania (2008) 'Sudanese Refugees in Uganda and Kenya', in Gil Loescher, James Milner, Edward Newman and Gary Troeller (eds), *Protracted Refugee Situations: Political, Human Rights and Security Implications*, Tokyo: United Nations University Press, 248–276.

Kaiser, Tania (2001) 'A beneficiary-based evaluation of UNHCR's programme in Guinea, West Africa', Geneva: UNHCR, Evaluation and Policy Analysis Unit, EPAU/2001/02, January.

Kamanga, Khoti (2005) 'The (Tanzania) Refugees Act of 1998: Some Legal and Policy Implications', *Journal of Refugee Studies*, Vol. 18, no. 1, 100–116.

Kamanga, Khoti (2002) 'International Refugee Law in East Africa: An Evolving Regime', *Georgetown Journal of International Affairs*, Winter/Spring, 25–35.

Kamara, Tom (2001a) 'Guinea: Confronting Insecurity in the Midst of Unstable Neighbours', WRITENET Paper No. 8/2000, UNHCR, February.

Kamara, Tom (2001b) 'West Africa: Problems and Prospects for Stability in the Mano River States', WRITENET Paper No. 02/2001, UNHCR, October.

Keller, Edmond and Donald Rothchild (eds) (1996) *Africa in the New International Order: Rethinking State Sovereignty and Regional Security*, Boulder, CO: Lynne Reiner Publishers.

Kelsall, Tim (1996) 'Continuity and change in the Tanzanian political system: the 1995 elections', Paper presented at the Political Studies Association Annual Conference, Glasgow, April.

Kenya (2007) Government of, 'The Refugees Act 2006', *Kenya Gazette Supplement No. 97 (Acts No. 13)*, Nairobi: Government Printer, 2 January.

Kenya (2003) Parliament of, *Hansard*, Nairobi, 20 November.

Kenya (1992) Government of, National Assembly 'Report of the Parliamentary Select Committee to investigate Ethnic Clashes in Western and Other Parts of Kenya, 1992', Nairobi: Government of Kenya, September.

Kenya (1990) Government of, Office of the Attorney General 'Draft – The Refugees Bill, 1990', Nairobi.

Khadiagala, Gilbert M. and Terrence Lyons (eds) (2001) *African Foreign Policies: Power and Process*, Boulder, CO: Lynne Rienner Publishers.

Khapoya, Vincent B. (1994) *The African Experience*, Englewood Cliffs, NJ: Prentice Hall.

Kibreab, Gaim (1991) *The State of the Art Review of Refugee Studies in Africa*, Uppsala Papers in Economic History, Research Report No. 26, Uppsala: Uppsala universitet.

Kibreab, Gaim (1985) *African Refugees: Reflections on the African Refugee Problem*, Trenton, NJ: Africa World Press.

Kironde, Apollo (1970) 'An African Evaluation of the Problem', in Hugh C. Brooks and Yassin el-Ayouty, *Refugees South of the Sahara: An African Dilemma*, Westport, CN: Negro Universities Press, 105–114.

Knickerbocker, Brad (2002) 'Biggest terror threat is from small arms', *Christian Science Monitor*, 4 December.

Krasner, Stephen D. (1985) *Structural Conflict: The Third World Against Global Liberalism*, Berkeley, CA: University of California Press.

Kraxberger, Brennan M. (2005) 'The United States and Africa: Shifting Geopolitics in an "Age of Terror"', *Africa Today*, Vol. 52, no. 1, Fall, 47–68.

Lancaster, Carol (2000) 'Africa in World Affairs', in John W. Harbeson and Donald Rothchild (eds), *Africa in World Politics: The African State System in Flux*, Third Edition, Boulder, CO: Westview Press, 208–234.

Landau, Loren B. (2003) 'Beyond the Losers: Transforming Governmental Practice in Refugee-Affected Tanzania', *Journal of Refugee Studies*, Vol. 16, no. 1, 19–43.

Landau, Loren (2002) 'The Humanitarian Hangover: Transnationalization of Governmental Practice in Tanzania's Refugee-Populated Areas', *Refugee Survey Quarterly*, Vol. 21, no. 1 and 2, 260–299.

Lawyers Committee for Human Rights (LCHR) (2002), *Refugees, Rebels and the Quest for Justice*, New York: LCHR.

Lawyers Committee for Human Rights (LCHR) (1995) *African Exodus: Refugee Crisis, Human Rights and the 1969 OAU Convention*, New York: LCHR.

Le Vine, Victor (2004) *Politics in Francophone Africa*, London: Lynne Rienner Publishers.

Lemarchand, René (1992) 'Africa's Troubled Transitions', *Journal of Democracy*, Vol. 3, no. 4, October, 98–109.

Lemarchand, René, and David Martin (1974) 'Selective Genocide in Burundi', Report No. 20, London: The Minority Rights Group.

Lewis, I. M. (1963) 'Pan-Africanism and Pan-Somalism', *The Journal of Modern African Studies*, Vol. 1, no. 2, 147–161.

Lischer, Sarah Kenyon (2005) *Dangerous Sanctuaries: Refugee Camps, Civil War, and the Dilemmas of Humanitarian Aid*, Ithaca: Cornell University Press.

Loescher, Gil (2001) *The UNHCR and World Politics: A Perilous Path*, Oxford: Oxford University Press.

Loescher, Gil (1993) *Beyond Charity: International Cooperation and the Global Refugee Crisis*, New York: Oxford University Press.

Loescher, Gil (1992) *Refugee Movements and International Security*, Adelphi Paper 268, London: Brasseys for The International Institute for Strategic Studies.

Loescher, Gil (1989) 'Introduction', in Gil Loescher and Laila Monahan (eds), *Refugees and International Relations*, Oxford: Clarendon Press, 1–33.

Loescher, Gil, Alexander Betts and James Milner (2008) *UNHCR: The Politics and Practice of Protection into the Twenty-First Century*, New York: Routledge.

Loescher, Gil and James Milner (2008a) 'Understanding the Problem of Protracted Refugee Situations', in Gil Loescher, James Milner, Edward Newman and Gary Troeller (eds), *Protracted Refugee Situations: Political, Human Rights and Security Implications*, Tokyo: United Nations University Press, 20–42.

Loescher, Gil and James Milner (2008b) 'A Framework for Responding to Protracted Refugee Situations', in Gil Loescher, James Milner, Edward Newman and Gary Troeller (eds), *Protracted Refugee Situations: Political, Human Rights and Security Implications*, Tokyo: United Nations University Press, 353–376.

Loescher, Gil and James Milner (2005) *Protracted Refugee Situations: Domestic and International Security Implications*, Adelphi Paper no. 375, London: Routledge for The International Institute for Strategic Studies.

Loescher, Gil, and James Milner (2003) 'The "Missing Link": The Need for Comprehensive Engagement in Regions of Refugee Origin', *International Affairs*, Vol. 79, no. 3, May, 583–617.

Loescher, Gil, James Milner, Edward Newman, and Gary Troeller (2007) 'Protracted Refugee Situations and the Regional Dynamics of Peacebuilding', *Conflict, Security and Development*, Vol. 7, no. 3, 491–501.

Loescher, Gil and Laila Monahan (eds) (1989) *Refugees and International Relations*, Oxford: Clarendon Press.

Loescher, Gil and John Scanlan (1986) *Calculated Kindness: Refugees and America's Half-Open Door*, New York and London: Free Press and Macmillan.

MacFarlane, S. Neil (1999) 'Taking Stock: The Third World and the End of the Cold War', in Louise Fawcett and Yezid Sayigh (eds), *The Third World beyond the Cold War: Continuity and Change*, Oxford: Oxford University Press, 15–33.

Mahiga, Augustine (1997) 'A Change in Direction for Tanzania', *Refugees*, no. 110, Winter, 14–15.

Malkki, Liisa H. (1995) *Purity and Exile: Violence, Memory and National Cosmology among Hutu Refugees in Tanzania*, Chicago: Chicago University Press.

Maluwa, Tiyanjana (1995) 'The Refugee Problem and the Quest for Peace and Security in Southern Africa', *International Journal of Refugee Law*, Vol. 7, no. 4, 653–674.

Martin, Guy (1995) 'International Solidarity and Cooperation in Assistance to African Refugees: Burden-Sharing or Burden-Shifting', *International Journal of Refugee Law*, Special Issue: OAU/UNHCR Addis Ababa Symposium on Refugees and Forced Populations Displacements in Africa, 8–10 September, 250–273.

Matlof, Judith (1996) 'Next Crisis in Central Africa: The Tanzania-Burundi Border', *The Christian Science Monitor*, 12 December.

Matthews, Graham (2004) 'Tanzania: Recent History', in *Africa South of the Sahara 2004*, 33rd Edition, London: Europa Publications, Taylor and Francis Group, 1114–1120.

Matthews, Jessica (1989) 'Redefining Security', *Foreign Affairs*, Vol. 68, no. 2, 162–177.

Matthews, Robert O. (1972) 'Refugees and Stability in Africa', *International Organization*, Vol. 26, no. 1, 62–83.

Matthews, Z.K. (1970) 'Refugees from Southern Africa', in Hugh C. Brooks and Yassin el-Ayouty, *Refugees South of the Sahara: An African Dilemma*, Westport, CN: Negro Universities Press, 163–172.

Mchome, Sifuni Ernest (ed.) (2001) 'Abstracts and Recommendations from the Second Workshop for the study conducted for the Prime Minister's Office, under the Special Programme for Refugee Affected Areas (SPRAA), within the European Union funded 'Review of Refugee Related Policies and Laws' project', Dar es Salaam: Centre for the Study of Forced Migration, March.

McGovern, Mike (2002) 'Conflit régional et rhétorique de la contre-insurgence: Guinéens et réfugiés en septembre 2000' *Politique Africaine*, no. 88, 84–102.

Melly, Paul (2003) 'Guinea: Early Warning Analysis', WRITENET Paper No. 19/2003, UNHCR, August.

Mendel, Toby D. (1997) 'Refugee Law and Practice in Tanzania', *International Journal of Refugee Law*, Vol. 9, no. 1, 35–59.

Menkhaus, Ken (2004) *Somalia: State Collapse and the Threat of Terrorism*, Adelphi Paper 364, London: Oxford University Press for The International Institute for Strategic Studies.

Messkoub, Mahmood (1996) 'The Social Impact of Adjustment in Tanzania in the 1980s: Economic Crisis and Household Survival Strategies', *Internet Journal of African Studies*, No. 1, April, http://www.bradford.ac.uk/research/ijas

Meyer, Sarah (2006) 'The 'refugee aid and development' approach in Uganda: empowerment and self-reliance of refugees in practice', *New Issues in Refugee Research*, Working Paper No. 131, Geneva, UNHCR, October.

Migdal, Joel S. (1988) *Strong Societies and Weak States: State-society relations and state capabilities in the Third World*, Princeton, NJ: Princeton University Press.

Milner, James (2006) 'The Militarization and Demilitarization of Refugee Camps and Settlements in Guinea, 1999–2004', in Robert Muggah (ed.), *No Refuge: The Crisis of Refugee Militarization in Africa*, London: Zed Books, with Astrid Christoffersen-Deb, 51–87.

Milner, James (2000) *Sharing the Security Burden: Towards the Convergence of Refugee Protection and State Security*, RSC Working Paper No. 4, Refugee Studies Centre, Oxford, May.

Mkandawire, Thandika (1999) 'Crisis Management and the Making of 'Choiceless Democracies'', in Richard Joseph (ed.), *State, Conflict, and Democracy in Africa*, Boulder, CO: Lynne Rienner Publishers, 119–136.

Mogire, Edward (2006) 'Preventing or Abetting: Refugee Militarization in Tanzania', in Robert Muggah (ed.), *No Refuge: The Crisis of Refugee Militarization in Africa*, London: Zed Books, 137–178.

Molefi, Joe (1984) 'Few Safe Havens for Apartheid's Exiles', *Africa Report*, Vol. 29, no. 1, January/February.

Morris, Eric and Stephen John Stedman (2008) 'Protracted Refugee Situations, Conflict and Security: The Need for Better Diagnosis and Prescription', in Gil Loescher, James Milner, Edward Newman and Gary Troeller (eds), *Protracted Refugee Situations: Political, Human Rights and Security Implications*, Tokyo: United Nations University Press, 69–84.

Mortimer, Robert (1984) *The Third World Coalition in International Politics*, Second Edition, London: Westview Press.

Mtango, Elly-Elikunda (1989) 'Military and Armed Attacks on Refugee Camps', in Gil Loescher and Liala Monahan (eds), *Refugees and International Relations*, Oxford: Oxford University Press, 87–121.

Musau, Jelvas (2001) 'Protecting Refugees in Dadaab: Processes, Problems and Prospects', *Forced Migration Review*, No. 11, October, 35–36.

Musokc, Issa Kaboko (1997a) 'From Hospitality to Total IIostility: Peasant Response to the Influx of Rwandan and Burundian Refugees in the Kagera and Kigoma Regions of Tanzania', Paper presented at the Annual Seminar on the Problem of Refugees in Eastern and Central Africa, Demographic Training Unit, University of Dar es Salaam, Tanzania, 5–6 June.

Musoke, Issa Kaboko (1997b) 'The Negative Environmental Impact of the Influx of Refugees in the Kagera and Kigoma Regions of Tanzania', Paper presented at the Annual Seminar on the Problem of Refugees in Eastern and Central Africa, Demographic Training Unit, University of Dar es Salaam, Tanzania, 5–6 June.

Naldi, Gino J. (1989) *The Organization of African Unity: An Analysis of Its Role*, London: Mansell.

Nnoli, Okwudiba (1978) *Self-Reliance and Foreign Policy in Tanzania: The Dynamics of the Diplomacy of a New State, 1961 to 1971*, London: NOK Publishers.

Noll, Gregor and Joanne van Selm (2003) 'Rediscovering Resettlement', *Insight*, No. 3, Washington DC: Migration Policy Institute, December.

Nowrojee, Binaifir (2000) 'In the Name of Security: Erosion of Refugee Rights in East Africa', *World Refugee Survey*, Washington: USCR.

Nowrojee, Binaifer, and Bronwen Manby (1993) 'Divide and Rule: State-sponsored Ethnic Violence in Kenya', New York: Human Rights Watch.

Nyamnjoh, Francis B. (2005) *Africa's Media: Democracy and the Politics of Belonging*, London: Zed Books.

O'Neill, William (2000) 'Conflict in West Africa: Dealing with Exclusion and Separation', *International Journal of Refugee Law*, Vol. 12, Special Supplementary Issue, 171–194.

O'Toole, Thomas (1978) *Historical Dictionary of Guinea (Republic of Guinea-Conakry)*, African Historical Dictionaries, No. 16, Netuchen, NJ: The Scarecrow Press, Inc.

Ofcansky, Thomas P., and Rodger Yaeger (1997) *Historical Dictionary of Tanzania*, Second Edition, African Historical Dictionaries, No. 72, London: The Scarecrow Press, Inc.

Ogata, Sadako (2005) *The Turbulent Decade: Confronting the Refugee Crises of the 1990s*, London: W. W. Norton and Company.

Okoth-Obbo, George (2001) 'Thirty Years On: A legal review of the 1969 OAU Refugee Convention', in A.A. Yusuf (ed.), *African Yearkbook of International Law*, London: African Association of International Law, 3–69.

Organisation guinéenne de défense des droits de l'homme et du citoyen (OGDH) (2000) 'Déclaration', 090/CD/OGDH, 13 September.

Organization of African Unity (OAU) and UNHCR (1998) 'Report of the Regional Meeting on Refugee Issues in the Great Lakes', Kampala, 8–9 May.

OAU (1990) *The Khartoum Declaration on Africa's Refugee Crisis*, Adopted by the OAU Seventeenth Extraordinary Session of the Commission of Fifteen on Refugees, Meeting in Khartoum, Republic of Sudan, 22–24 September.

Orwa, Katete (1989) 'Foreign Policy, 1963–1986', in W.R. Ochieng' (ed.), *A Modern History of Kenya: 1895 – 1980*, Nairobi: Evans Brothers (Kenya) Limited, 219–244.

Oularé, Ali and Fodé Keita with Sadigou Tounkara (1992) 'Enquête socio-economic sur la situation des réfugiés libériens et sierra-leonais en Guinée Forestiere', Conakry, University of Conakry for UNHCR, Branch Office for Guinea, November.

Oxfam (2005) *Foreign Territories: The Internationalisation of EU Asylum Policy*, Oxford: Oxfam GB.

Parker, Alison (2002) *Hidden in Plain View: Refugees living without protection in Nairobi and Kampala*, New York: Human Rights Watch.

Pérouse de Montclos, Marc-Antoine (2001) 'Elections among the Kenya Somali: A Conservative but Marginalised Vote', in Marcel Rutten, Alamin Mazrui and François Grignon, *Out for the Count: The 1997 General Elections and Prospects for Democracy in Kenya*, Kampala: Fountain Publishers, 296–314.

Pérouse de Montclos, Marc-Antoine (1998) 'Le poids de l'histoire et le choc des cultures: les réfugiés somaliens du Kenya confrontés à la raison d'État', in Véronique Lassailly-Jacob (ed.), *Communautés déracinées dans les pays du Sud*, autrepart / Les Cahiers des sciences humaines, Paris: Orstom, 155–171.

Pérouse de Montclos, Marc-Antoine, and Peter Mwangi Kagwanja (2000) 'Refugee Camps or Cities? The Socio-economic Dynamics of the Dadaab and Kakuma Camps in Northern Kenya', *Journal of Refugee Studies*, Vol. 13, no. 2, 205–222.

Pinkney, Robert (2003) *Democracy in the Third World*, Second Edition, Boulder, CO: Lynne Rienner Publishers.

Poku, Nana and David T. Graham (eds) (1998) *Redefining Security: Population Movements and National Security*, London: Praeger Publishers.

Prunier, Gérard (1998) 'The Rwandan Patriotic Front', in Christopher Clapham (ed.), *African Guerrillas*, Oxford: James Currey Ltd., 119–133.

Prunier, Gérard (1995) *The Rwanda Crisis: History of a Genocide*, London: Hurst and Company.
Putnam, Robert D. (1988) 'Diplomacy and Domestic Politics: the Logic of Two Level Games', *International Organization*, Vol. 42, no. 3, Summer, 427–460.
Rake, Alan (2004) 'Kenya: Recent History', in *Africa South of the Sahara*, 33rd Edition, London: Europa Publications, 548–557.
Ravenhill, John (1990) 'The North-South Balance of Power', *International Affairs*, Vol. 66, no. 4, 731–748.
Reed, Wm. C. (1998) 'Guerrillas in the Midst: The Former Government of Rwanda (FGoR) & the Alliance of Democratic Forces for the Liberation of Congo-Zaire (ADFL) in Eastern Zaire', in Christopher Clapham (ed.), *African Guerrillas*, Oxford: James Currey Ltd., 134–154.
Refugee Consortium of Kenya (RCK) (2006) 'The Refugee Bill 2006: Improving Security and the State of Migration in Kenya', Nairobi: RCK.
Refugee Consortium of Kenya (RCK) (2004) 'The Refugees Bill 2003: Comments on the Parliamentary Debates: 1st and 2nd Readings October-November 2003', Nairobi: RCK.
Refugee Consortium of Kenya (RCK) (2003a) 'Refugee Management in Kenya', *Forced Migration Review*, Number 16, January, 17–19.
Refugee Consortium of Kenya (2003b) 'Refugee Rights in the Context of the War Against Terrorism', *Refugee Insights*, April, 3–5.
Refugee Council USA (2003) 'US Refugee Admissions Program for Fiscal Year 2004: Recommendations of The Refugee Council USA', Washington DC, May.
Reno, William (1998) *Warlord Politics and African States*, London: Lynne Rienner Publishers.
Rivière, Claude (1977) *Guinea: The Mobilization of a People*, Translated from the French by Virginia Thompson and Richard Adloff, Ithaca: Cornell University Press.
Robinson, W. Courtland (1998) *Terms of Refuge: The Indochinese Exodus and the International Response*, London: Zed Books.
Rogge, John (1994) 'Repatriation of Refugees', in Tim Allen and Hubert Morsink (eds), *When Refugees Go Home*, London: James Currey Ltd.
Rogge, John (1987) *Refugees: A Third World Dilemma*, Totwa, NJ: Rowman and Littlefield.
Rotberg, Robert (2004) 'The Failure and Collapse of Nation-States: Breakdown, Prevention, and Repair', in Robert Rotberg (ed.), *When States Fail: Causes and Consequences*, Princeton: Princeton University Press, 1–45.
Rubin, Neville (1974) 'Africa and Refugees', *African Affairs*, Vol. 73, no. 292, 290–311.
Ruthström-Ruin, Cecilia (1993) *Beyond Europe: The Globalization of Refugee Aid*, Lund: Lund University Press.
Rutinwa, Bonaventure (2002a) 'The Marginalisation of Local Relief Capacity in Tanzania', in Monica Kathina Juma and Astri Suhrke (eds), *Eroding Local Capacity: International Humanitarian Action in Africa*, Uppsala: Nordiska Afrikainstitutet, 73–93.
Rutinwa, Bonaventure (2002b) 'Prima facie status and refugee protection', *New Issues in Refugee Research*, Working Paper No. 69, Geneva: UNHCR, October.

Rutinwa, Bonaventure (1999) 'The end of asylum? The changing nature of refugee policies in Africa', *New Issues in Refugee Research*, Working Paper No. 5, Geneva: UNHCR, May.

Rutinwa, Bonaventure (1996) 'The Tanzanian Government's Response to the Rwandan Emergency', *Journal of Refugee Studies*, Special Issue, Vol. 9, no. 3, 291–302.

Rutinwa, Bonaventure, and Khoti Kamanga (2003) 'The Impact of the Presence of Refugees in Northwestern Tanzania', Report by the Centre for the Study of Forced Migration, University of Dar es Salaam, September.

Rwelamira, M. R. (1989) 'Two Decades of the 1969 OAU Convention Governing the Specific Aspects of the Refugee Problem in Africa', *International Journal of Refugee Law*, Vol. 1, no. 4, 557–561.

Samatar, Abdi Ismail and Ahmed I. Samatar (2002) *The African State: Reconsiderations*, Portsmouth, NH: Heinemann.

Samatar, Said S. (1984) 'The Somali Dilemma: Nation in Search of a State', in A.I. Asiwaju (ed.), *Partitioned Africans: Ethnic Relations across Africa's International Boundaries, 1884- 1984*, London: Hurst and Company.

Shacknove, Andrew (1993) 'From Asylum to Containment', *International Journal of Refugee Law*, Vol. 5, no. 4, 516–533.

Shuck, Peter (1997) 'Refugee Burden-Sharing: A Modest Proposal', *Yale Journal of International Law*, Vol. 22, no. 2, 243–297.

Skran, Claudena (1995) *Refugees in Inter-War Europe: The Emergence of a Regime*, Oxford: Clarendon Press.

Smillie, Ian, and Larry Minear (2003) *The Quality of Money: Donor Behaviour in Humanitarian Financing*, Sommerville, MA: Humanitarianism and War Project, The Feinstein International Famine Centre, Tufts University, April.

Smith, Merrill (2004) 'Warehousing Refugees: A Denial of Rights, a Waste of Humanity', in *World Refugee Survey 2004*, Washington: USCR, 34–56.

Snyder, Jack (2000) *From Voting to Violence: Democratization and Nationalist Conflict*, The Norton Series in World Politics, London: W. W. Norton and Company.

Sommers, Marc (2001) *Fear in Bongoland: Burundian Refugees in Urban Tanzania*, Refugee and Forced Migration Studies, Volume 8, Oxford: Berghahn Books.

Somerville, Keith (1999) 'Africa After the Cold War: Frozen Out or Frozen in Time?', in Louise Fawcett and Yezid Sayigh (eds), *The Third World beyond the Cold War: Continuity and Change*, Oxford: Oxford University Press, 134–169.

South Africa (2004) Government of, Permanent Mission to Geneva 'Statement on behalf of the African Group at the Second Meeting of the Forum of the HCR on Convention Plus', Geneva, 12 March.

South Africa (2003) Government of, Permanent Mission to Geneva 'Statement on behalf of the African Group at the First Meeting of the Forum of the HCR on Convention Plus', Geneva, 27 June.

Spencer, Sarah (ed.) (2003) *The Politics of Migration: Managing Opportunity, Conflict and Change*, Oxford: Blackwell Publishing.

Sperl, Stefan and Irinel Bradisteanu (2004) 'Refugee resettlement in developing countries: The experience of Benin and Burkina Faso, 1997 – 2003: An independent evaluation', Geneva: UNHCR, Evaluation and Policy Analysis Unit and Resettlement and Special Cases Section, EPAU/2004/04-Rev.1, April.

Stedman, Stephen John and Terrence Lyons (2004) 'Conflict in Africa', in E. Gyimah-Boadi (ed.), *Democratic Reform in Africa: The Quality of Progress*, Boulder, CO: Lynne Rienner Publishers, 141–158.

Stedman, Stephen John and Fred Tanner (eds) (2003) *Refugee Manipulation: War, Politics and the Abuse of Human Suffering*, Washington, DC: Brookings Institution.

Stein, Barry N. (1987) 'ICARA II: Burden Sharing and Durable Solutions', in John R. Rogge (ed.), *Refugees: A Third World Dilemma*, Totowa, NJ: Rowman and Littlefield, 47–59.

Suhrke, Astri (1998) 'Burden-Sharing during Refugee Emergencies: The Logic of Collective versus National Action', *Journal of Refugee Studies*, Vol. 11, no. 4, 1–20.

Suhrke, Astri, Michael Barutciski, Peta Sandison and Rick Garlock (2000) 'The Kosovo refugee crisis: An independent evaluation of UNHCR's emergency preparedness and response', Geneva: UNHCR, Evaluation and Policy Analysis Unit, EPAU/2000/001, February.

Sundet, Geir (1996) 'Democracy in Transition: The 1995 Elections in Tanzania', *Human Rights Report*, No. 8, Oslo: Norwegian Institute of Human Rights, June.

Tanzania (2003) Government of the United Republic of, Ministry of Home Affairs 'The National Refugee Policy', Dar es Salaam, September.

Tanzania (2000) Government of the United Republic of, Permanent Mission to the United Nations 'Statement by Ambassador Hassan Kibelloh, Permanent Secretary, Ministry of Foreign Affairs and International Cooperation of the United Republic of Tanzania in the General Debate of the 55th Session of the United Nations General Assembly', New York, 22 September.

Tanzania (1999) Government of the United Republic of, 'The Refugees Act, 1998', Dar es Salaam.

Tanzania (1998) Government of the United Republic of, 'Statement by Mr. Bernard Mchomvu, Permanent Secretary in the Ministry of Home Affairs, to the 49th Session of the EXCOM on International Solidarity and Burden Sharing in All its Aspects: National, Regional and International', Geneva, 6 October.

Tanzania (1997) Government of the United Republic of, Prime Minister's Office 'Programming Mission for Rehabilitation of Refugee Affected Areas and Development Programme in Kigoma Region', Dar es Salaam, April.

Tanzania (1995a) Government of the United Republic of, 'Statement by Hon. Judge E. Mweisumo, Deputy Minister for Home Affairs (Tanzania) to the UNHCR Executive Committee, Forty-Sixth Session, October, 1995', Geneva, October.

Tanzania (1995b) Government of the United Republic of, Ministry of Foreign Affairs and International Cooperation 'Speech delivered by Hon. Joseph Rwegasira, Minister for Foreign Affairs and International Cooperation when opening an international workshop on the refugee crisis in the Great Lakes Region held on 16th to 19th August, 1995 in Arusha', Arusha, 16 August.

Tanzania (1990) Government of the United Republic of, Ministry of Home Affairs 'Opening speech by the Minister for Home Affairs, Hon. Nalatla L. Kiola, MP, to a Symposium Organized by Africa Refugee Study Centre in Arusha', 30 July.

Tanzania (1972) Government of the United Republic of, Ministry of Home Affairs 'Speech by the Minister for Home Affairs during 1972/73 Budget Session', Dar es Salaam, undated (likely 1972).

Tanzania (1966) Government of the United Republic of, 'Refugees (Control) Act, 1965', Dar es Salaam.

Tarrow, Sidney (1994) *Power in Movement: Social movements, collective action and politics*, Cambridge: Cambridge University Press.

Taylor, Ian and Paul Williams (2004) 'Understanding Africa's Place in World Politics', in Ian Taylor and Paul Williams (eds), *Africa in International Politics: External Involvement on the Continent*, London: Routledge, 1–22.

Tazreiter, Claudia (2004) *Asylum Seekers and the State: The Politics of Protection in a Security-Conscious World*, Aldershot: Ashgate.

Temu, Andrew E., and Jean M. Due (2000) 'The Business Environment in Tanzania after Socialism: Challenges of Reforming Banks, Parastatals, Taxation and the Civil Service', *Journal of Modern African Studies*, Vol. 38, no. 4, 683–712.

Terry, Fiona (2002) *Condemned to Repeat?: The Paradox of Humanitarian Action*, Ithaca: Cornell University Press.

Throup, David (1997) 'The Colonial Legacy', in Oliver Furley (ed.), *Conflict in Africa*. London: Tauris Academic Studies, 237–274.

Throup, David and Charles Hornsby (1998) *Multi-Party Politics in Kenya*, Oxford: James Currey Ltd.

Tordoff, William (2002) *Government and Politics in Africa*, Fourth Edition, London: Palgrave Macmillan.

Tunga, N.R.T. (1987) 'Ujamaa Socialism and Rwandese Refugees' Settlement in Mwesi, Tanzania', Paper prepared for the Conference on The Management of Planned and Spontaneous Refugee Settlements in Africa, Dar es Salaam, April.

Turner, Simon (1999) 'Angry young men in camps: gender, age and class relations among Burundian refugees in Tanzania', *New Issues in Refugee Research*, Working Paper No. 9, Geneva: UNHCR, June.

Turner, Simon (2004) 'Under the Gaze of the 'Big Nations': Refugees, Rumours and the International Community in Tanzania', *African Affairs*, Vol. 103, 227–247.

Turton, David (1996) 'Migrants and Refugees', in Tim Allen (ed.), *In Search of Cool Ground: War, Flight, and Homecoming in Northeast Africa*, Trenton, NJ: Africa World Press, 96–110.

Turton, E.R. (1972) 'Somali Resistance to Colonial Rule and the Development of Somali Political Activity in Kenya 1893 – 1960', *The Journal of African History*, Vol. 13, no. 1, 119–143.

Ullman, Richard (1983) "Redefining Security", *International Security*, Vol. 8, no. 1, Summer, 129–53.

UN Development Programme (UNDP) (1994) *Human Development Report 1994*, Oxford: Oxford University Press.

UN Environment Programme (UNEP) (2000) 'Environmental Impact of Refugees in Guinea: Report to the Secretary General on the findings and recommendations of the pre-assessment on the environmental impact of refugees in Guinea', Nairobi: UNEP Regional Office for Africa, March.

UN General Assembly (UNGA) (1988) 'International Conference on Indo-Chinese Refugees', Resolution 43/119, 8 December.

UNGA (1982) 'International Conference on Assistance to Refugees in Africa', Resolution 37/197, 18 December.

UNGA (1981) 'International Conference on Assistance to Refugees in Africa', Resolution 36/124, 14 December.

UNGA (1980) 'International Conference on Assistance to Refugees in Africa', Resolution 35/42, 25 November.

UN High Commissioner for Refugees (UNHCR) (2008a) 'Supplementary Appeal: Comprehensive Solutions for Burundian Refugees in Tanzania's Old Settlements', Geneva: UNHCR, 12 February.

UNHCR (2008b) 'Q&A: Prime Minister Pinda on Tanzania's Protracted Refugee Situations', Geneva, 19 December 2008.

UNHCR (2007a) *Global Report 2006*, Geneva: UNHCR, June.

UNHCR (2007b) *Global Appeal 2008–2009*, Geneva: UNHCR, December.

UNHCR (2007c) *2005 UNHCR Statistical Yearbook*, Geneva: UNHCR, April.

UNHCR (2007d) 'Press Release: UNHCR Calls on Kenya to Halt Somali Returns', 3 January.

UNHCR (2006) *The State of the World's Refugees: Human Displacement in the New Millennium*, Oxford: Oxford University Press.

UNHCR (2005a) *Global Report 2004*, Geneva: UNHCR, 2005.

UNHCR (2005b) 'News Story: When going home is not an option: Local integration in Guinea', 20 July.

UNHCR (2005c) *Statistical Yearbook 2003: Refugees, Asylum-seekers and Other Persons of Concern - Trends in Displacement, Protection and Solutions*, Geneva: UNHCR, May.

UNHCR (2004a) *Global Appeal 2005*, Geneva: UNHCR.

UNHCR (2004b) *Global Report 2003*, Geneva: UNHCR.

UNHCR (2004c) 'UNHCR Briefing Notes: Africa Dialogue; Food Aid Crisis; Chad; Western Sahara; Ingushetia', 5 March.

UNHCR (2003a) *Global Report 2002*, Geneva: UNHCR.

UNHCR (2003b) 'UNHCR Briefing Notes: Asylum Statistics; Iran; Sierra Leone Repatriation', 3 December.

UNHCR (2003c) 'UNHCR Briefing Notes: Liberia, Sudanese Refugees in Uganda, Sudanese Refugees in Chad', 9 September.

UNHCR (2003d) 'Press Release: WFP and UNHCR Call for Urgent Aid for Refugees in Africa', 14 February.

UNHCR (2002a) *Global Report 2001*, Geneva: UNHCR, 2002.

UNHCR (2002b) 'UNHCR Briefing Notes: Guinea', 12 November 2002.

UNHCR (2002c) 'UNHCR Briefing Notes: Cote d'Ivoire; Liberians in Sierra Leone and Guinea; Tanzania/Rwanda; High Commissioner to visit Arabian Peninsula', 11 October.

UNHCR (2002d) 'West Africa Update', 7 March.

UNHCR (2002e) 'Press Release: UNHCR Receives Report on Nairobi Investigation', 25 January.

UNHCR (2001a) *Global Report 2000*, Geneva: UNHCR.

UNHCR (2001b) 'UNHCR Briefing Notes: FYR of Macedonia/Serbia, Chechnya, West Africa, Pakistan/Afghanistan', 7 August.

UNHCR (2001c) 'UNHCR Briefing Notes: FYR of Macedonia/Fed. Rep. of Yugoslavia, Guinea, Harmonisation of EU's asylum policies', 25 May.

UNHCR (2001d) 'Press Release: UNHCR Urges Guinea to Open Borders to Asylum Seekers', 17 May.

UNHCR (2000a) *The State of the World's Refugees: Fifty Years of Humanitarian Action*, Oxford: Oxford University Press.

UNHCR (2000b) *Global Report 1999*, Geneva: UNHCR.

UNHCR (2000c) 'UNHCR Guinea Update 27 Dec 2000', 27 December.

UNHCR (2000d) 'UNHCR Briefing Notes: Guinea Update', 26 December.

UNHCR (2000e) 'Press Release: UNHCR Office Destroyed in Guinea Fighting', 7 December.

UNHCR (2000f) 'Press Release: UNHCR Alarmed by Deteriorating Situation in Guinea', 6 December.

UNHCR (2000g) 'Press Release: UNHCR Worker Released in Liberia', 28 September.

UNHCR (2000h) 'UNHCR Guinea Update 18 Sep 2000', 18 September.

UNHCR (2000i) 'Press Release: UNHCR Worker Killed, One Missing in Guinea Attack', 17 September.

UNHCR (2000j) 'UNHCR Briefing Notes: Guinea, Pakistan', 15 September.

UNHCR (2000k) 'UNHCR Briefing Notes: Timor, Guinea', 12 September.

UNHCR (1998a) 'Statement by Mrs. Sadako Ogata, United Nations High Commissioner for Refugees, at the 1998 Substantive Session of ECOSOC', New York, 28 July.

UNHCR (1998b) 'The Rehabilitation of Refugee-Impacted Areas in the Great Lakes Region', in OAU and UNHCR, 'Report of the Regional Meeting on Refugee Issues in the Great Lakes', Kampala, 8–9 May.

UNHCR (1997a) *The State of the World's Refugees: A Humanitarian Agenda*, Oxford: Oxford University Press.

UNHCR (1997b) 'Great Lakes Chronology', *Refugees*, No. 110, Winter, 8.

UNHCR (1983a) 'Informal Meeting on Military Attacks on Refugee Camps and Settlements in Southern Africa and Elsewhere', EC/SCP/27, 6 June.

UNHCR (1983b) 'Report of Ambassador Felix Schnyder on Military Attacks on Refugee Camps and Settlements in Southern Africa and Elsewhere', EC/SCP/26, 15 March.

UNHCR, Africa Bureau (2001) 'Addressing Protracted Refugee Situations in Africa', Paper prepared for the Informal Consultations on New Approaches and Partnerships for Protection and Solutions in Africa, Geneva, 14 December.

UNHCR, Central Evaluation Section (1994) 'Review of UNHCR's Kenya-Somalia Cross-Border Operation', EVAL/CROS/14, Geneva: UNHCR, December.

UNHCR, Dadaab (2002) 'Assessment of the Security Situation in Dadaab from 1998 to 2002', Dadaab, December.

UNHCR, Department of International Protection (2004) 'Resettlement Handbook', Geneva, November.

UNHCR, Donor Relations (2002) 'Impact of Budgetary Reductions: Preliminary Note', Geneva: UNHCR, 25 September.

UNHCR, Environmental Unit (1998) 'Towards Sustainable Environmental Management Practices in Refugee-Affected Areas (TSEMPRAA): Country Reports: Côte d'Ivoire and Guinea', Geneva, August.

UNHCR, Evaluation and Policy Analysis Unit (EPAU) (2001) 'Evaluation of the Dadaab firewood project, Kenya', Geneva: UNHCR, EPAU/2001/08, June.

UNHCR, Executive Committee of the High Commissioner's Programme (ExCom) (2004a) 'Economic and Social Impact of Massive Refugee Populations on Host Developing Countries, as well as Other Countries', EC/54/SC/CRP.5, 18 February.

UNHCR, ExCom (2004b) 'Protracted Refugee Situations', EC/54/CRP.14, 10 June.

UNHCR, ExCom (2003a) 'Economic and Social Impact of Refugee Populations on Host Developing Countries, as well as Other Countries', EC/53/SC/CRP.4, 10 February.

UNHCR, ExCom (2003b) 'Framework for Durable Solutions for Refugees and Persons of Concern', EC/53/SC/INF.3, 16 September.

UNHCR, ExCom (2003c) 'The Strategic Use of Resettlement', EC/53/SC/CRP.10/ Add. 1, 3 June.

UNHCR, ExCom (2002a) 'Agenda for Protection: Addendum', AC.96/965/Add.1, 26 June.

UNHCR, ExCom (2002b) 'Economic and Social Impact of Refugee Populations on Host Developing Countries as well as Other Countries: Partnerships with Bilateral Development Agencies', EC/52/SC/CRP.10, 31 May.

UNHCR, ExCom (2001) 'New Directions for Resettlement Policy and Practice', EC/51/SC/INF.2, 14 June.

UNHCR, ExCom (1998a) 'Annual Theme: International Solidarity and Burden-Sharing in all its Aspects: National, Regional and International Responsibilities for Refugees', A/AC.96/904, 7 September.

UNHCR, ExCom (1998b) 'Economic and Social Impact of Massive Refugee Populations on Host Developing Countries, as well as Other Countries: A Quantitative Assessment on the Basis of Special Case Studies', EC/48/SC/ CRP.40, 3 August.

UNHCR, ExCom (1998c) 'Report of the Forty-Ninth Session of the Executive Committee of the High Commissioner's Programme', A/AC.96/911, 12 October.

UNHCR, ExCom (1997) 'Social and Economic Impact of Large Refugee Populations on Host Developing Countries', EC/47/SC/CRP.7, 6 January.

UNHCR, Global Consultations on International Protection (2002) 'Strengthening and Expanding Resettlement Today: Dilemmas, Challenges and Opportunities', EC/GC/02/7, 25 April.

UNHCR, Global Consultations on International Protection (2001a) 'The Civilian Character of Asylum: Separating Armed Elements from Refugees', EC/GC/01/5, 19 February.

UNHCR, Global Consultations on International Protection (2001b) 'Mechanisms of International Cooperation to Share Responsibilities and Burdens in Mass Influx Situations', EC/GC/01/7, 19 February.

UNHCR, Guinea (2001) 'Republic of Guinea: Update on resettlement activities and populations in need of resettlement', Prepared for the Annual Tripartite Consultations on Resettlement, Geneva, 20 – 21 June 2001, undated (likely 17 June 2001).

UNHCR, High Commissioner's Forum (2004a) 'Making Comprehensive Approaches to Resolve Refugee Problems more Systematic', FORUM/2004/7, 16 September.

UNHCR, High Commissioner's Forum (2004b) 'Convention Plus: Targeting Development Assistance to Achieve Durable Solutions for Refugees', FORUM/2004/3, 17 February.

UNHCR, Inspection and Evaluation Service (1997) 'Refugee Camp Security in the Great Lakes Region', EVAL/01/97, Geneva: UNHCR, April.

UNHCR, Inspection and Evaluation Service (1996) 'A review of UNHCR's Women Victims of Violence project in Kenya', Geneva: UNHCR, March.

UNHCR, Inspector General's Office (2000) 'Summary report of the inquiry into the death of one UNHCR Staff Member and the abduction of another in Macenta, Guinea, on 17 September 2000', Geneva, 8 December.

UNHCR, Kenya (1998) 'Last Coast Province Refugee Camp Closes' Press Release, Nairobi: UNHCR, 22 December.

UNHCR, Population Data Unit (2002) 'Selected Indicators Measuring Capacity and Contributions of Host Countries', Geneva: UNHCR, April.

UNHCR, Resettlement Section (2007) 'Projected Global Resettlement Needs: 2008', Geneva, June.

UNHCR, Resettlement Section (2004) 'Projected Global Resettlement Needs: 2005', Geneva, June.

UNHCR, Resettlement Section (2003a) 'Easy Guide to Refugee Resettlement Programmes', Geneva, June.

UNHCR, Resettlement Section (2003b) 'Resettlement Statistics 2002', Geneva, June.

UNHCR, Resettlement Section (2003c) 'UNHCR: Projected Global Resettlement Needs: 2004', Geneva, 18 June.

UNHCR, Technical Support Service (1990a) 'Guinea: Emergency Assistance and Emergency Management – Liberian refugee emergency: 23 February–23 March 1990', TSS Mission Report 90/09, Geneva, undated (likely March 1990).

UNHCR, Technical Support Service (1990b) 'Guinée: Assistance d'Urgence aux Réfugiés du Liberia: 25 février-15 mars 1990', TSS Mission Report 90/05, Geneva, undated (likely March 1990).

UN-OCHA (2003) 'Guinea: Consolidated Appeals Process (CAP) 2004', Geneva, November.

UN-OCHA (2001) 'Guinea: Consolidated Inter-Agency Appeal 2002', Geneva, November.

UN-OCHA (2002) 'West Africa: Consolidated Inter-Agency Appeal 2001', Geneva, November.

UN-OCHA, IRIN (2005) 'Guinea: Living on the edge', IRIN Web special, January, http://www.irinnews.org/webspecials/Guinea/default.asp.

UN Secretary-General (UNSG) (2001) 'Report of the Secretary-General on the activities of the Office of Internal Oversight Services: Investigation into allegations of refugee smuggling at the Nairobi Branch Office of the Office of the United Nations High Commissioner for Refugees', New York: United Nations General Assembly, Fifty-sixth session, Agenda item 130, 21 December.

UN Security Council (UNSC) (2002) 'Letter dated 19 April 2002 from the Chairman of the Security Council Committee established pursuant to resolution 1343 (2001) concerning Liberia address to the President of the Security Council', S/2002/470, New York, 19 April.

UNSC (2001a) 'Press Release: UN High Commissioner for Refugees Asks Security Council to Strengthen Mission in Sierra Leone', SC/7029, New York, 8 March.

UNSC (2001b) 'Letter dated 19 January from the Secretary-General addressed to the President of the Security Council', S/2001/64, New York, 19 January.

UNSC (2000a) 'Press Release: Security Council Condemns Incursions into Guinea by Liberia and Sierra Leone Rebels', SC/6980, New York, 21 December.
UNSC (2000b) 'Press Release: Presidential Statement Expresses Concern at Fragile Situation in Sierra Leone and Instability in Wider Region', SC/6946, New York, 3 November.
UNSC (2000c) 'Report of the Security Council mission to Sierra Leone', S/2000/992, New York, 16 October.
United States of America (USA) (2004a), Government of the, Department of State, Bureau of Population, Refugees and Migration 'Fact Sheet: Refugee Admission Programme for Africa', Washington DC, 16 January.
USA (2004b) Government of the, Department of State, Bureau of Population, Refugees and Migration 'US Refugee Admissions Program News', Vol. 2, no. 2, 15 June.
USA (2003) Government of the, Department of State, Bureau of Population, Refugees and Migration 'Cumulative Summary of Refugee Admissions: As of October 1, 2003', Washington DC, 15 November.
USA (2002) Government of the, Department of the Treasury 'Fact Sheet: Designation of Somalia and Bosnia-Herzegovina Branches of Al-Haramain Islamic Foundation', 11 March.
USA (2001a) Government of the, Department of State 'Press Release: US Contributes Additional $5 Million to Humanitarian Emergency in Guinea', Washington, 8 February.
USA (2001b) Government of the, Department of State 'Press Release: US Legislator Says Liberia's Taylor Is 'Menace to West Africa'', *Washington File*, 15 March.
USA (2001c) Government of the, Department of State, Bureau of Population, Refugees and Migration 'Fact Sheet: US Refugee Admissions and Resettlement Programme', Washington DC, 17 October.
USA (1998) Government of the, United States Mission to International Organizations Geneva 'United States Plenary Statement to the UNHCR Executive Committee 49th Session 1998', Geneva, 5 October.
US Committee for Refugees (USCR), *World Refugee Survey*, Washington: USCR, annual.
USCR (2000a) 'Press Release: USCR Calls on the International Community to Protect Sierra Leonean and Liberian Refugees' Right to Asylum in Guinea', Washington, 22 December.
USCR (2000b) 'Press Release: Escalation of Attacks in Guinea Endangers Refugees; Poses Serious Challenges for UNHCR', Washington, 8 December.
USCR (2000c) 'Killings of Humanitarians Underscore Insecurity for Aid Workers', *Refugee Reports*, Vol. 21, no. 9.
USCR (2000d) 'Press Release: Threat of Widening War in West Africa: 400,000 Refugees in Guinea Are Vulnerable', Washington, 19 October.
USCR (2000e) 'Press release: Sierra Leone and Liberia Violence Spills into Guinea: Backlash Endangers Hundreds of Thousands of Refugees', Washington, 13 September.
Van Damme, Win (1999) 'Field Reports: How Liberian and Sierra Leonean Refugees Settled in the Forest Region of Guinea (1990 – 96)', *Journal of Refugee Studies*, Vol. 12, no. 1, 36–53.
Van Damme, Win (1995) 'Do Refugees Belong in Camps? Experience from Goma and Guinea', *The Lancet*, Vol. 346, 5 August, 360–362.

Van der Meeren, Rachel (1996) 'Three Decades in Exile: Rwandan Refugees 1960–1990', *Journal of Refugee Studies*, Vol. 9, no. 3, 252–267.

Van Hoyweghen, Saskia (2002) 'Mobility, Territoriality and Sovereignty in Post-Colonial Tanzania', *Refugee Survey Quarterly*, Vol. 21, no. 1 and 2, 300–327.

Veney, Cassandra (2007) *Forced Migration in East Africa: Democratization, Structural Adjustment, and Refugees*, Basingstoke: Palgrave Macmillan.

Verdirame, Guglielmo (1999) 'Human Rights and Refugees: The Case of Kenya', *Journal of Refugee Studies*, Vol. 12, no. 1, 54–77.

Vidal, John (1999) 'Black need, but only whites receive: Race appears to be skewing the west's approach to aid', *The Guardian (UK)*, 12 August.

Waever, Ole (1995) 'Securitization and Desecuritization', in R.D. Lipschutz (ed.), *On Security*, New York: Columbia University Press, 46–76.

Wange, Samuel M., and Brian Van Arkadie (2000) *Overcoming Constraints on Tanzanian Growth: Policy Challenges Facing the Third Phase Government*, Dar es Salaam: Mkuki na Nyota Publishers for the Economic and Social Research Foundation.

Weber, Max (1994) 'The Profession and Vocation of Politics', in Peter Lassman and Ronald Speirs (eds), *Weber: Political Writings*, Cambridge: Cambridge University Press, 309–369.

Weiner, Myron (1995) *The Global Migration Crisis: Challenge to States and to Human Rights*, New York: HarperCollins.

Weiner, Myron (1993) 'Security, Stability and International Migration', in Myron Weiner (ed.), *International Migration and Security*, Boulder, CO: Westview Press, 1–35.

Whitaker, Beth Elise (2002a) 'Changing Priorities in Refugee Protection: the Rwandan repatriation from Tanzania', *Refugee Survey Quarterly*, Vol. 21, no. 1 and 2, 328–344.

Whitaker, Beth Elise (2002b) 'Refugees in Western Tanzania: The Distribution of Burdens and Benefits Among Local Hosts', *Journal of Refugee Studies*, Vol. 15, no. 4, 339–358.

Whitaker, Beth Elise (1999) 'Changing opportunities: refugees and host communities in western Tanzania', *New Issues in Refugee Research*, Working Paper No. 11, Geneva: UNHCR, June.

Widner, Jennifer A. (1992) *The Rise of the Party-State in Kenya: From 'Harambee!' to 'Nyayo!'*, Berkeley: University of California Press.

Williams, David (2000) 'Aid and Sovereignty: Quasi-States and the International Financial Institutions', *Review of International Studies*, Vol. 26, no. 4, 557–573.

Williams, Paul D. (2007) 'Thinking about Security in Africa', *International Affairs*, Vol. 83, no. 6, 1021–1038.

Wright, Stephen (1999) 'The Changing Context of African Foreign Policies', in Stephen Wright (ed.), *African Foreign Policies*, Boulder, CO: Westview Press, 1–22.

Woodward, Peter (1984) 'Relations between Neighbouring States in North-East Africa', *The Journal of Modern African Studies*, Vol. 22, no. 2, June, 273–285.

World Bank (2000) 'News Release No. 2001/193/S: The World Bank and IMF Support Debt Relief for Guinea under the Enhanced HIPC Initiative', Washington, 22 December.

World Food Programme (WFP) (2003) 'News Release: WFP and UNHCR Call for Urgent Aid for Refugees in Africa', Geneva, 14 February.

World Food Programme (WFP) (2000) 'Press Release: Funding Shortfall Threatens WFP's Response to West Africa Crisis', Rome, 15 November.

World Food Programme (WFP) (1996) 'Protracted Emergency Humanitarian Relief Food Aid: Toward 'Productive Relief': Programme Policy Evaluation of the 1990–1995 period of WFP-assisted refugee and displaced persons operations in Liberia, Sierra Leone, Guinea and Côte d'Ivoire: Mission Report', Rome, October.

Yeager, Rodger, (1982) *Tanzania: An African Experiment*, Boulder, CO: Westview Press.

Young, Crawford (2000) 'The Heritage of Colonialism', in John W. Harbeson and Donald Rothchild (eds), *Africa in World Politics: The African State System in Flux*, Third Edition, Boulder, CO: Westview Press, 23–42.

Young, Crawford (1999) 'The Third Wave of Democratization in Africa: Ambiguities and Contradictions', in Richard Joseph (ed.), *State, Conflict, and Democracy in Africa*, Boulder, CO: Lynne Rienner Publishers, 13–38.

Zakaria, Fareed (1997) 'The Rise of Illiberal Democracy', *Foreign Affairs*, Vol. 76, no. 6, November/December, 22–43.

Zarjevski, Yéfime (1988) *A Future Preserved: International Assistance to Refugees*, Oxford: Pergamon Press.

Zartman, I. William (ed.) (1995) *Collapsed States: The Disintegration and Restoration of Legitimate Authority*, Boulder, CO: Lynne Reinner Publishers.

Zetter, Roger (1991) 'Labelling Refugees: Forming and Transforming a Bureaucratic Identity', *Journal of Refugee Studies*, Vol. 4, no. 1, 39–62.

Zolberg, Aristide R., Astri Suhrke, and Sergio Aguayo (1989) *Escape from Violence: Conflict and the Refugee Crisis in the Developing World*, Oxford: Oxford University Press.

Index

Note: "t" tables; "f" figures; "m" maps and "n" notes